Work Time

WORK TIME
Conflict, Control, and Change

Cynthia L. Negrey

polity

First published in 2012 by Polity Press

Polity Press
65 Bridge Street
Cambridge CB2 1UR, UK

Polity Press
350 Main Street
Malden, MA 02148, USA

ISBN-13: 978-0-7456-5425-6   .
ISBN-13: 978-0-7456-5426-3(pb)

A catalogue record for this book is available from the British Library.

Typeset in 10.5 on 12 pt Sabon
by Toppan Best-set Premedia Limited
Printed and bound in Great Britain by MPG Books Group Limited, Bodmin, Cornwall

For further information on Polity, visit our website: www.politybooks.com

Contents

List of Figures, Tables, and Boxes

Figures

Tables

Boxes

Acknowledgments

Quizzical looks. Blank stares. These were common reactions, from students especially, but also from friends, family, and even a few colleagues, when, upon inquiry, I said the book I'm writing is about work time. The notion wasn't immediately intuitive, but with a bit of explanation – history of the 40-hour workweek, growth of part-time jobs, work–family issues – they got it. Among the students, perhaps, this is just an expression of an immature work life. But, more likely, I think, these reactions are a microcosm of a society in which work time is taken for granted and not a well-developed subject of public discourse. Scratch the surface, however, and everyone has a story, or knows someone else's story: overworked and stressed out; an undesirable work schedule; stuck in a part-time job; child-care problems; it's better in Europe. These personal troubles are the stuff of everyday conversation. But, ordinarily, people don't think of them more broadly and abstractly as matters of labor market structure, or even as something we might hope to change.

This book originated as a memo and a short working paper. The memo was a review more than a decade ago of an American Sociological Association collection of syllabi in the Sociology of Work in which I pondered: why don't more instructors cover work time in their classes? Preoccupied with the next deadline, I filed the memo away to uncover it several years later while purging old files. The memo contained a list of topics on work time that, upon rediscovery, eventually led me on the path that ends here. The working paper, "A New Shorter Full-time Norm," was written about 10 years ago when, on leave from the University of Louisville, I was a study director at the Institute for Women's Policy Research in Washington, DC. IWPR member Clara G. Schiffer had a passion for work time and funded my work on the paper, which informed small portions of chapters 3, 4, 5, and 6 herein. I'm grateful to Ms Schiffer and IWPR, especially Heidi Hartmann and Barbara Gault, for providing the resources and time to draft that paper.

Early on, Carmen Sirianni encouraged my budding interest in work time. Peter Meiksins reinforced it. Both commented on a synopsis of this book and reassured me of its value. Keen insights from William Finlay, Arne Kalleberg, Amy Wharton, and the anonymous reviewers helped me expand select content, refine themes, and reorganize some major ideas. At Polity, Commissioning Editor for Sociology Jonathan Skerrett pushed me analytically and imposed a word limit that challenged me to tighten details, and tighten again. It is a far better product for that discipline. I also thank Beatrice Iori and Helen Gray, production and copy editors respectively, for the attention and care they gave my manuscript.

Last, but certainly not least, I thank my family, friends, and colleagues, who respected my writing time, asked about my progress, and probably listened to more than they bargained for (!) over many years.

Introduction

A displaced full-time manufacturing worker works two part-time jobs in retail, earning 50 percent less per hour than his manufacturing wage. Package handlers strike over too many part-time jobs and too few full-time opportunities at UPS. Auto workers, required to work 12- to 14-hour days, often seven days a week, go on strike over excessive hours. An Asian company acquires an American musical instrument manufacturer, lowering wages and mandating overtime. A tech worker works more than 50 hours a week as a contract employee. But he worries about job insecurity and prefers a regular, full-time job. Another contract worker likes the arrangement because of flexibility to work at home. A student works part time and plans to work full time after finishing school. A professor, who worked 50 hours a week his entire career, opts for phased retirement and cuts his work time in half for a few years before exiting the university. A temp worker re-entering the labor force after many years hopes the experience will help her get a regular, full-time job. A single mother withdraws her child from day care because it costs more than she earns, then works nights and weekends when a relative can care for her child. A part-time retail worker's hours return to 25 after having worked 40-hour weeks during the holiday season. A parent laments that he cannot attend his children's school events because his work schedule is inflexible. Meatpacking workers seek accommodations for break times for religious observance. Government workers can work four 10-hour days to reduce commutes when gasoline is $4.00 per gallon. Less than six months later they are required to take periodic unpaid furloughs during the 2008 budget crunch.

These are several examples of choices workers make, or have imposed on them, and ways in which they experience work time in various occupations, organizations, and industries. They are personal experiences, but each is a representation of broader organizational strategies and social issues.

In *The Sociological Imagination*, Mills (1959) argued that personal experiences, or private troubles, are often individual manifestations of public issues. Unemployment is a good example. Although inadequate training, education, or experience can be the cause of an individual's inability to get a job, often unemployment stems from problems in the larger economy – overproduction by industries and companies, for example, or producers' and consumers' inability to obtain credit to do business and make purchases – and individuals experience job loss, financial difficulties, and personal and family stress. Many Americans today experience private troubles associated with work time: they feel overworked, have conflicts between their job and family responsibilities, have too little income and not enough work. It's easy to blame private troubles on oneself: I work too much because I'm too dutiful – I need to "just say no"; I need to manage my time better so I can be effective at my job and less stressed at home; maybe I should get a degree so I can get a better job with better hours and pay.

An "On the Job Advice" column from *The Indianapolis Star* took this private troubles approach in advising readers to "[w]ork smarter, not harder" and "[s]et aside personal and family time" as professional New Year's resolutions. The writer recommended analyzing the workday to determine where time is being used inefficiently in order to become more productive without working longer. On the personal and family side, she recommended reading a book, watching a movie and dining with one's family, and using vacation days (Phillips 2008). This book is a meditation on these matters and more, but I depart from the private troubles approach by investigating work time as a public issue. What are recent and longer-term work-time trends? What are the historical, cultural, public policy, and business sources of our current work-time practices? How do US trends and practices compare to other nations? Once the sources of these conventions, and cross-national variations, are understood, what are the possibilities for change to better distribute work time across people, within our daily lives, and throughout our lifetimes?

I became interested in work time as a graduate student in Michigan in the early 1980s. The United States was then in the throes of the deepest recession since the Great Depression, and the industrial Midwest was affected disproportionately because its economy was based on traditional manufacturing industries like automobiles, steel, and machine tools. The twin recessions of 1979 to 1982 foreshadowed structural economic difficulties that persist, particularly job loss associated with global competition and production. With double-digit unemployment in the early 1980s, I became fascinated by the notion of work-time reduction to redistribute jobs and ease unemployment. In my research, I learned that scholars, policymakers, labor activists, and other critical thinkers touted this idea in the 1930s and 1960s.

While I was curious about work time and unemployment, I became aware that part-time and temporary jobs in the US were increasing at a rate faster than full-time employment. This trend was setting up a structural condition whereby there would not be enough full-time jobs for everyone who wanted them. Some workers would be forced into and become stuck in part-time or temporary jobs. Knowing that part-time and temporary jobs generally pay less than full-time jobs, a growing percentage of the American workforce would be condemned to working poverty.

Yet there was another factor in this complex web of work time. Some workers, especially women, want part-time jobs to integrate employment and family care. Since the 1980s, other forms of employment have emerged to help parents reconcile jobs with family life, such as job sharing, compressed workweeks, and flexible scheduling. These changes contributed to the emergence of employer-provided work–family benefits at some workplaces and a large scholarship on work–life issues in sociology, business, psychology, family studies, and other fields.

The recent Great Recession, the deepest since the Great Depression, re-created many of the conditions of the deep twin recessions of 1979 to 1982, although the twin recessions were centered in manufacturing and the Great Recession was centered in housing and finance, now in a more globally integrated, technology-mediated economy. US unemployment nationwide was near 10 percent in October 2009, the highest it had been since 1983. The Great Recession exerted downward pressure on hours, but average weekly hours among non-supervisory workers in private nonagricultural industries have actually been declining since 1965 – about five hours to under 34 in 2007, before the Great Recession (US Department of Labor, Bureau of Labor Statistics, Table B-47, Hours and Earnings in Private Nonagricultural Industries, 1960–2008). Part-time and temporary work remain integral features of the labor market and organizational strategies of flexibility, and workers continue to juggle employment and family care in more or less satisfactory ways. Many public-sector workers have been required to take unpaid furloughs as an alternative to layoffs as governments and schools cope with tighter budgets. UPS pilots averted 300 layoffs by volunteering for enough unpaid time off to save the company $90 million through 2011, and mechanics there considered early retirement, job sharing, reduced hours, or other cost-cutting measures (Howington 2009). Renewed discussion of short-time compensation, which provides prorated unemployment benefits to workers whose hours have been cut to avoid layoffs and is an important part of the social safety net in Germany, France, and a number of other European countries, emerged among policy experts in the US as the Great Recession pushed well into its second year. Short-time compensation is available in only 17 US states and is little used in the majority of them (Abraham and Houseman 2009).

In 2011, jobless recovery – economic growth with high unemployment – continues for the foreseeable future. The recessions of 1991 and 2001 also ended initially in jobless recoveries. There was jobless recovery in the mid-1930s, too. But the 1930s crisis was met in part with a legislative reduction of work time to 40 hours per week in the form of the Fair Labor Standards Act of 1938. Legislative adjustment of work time is not on the agenda in this crisis period, to date, in the US. Some European countries have raised the retirement age to reduce retirement spending and offset public debt crises.

Beyond unemployment and non-standard jobs, why a book about work *time*? In the developed economies, most people work for pay, and work schedules structure time. Work schedules are largely determined by occupations, and because occupations differ, schedules vary. These variations influence how people experience time and, even, whom we have opportunities to know. Unpaid work and leisure routines may (or may not) differ from paid work routines. In developing countries, cultural change occurs as more of the population transitions to routines of market work. In these respects, the study of work time is timeless.

This book is a broad overview of the evolution and current state of work time, primarily in the US, which bears some similarities to other nations, but there are important differences too. It addresses specific questions. How many hours do we work? When do we work? How regularly do we work? Who determines how time is spent and measured? How do we experience work time? What differences do social class, gender, and age make? How do electronic technologies affect work time? How does work time in the US compare to other countries? Cross-national comparison is particularly meaningful because Americans work among the most hours in the world, and the US is among the least generous developed countries regarding vacation time and public policies that support employed parents. The basic argument is that, like all time in human society (Bluedorn 2002), work time is socially constructed – through cultural norms, public policy, within organizations, and via negotiations in households and workplaces. Today's legal standard workweek of 40 hours in the US is the product of workers' struggles, organizational changes, and legislative reforms over the course of the nineteenth and early twentieth centuries. Because work time is unevenly distributed, it shapes opportunities across social classes, genders, and age groups. For example, the American working class, like that of other developed economies, has feminized since the 1930s due to increasing numbers of women becoming employed after World War II at all occupational levels. As a consequence of deindustrialization in recent decades, workers, especially men, have been displaced from manufacturing jobs into low-level white-collar and service occupations. Men's and women's lives have converged, particularly in that they both work outside the home; men contribute more to household work and family care than in the past; and their total work time (paid and unpaid) is similar. Yet gender-typed differences in work and family care persist (Cobble 2007), as do work–life tensions.

Unlike the US, some European countries have used public policy to devise a "pro-social" workweek, while others, like the US, have few regulations and tend to let employers control work time. But even in the US a new class politics is evident, the product of women's activism in the labor movement – particularly within public- and service-sector unions – which has been a platform for demanding paid family leave, more affordable child care, and paid sick leave (Firestein and Dones 2007; Hartmann and Lovell 2009; Nussbaum 2007). Business competition, budget pressures in the public sector, and workers' desires for quality time and adequate compensation will continue to make work time a timeless subject.

History, culture, public policy, organization, and the household are necessary contexts for understanding work time. Chapter 1 begins by examining the work routines of hunter-gatherers to think critically about work time and necessity at the most basic level. The transition from church time to clock time in fourteenth-century Europe foregrounds an examination of commodified time in industrial capitalism. While a clock-oriented industrial time sense persists and has generalized outside factories, today we live in a service society in which most work occurs outside factories. Our individual experiences of time may be sufficiently diverse because of occupational and organizational differentiation that, beyond the universal clock, a single collective time sense may not exist. In some occupations, a task-oriented time sense prevails. Ideologies about and experiences of work time are also embedded in the gender division of labor. Therefore, a theoretical exploration of gender and work time complements the class-oriented analysis of commodified time.

Chapter 2 resurrects workers' and social reformers' activism and legislative efforts that reduced the statutory workweek, ultimately to 40 hours, in the US. This history is not widely appreciated, and there is a tendency to assume 40 hours is a "natural" length of the workweek. Even more obscure, the 40-hour week was the outcome of an ever so close, almost successful, but failed effort to establish a 30-hour week to create jobs after high unemployment of long duration in the Great Depression.

Since then, the 40-hour workweek has become a rigid legal norm in the US, but changes in the labor market and occupational structure have affected the distribution of work time across workers. Growth in long-hours professional and managerial jobs has accompanied growth in non-standard short-hours jobs, creating a bifurcated distribution of work time. These trends, along with annual hours, are examined in chapter 3, as are increases in recent decades in part-time, temporary, and contract employment. Such "non-standard" work is laden with contradiction in that it can be a source of flexibility and control of time for workers, but control is offset by low wages and few if any benefits. Nor are all workers satisfied with their work hours.

Gender is woven throughout. Historically, protective labor legislation for women (and children) was used by activists as an "entering wedge" to gain limits on work time for all workers. Non-standard work today is distributed unevenly across women and men, and there are gender differences among those who work long or short workweeks, and in work-hours preferences. However, gender relations are most pronounced in chapter 4, where work–family integration is discussed. There I examine the gender division of labor in the household: how this division of labor contributes to a widespread sense of time scarcity; and adaptations of individuals, households, businesses, and public policy to foster work–family integration. Chapter 4 also introduces the notion of work–life, which focuses less on employed parents and more on a broad array of workers' experiences of integrating and managing the boundary between work and the rest of life.

European countries are far ahead of the US in enacting public policies that reconcile work–family, albeit imperfectly. Some practices reinforce gender inequity, whereas others deliberately encourage gender equity. These European cases, covered extensively in the scholarly literature, provide valuable lessons for the US. Chapter 5 takes a global perspective, situating European policy within European work-time regimes more generally and contrasting their shorter workweeks to the long weeks in developing countries.

Chapter 6 looks ahead in considering the electronic frontier of work time, as well as contradictory strategies to customize work time in employees' and employers' interests. I encourage bold critical thought about work time on a number of fronts: current sluggish job growth, work–life integration, and long-term environmental sustainability. Alternative fuels and technologies and "green" consumer practices are essential components of a new "green" economy. Should work time be part of that vision too?

Conflict, control, and change are analytic themes with multiple meanings. Conflict over work time occurs in different areas: between employers and workers (e.g., how much, when, and how intensely to work); couples in their homes when juggling the demands of paid work and family care; and organizational practices, societal work-time trends, and extant public policies. Control refers to employers' efforts to control workers' time and productivity on the job; workers' desires to control their time to control their lives; and public policies that aid or undermine employers' efforts and workers' desires. Change refers to the historical evolution of work-time conventions, present trends, future trajectories, and unpredictable ruptures that may result from unanticipated events.

In every area of scholarship, a time comes when it is fruitful to abstract from the minutiae of individual studies for purposes of broad examination. That is the main goal of this book. The work-time literature in the social sciences has grown in the past 30 years, much of it focused on work–family or work–life integration and labor market trends. Organization specialists are turning their attention to temporal structures within organizations. Scholars' attention to work time expresses not only their personal interests, motivations, and expertise, but also reflects broader social concerns. Yet rarely are these literatures brought under a single umbrella to inform each other or situated in the long historical trajectory of work time and reform activism. I hope my attempt at integration will be useful as more researchers pursue work time as an area of study and instructors cover it in their courses. And I hope all of us together can stimulate widespread discussion of the time of work in our lives.

1
From Field to Factory and Beyond

As human societies developed from pre-industrialism to industrialism and beyond, work sites expanded from fields, homes, and monasteries to shops, factories, classrooms, offices, laboratories, and more. Work routines and hours changed, too, as work sites, products, and services became more diverse. Ideologies and conventions regarding work time have changed as well. Here we trace macro-level changes in work time from hunter-gatherers to pre-industrial agricultural society, capitalist industrial society, and today's service and information economy. Along the way we observe changes in how societies think about time, particularly in relationship to nature and the development of the clock, the association of time with money, and time as a gendered resource.

The social sciences are compelling because they provide tools for systematic study of social institutions and practices and allow us to gain knowledge that very frequently challenges conventional wisdom (Berger 1963). Work time in hunter-gatherer societies is a good example. It's a common (mis)perception that humans worked longer and harder as pre-industrial hunter-gatherers, horticulturalists, pastoralists, and agriculturalists. It's customary to think of modern technology as labor saving, and assume, wrongly perhaps, that pre-industrial humans surely must have worked constantly without the technologies we take for granted today. Modern technologies have indeed allowed us to produce more with less, but instead of achieving some admittedly indeterminate level of comfort and balancing work and rest, we use technologies to produce more and more – and, in the aggregate, we work long hours.

Hunter-gatherers are poor by modern standards, yet Sahlins (1972: 10–12) saw material plenty in their absolute poverty. In the non-subsistence sphere beyond the basic necessities of food and water, wants are generally easily satisfied. Homespun products of stone, bone, wood, and skin are easily acquired, available in abundance, and shared by all. Their nomadic existence discourages acquisition of material goods: they can move only that which they can carry. Wealth is an encumbrance. In this sense, the notion of human scarcity is a bourgeois construction of the market economy. Few in the developed world today would want to live off the land in the mode of hunter-gatherers or return to agrarian subsistence, but the affluent among us could surely do with less (economic conditions at the time of this writing are forcing many to do just that) and perhaps work fewer hours. Let's hold that thought and return to it in chapter 6.

Original Affluence?

How long and hard did hunter-gatherers work for the necessities of life? Broad generalizations about work time in subsistence societies are difficult to make due to small sampling frames, small numbers, and cultural differences of societies studied and different research methods. Gershuny (2000: 61) acknowledges the contributions of anthropological and historical interpretations of time in hunting and gathering (and medieval) societies, but challenges their validity because our knowledge might be based on relatively successful societies that left records or survived long enough to be studied. But were they exceptional in this regard and thus atypical?

Sahlins (1972: 14) argued "a good case can be made that hunters and gatherers work less than we do; and, rather than a continuous travail, the food quest is intermittent, leisure abundant, and there is a greater amount of sleep in the daytime per capita per year than in any other condition of society." Evidence from McCarthy and McArthur's study during the 1948 American-Australian Scientific Expedition to Arnhem Land (Mountford 1960 as cited by Sahlins 1972: 15–19) is that the average time per person per day devoted to the appropriation and preparation of food (including weaponry repair) was four or five hours, stopping when they procured enough for the time being, leaving time to spare. Nor did they maximize the available labor and disposable resources. Economic activity was not physically demanding; they worked to exhaustion rarely. Yet their dietary intake was adequate by standards of the National Research Council of America at 2,160 calories per day per capita (over a four-day period of observation) and 2,130 calories (over 11 days) at two sites, Fish Creek and Hemple Bay. These were free-ranging native Australians, living outside mission or other settlements during the period of study, although this was not necessarily their permanent or ordinary circumstance.

Fish Creek was an inland camp in western Arnhem Land, consisting of nine adults (six men and three women). It was studied at the end of the dry season, when the supply of vegetation was low. Kangaroo hunting was rewarding, although the animals became increasingly wary under steady stalking, according to the researchers. In inland hunting, as at Fish Creek, one day's work may yield two days' sustenance. Fish Creek generated enough surplus that it supported a virtually full-time 35-to-40-year-old craftsman. Much of the group's spare time was passed in rest and sleep, averaging 3 hours 15 minutes of daytime rest and sleep among both men and women during 14 days of observation.

Hemple Bay was a coastal occupation on Groote Eylandt, with eight adults (four men and four women) and five children. Vegetation was plentiful; fishing was variable, but on the whole good by comparison with other coastal camps visited by the expedition. Fishing perhaps produces smaller if steadier returns than hunting, enjoining somewhat longer and more regular efforts. Providing for children may also account for more time obtaining food at Hemple Bay. The use of metal tools or the reduction of local pressure on food resources by depopulation may have raised productivity above aboriginal levels, although the two groups observed may have been less skilled than their ancestors.

Sahlins (1972) concluded that the work habits in the two camps in Arnhem Land were similar to those of other hunter-gatherers. Among the Dobe Bushmen, for example, who occupied an area of Botswana where !Kung Bushmen had been living for at least 100 years, a day's work was about six hours, and they worked at food procurement about two and a half days per week. Thus, the workweek there was approximately 15 hours, or an average of 2 hours 9 minutes per day. An intensive four-week study of the Dobe Bushmen had been conducted in July and August 1964, during a period of transition from more to less favorable seasons of the year. The camp was populated by 41 people, about the average size of such settlements. The Dobe Bushmen encountered an abundance of vegetation, particularly the energy-rich mangetti nut, and metal had been available since the late nineteenth century. The ratio of food producers to the general population was estimated to be 2:3, but the food producers were estimated to work only 36 percent of the time (Sahlins 1972: 20–1). The daily per capita subsistence yield was 2,140 calories. Because subsistence work required a relatively small amount of time, the majority of the Dobe Bushmen's time was spent resting or visiting other camps (Sahlins 1972: 23). Similar evidence of the "characteristic paleolithic rhythm of a day or two on, a day or two off" (Sahlins 1972: 23) exists for nineteenth-century Australian aboriginal tribes as well as the African Hadza at the mid-twentieth century. The Hadza men were said to be more concerned "with games of chance than with chances of game" and, despite being surrounded by cultivators, chose not to take up agriculture themselves, preferring to preserve their leisure (Sahlins 1972: 27).

Trust in the abundance of nature's resources rather than despair at the inadequacy of human means created "lazy travelers" (Smyth 1878: 125, as cited by Sahlins 1972: 29) whose nomadic lifestyle was only in part a flight from starvation. Sahlins's sympathetic account of hunter-gatherers sees their wanderings not as anxious, but more like "a picnic on the Thames" (1972: 29–30). Their intermittent work rhythm created an objectively low standard of living with few possessions, but they were not poor per se. Gender inequity of work time did exist, however. Because plant cultivation tended to be more reliable than hunting, and women did the gathering, women worked more regularly than men and provided more of the food supply (Sahlins 1972: 35, 37).

More recently, scholars have challenged Sahlins's notions of original affluence and leisurely work routines. These studies show wide variation in work hours and in some cases more hours than Sahlins's original affluence would suggest. These differences might be due to cultural factors or differences in research methods. Hill et al. (1985), for example, counted almost seven hours per day of food acquisition on normal activity days among mission-resident northern Ache men in Eastern Paraguay, based on observation of nine foraging trips of 5–15 days over a six-month period from October 1981 to April 1982 – a considerably longer sampling frame than the seven days and 14 days of the McCarthy and McArthur studies. Ache men spent most of their time searching for or in pursuit of game, with little variation from day to day or man to man. There was more variation in "miscellaneous work," especially tool manufacture and repair, cleaning camp, and building huts. The Ache worked more hours than any of 14 horticultural societies in Hame's survey, cited by Hill et al., and more hours than four other hunter-gatherer societies for which Hill et al. had quantitative data. The Ache, however, consumed more calories per day per capita and more protein, and weighed more than any other group in their height range (Hill et al. 1985: 45).

Hali men in rural Papua New Guinea spent 2.79 hours and Hali women 4.5 hours per day on subsistence activity, in line with Sahlins's evidence. Hali women's hours were longer than men's because they lived with their children separately from their husbands and were responsible for providing for their children. Women farmed and reared pigs; men cultivated sweet potatoes but only for themselves (Umezaki et al. 2002).

A review of 15 studies of agrarian household economies published from 1939 to 1978 (Minge-Klevana 1980) showed men's total ("outside" and "inside") work hours ranged from 3.9 among the Kayapo to 11.1 in Muhero. Women's total ranged from 4.9 hours among the Kayapo to 13.65 in Medieres.

Subsistence routines provide a baseline against which to compare modern work time. Subsistence work was more strictly gender differentiated and governed by natural and seasonal rhythms. Nature, season, and gender are still factors, but modern humans contend with the clock. How the clock became so important requires we visit the Middle Ages and the emergence of capitalism.

Medieval Church Time, Modern Clock Time

Work and time are essential aspects of social structure and function, and control of time, and power over time, are essential components in the functioning of societies (Le Goff 1980: xii–xiii; Harvey 1985: 7). The transition from church time to clock time in the Middle Ages provides compelling evidence for this thesis. Changes in labor time and the conditions of intellectual and economic production accompanied the secularization of human activity (Le Goff 1980: 30).

Christianity is frequently judged to have fundamentally transformed the notion of time. Medieval clerics regarded time in light of biblical texts and Christian tradition: time begins with God and is dominated by Him. Divine action is so naturally connected with time that time cannot pose a separate and distinct problem; it is rather the necessary and natural condition of every divine act. For the early Christians, eternity was not opposed to time; nor was it the absence of time, but merely the extension of time to infinity. The appearance of Christ gave time a historic dimension or center, and the concept of salvation transformed the sense of time's end. During the twelfth century, however, the traditional framework of Christian thought on time was shaken, by merchants who experienced a connection between time and space that undermined the Church's concept of time (Le Goff 1980: 30–4).

The invention of the mechanical clock in medieval Europe was comparable in social and economic significance to movable type, which eventually turned Europe from a weak, peripheral outpost of Mediterranean civilization into a hegemonic aggressor (Landes 1983: 6, 12; Bluedorn 2002: 9–11). Interest in time measurement led to the invention of the clock, not the other way around, motivated in part by setting prayer times to specific hours of the day and religious concern for punctuality among monks. Benedictine monks in the sixth century had first introduced fixed and pre-set times for each of their activities, a practice revolutionary in its time (Whipp et al. 2002: 13; Zerubavel 1981). Monasteries were the largest productive enterprises of medieval Europe, and the new monastic Orders of the eleventh and twelfth centuries enforced higher standards of punctuality. The purpose of such rationalized conduct was to overcome the natural state; it trained monks objectively as workers in the service of God. Gradually, this concern for rational action and proper timekeeping diffused to the countryside and marketplace until, by the end of the fourteenth century, it became a duty, an integral part of Protestant righteous conduct (Weber 1958; Whipp et al. 2002: 13). New sources of demand for clocks emerged outside the monasteries, especially among the ambitious urban bourgeoisie (Landes 1983: 58–71).

Like the peasants, the merchants were at first subjected to seasonal cycles and unpredictability of the weather. They sought to control this natural order through prayer and superstitious practice. Once merchants organized commercial networks, however, time became an object of measurement. Duration of travel, price inflation or deflation in the course of a commercial transaction, fluctuations in the commercial price of silver, and their workers' labor time all required merchants' attention and became the object of increasingly explicit regulation. Historical documents such as account sheets, travel diaries, manuals of commercial practice, and letters of exchange all show how important the exact measurement of time was becoming to the orderly conduct of business. The material reality of merchants' business superimposed a new, measurable, predictable time on that of the eternally renewed, unpredictable natural environment (Le Goff 1980: 35).

Prior to clocks, bells were used to chime the hours of commercial transactions and work hours, such as in 1355 when the royal governor of Artois authorized the people of Aire-sur-la-Lys, a center of textile trade, to build a belfry whose bells would chime for the aforementioned purposes. As clocks were erected opposite church bell towers, they came to symbolize a great revolution to the complexity of urban labor time (Le Goff 1980: 35–6, 44).

The unit of labor time in the medieval West was the day.[1] Initially, this was the rural workday – as in "journal," a French dialect word for the amount of land that can be plowed in one day, or "jour." The urban workday was defined with reference to variable natural time, from sunrise to sunset, marked off in an approximate way by religious time borrowed from Roman antiquity. Within this basic framework, few conflicts arose over work time with the exception of night labor. In the natural and rural context, night labor was a sort of urban heresy, generally prohibited and subject to fines. On the whole, labor time was still the time of an economy dominated by agrarian rhythms, free of haste, inexact, and unconcerned by productivity (Le Goff 1980: 44).

From the end of the thirteenth century, this system of labor time was under challenge, and conflicts over night work contributed to stricter definition, measurement, and use of the workday, as well as social conflicts over the duration of work. At first it was the workers who wanted a longer workday, to increase their wages during the first monetary crisis when prices rose and wages fell. The problem was especially acute in the textile sector, where wages were a significant factor in production costs and employers' profits. In Paris, Philip the Fair authorized night work on January 19, 1322. In response, employers sought to regulate the workday more closely and to combat workers' cheating. Work bells, rung by hand by pulling a rope attached to the bell, proliferated. Worker uprisings were subsequently aimed at silencing the "werkglocken" in an expression of resentment and mistrust of those who controlled them (Landes 1983: 73–5; Le Goff 1980). Because of these revolts, textile employers took harsh measures to protect the work bell. Workers who seized the bell to use it as a signal of revolt would incur the heaviest fines: 60 Parisian pounds for anyone who rang the bell for popular assembly and for anyone who came armed; and the death penalty for anyone who rang the bell to call for revolt against the king, the aldermen, or the officer in charge of the bell. Urban and suburban vineyard day laborers, on the other hand, agitated for a reduction of the workday, a confrontation that led to a trial before the Parlement of Paris (Le Goff 1980: 45–7).

Work bells associated time not to events per se but to regular, normal time. Rather than the uncertain clerical hours of the church bells, there were the certain hours of business. Time came to be integrated into daily life. Creating a better measure of labor was an important factor in the process of the secularization of time (Le Goff 1980: 48).

The invention and spread of mechanical clocks contributed decisively to the notion of "certain hours." During the first half of the fourteenth century city clocks were distributed throughout major urban areas in northern Italy, Catalonia, northern France, southern England, Flanders, and Germany. Despite the fact that the new clocks were fragile, capricious, irregular, and frequently out of order, the 60-minute hour came to be firmly established. It replaced the day as the fundamental unit of labor time. In this sense, the workday gave way to a concept of work hours. During this era, time associated with natural rhythms, agrarian activity, and religious practice remained the primary temporal framework; and the new clock-oriented urban time was non-unified and unsynchronized within and across regions. Travelers in the fifteenth and sixteenth centuries experienced confusion and disorder caused by the changing origin of time from one city to the next (Le Goff 1980: 49). Although rural/urban and religious/secular splits in the concept and practice of time are identifiable in the Middle Ages, by the fourteenth century the notion of "wasting time" was becoming a serious sin – thus, religious belief spurred on productivity – and at the dawn of the Renaissance merchants were no longer confronted with the admonition that time is a gift from God that cannot be sold (Le Goff 1980: 50–1). Weber overlooked this chronometric aspect of the Protestant ethic. What the clock was to the cloistered ascetics of the Middle Ages, the watch became to the in-the-world ascetics of post-Reformation Europe (Landes 1983: 90–2). Probably dozens of clockmakers were active in Europe by the end of the fourteenth century. In the fifteenth century, miniaturization enabled portability and punctuality and wearing watches became fashionable. The shifting balance of production and use of timekeepers were symptoms of and factors in the displacement of the center of commercial and industrial activity from Southern to Northern Europe in the sixteenth and seventeenth centuries (Landes 1983: 7,

81–92). The temporal foundation for market capitalism had been laid, and the chronological net around daily life tightened (Simmel 1950, 1978; Harvey 1985: 6–7).

Clock time was gradually adopted worldwide, and, by the end of the nineteenth century, it was imposed across the globe as standard time, ending the myriad local times and dates used by the peoples of the world. In 1883, the more than 200 local times from Washington, DC, to San Francisco were rationalized, easing the scheduling of rail transport (Kern 1983; Harvey 1985: 8). Greenwich Mean Time, and the division of the earth into 24 equal zones, one hour apart, by 1884, constituted the beginning of the global day. The development of world time was an essential precondition for global trade, finance, transport, and communication (Whipp et al. 2002: 13–14). Night work has been common in factories since the Industrial Revolution to maximize the productivity of machines, but today virtual workdays and nights may be reversed, as among call center workers in India who serve the West (Poster 2007).

Commodified Time

Modern work time must be understood within modern capitalism. The essence of capitalist work relations is the wage–labor exchange (Edwards 1979). Workers sell their ability to work in exchange for wages. Because work occurs within the dimension of time, workers in effect sell their time in exchange for wages and, once sold, workers' time and labor belong to the employer. In this exchange, time and labor are commodified, and therein lies the root of employers' efforts to ensure that all time purchased is filled with productive work. Employers want the most for their money (Marx 1977; Whipp et al. 2002; Zerubavel 1981).

Marx (1971) believed all economic activity reduces to economy of time. As he (Marx 1977) argued, commodity values are measured by the amount of labor time socially necessary for their production. Use value is a property of commodities' substance and function, independent of labor time, and it differs qualitatively. What equates them quantitatively, however, can only be the labor that produced them, which can only be measured by its duration. Therefore, each commodity represents the labor time expended in its direct production and the production of its inputs; for example, an intricate lace garment is worth more than a plain cotton garment, even if the raw materials cost the same.

Profit-seekers (and other cost-conscious organizations) desire to produce commodities that "contain" more value than the sum of the commodity values used in their production. This surplus value derives from surplus labor, labor expended by workers beyond that necessary for subsistence. Work time is composed of both this necessary and surplus time.

To achieve productivity gains, employers can lengthen the workday, for example, requiring workers to produce more by working longer hours, or they can introduce machinery or other improvements that increase productivity within a fixed period of time. Scientific management's obsession with time and motion to exact precision and efficiency in workers' movements, inventory storage, and production area layout is another example (Clawson 1980; Robinson and Godbey 1997: 30–1), as are other forms of time management that prescribe the ways people should use their time at work (Perlow 1999). Productivity gains, however, do not necessarily result in reductions of work time. Because capitalism must grow to survive, reducing work time is anathema to the creation of surplus value and profit. Process and technology improvements permit the production of more with less labor, but capitalism's growth imperative converts what could be disposable time to surplus labor time (Marx 1971: 144), unlike the hunter-gatherers discussed above who spend their time beyond subsistence work at leisure. In Cleaver's (1979: 119) words, "Any time spent by the working class that is not work ... is dead time for capital ... For the working class, on the other hand, labor time is time lost."

Industrial Time-discipline

Clock-oriented factory time did not emerge naturally, automatically, or without resistance (Adam 1990: 111; Marx 1977; Rubin 2007b: 4; Thompson 1967); it was imposed by factory owners in an effort to synchronize and control labor. Significant changes in the apprehension and social definition of time occurred in the period from 1300 to 1650 (Le Goff 1980; Thompson 1967), marking the transition in England from an agricultural to an industrial time-sense (Adam 1990; Rubin 2007a; Thompson 1967). In his classic essay, historian E. P. Thompson (1967) asked how far, and in what ways, did the shift in time-sense affect labor discipline, and how far did it influence the inward apprehension of time of working people? If the transition to industrial society entailed a restructuring of work habits – new discipline, new incentives, indeed, new human nature – how far was this related to inward notations of time?

In non-industrialized societies time is attached to and measured against natural phenomena: daybreak; nightfall (Landes 1983: 1; Thompson 1967); cooking time, as in "a rice-cooking" in Madagascar (Thompson 1967: 58), orientation to the tides among fishing and seafaring peoples. These represent task-oriented time. The peasant or laborer attends to an observed necessity, and there is little demarcation between work and life. From the perspective of the observer who is accustomed to labor timed by the clock, task-oriented time may appear wasteful and inefficient. Yet, in some settings today, a clock orientation may be at odds with the labor process of the job itself.

Examples of task-oriented time continue to be evident in modern societies. Farmers plant and harvest by the seasons and in the past had to work in daylight. Today, artificial lighting on combines permits them to work in darkness. Musicians and other entertainers work regularly or intermittently on projects. Professors juggle one task after another as they teach classes, grade papers, advise students, meet in committees, and write scholarly papers; and, on the other side of the desk, students similarly approach assignments with a task orientation framed by deadlines. Parents respond to children's needs as they ebb and flow. Integrating work and family today is not only a matter of negotiating competing schedules of paid work and home, but includes dealing with conflicting time orientations – the clock-oriented realm of paid work and the more task-oriented realm of the household. Increasingly, however, the household is being forced to adapt to and adopt the clock-oriented time of the world of paid work, schools, sporting events, and lessons, for example, as more facets of life are scheduled. Much social science research has been devoted to questions pertaining to the spillover effects of work and home, how people integrate employment and family duties, and work–life boundaries, which will be discussed in chapter 4.

In early industrialism, workers resisted the new work regimes in factories despite having no choice but to work. In chapter 28 of *Capital*, volume 1, Marx provided an account of legislation and repressive state actions to force the proletariat to work in the new factories. In some areas, new tax policies, requiring payment of taxes with money that could be obtained only by working for wages, forced displaced peasants to seek factory jobs. The factories, however, could not absorb all of the "free and rightless proletariat" (Marx 1977: 896); consequently, legislation against vagabondage was enacted and enforced throughout Western Europe to bind the proletariat ideologically if not directly to factory employment. In England, "vagabonds" (other than those who were too old and/or unable to work, who were given beggar's licenses) were whipped, imprisoned, mutilated (e.g., by slicing off part of an ear), branded, made slaves, and/or executed. While these class struggles were about whether individuals would spend their time working in factories at all, later struggles developed over the length of the workday.

In chapter 10 of *Capital*, volume 1, Marx details struggles over the length of the workday and night work, and illustrates abuses associated with child labor and overwork. By the time he wrote *Capital*, 10 hours had become the average length of the workday (eight hours on Saturday) in England. The length of work time is not a guarantee of a particular quantity of labor, however. This is why Marx gave to labor the name "variable capital." Employers buy "labor power" for a given period and hope to obtain the average labor. The uncertainty associated with variable capital drives employers to devise methods to maximize labor output, such as the use of piece wages, the application of machinery and technology, and work "speed up."[2] The class struggle at the point of production is over how intensely workers will work during the time on the job, and who controls how and at what pace the work is done. In response to employers' efforts to increase productivity, workers have also devised countless strategies of resistance: talking (or texting) on the phone, extra coffee breaks, reading magazines or newspapers, surfing the Internet, socializing with other workers, rate setting, stopping the line, and the like.

This clock-oriented workplace concept of time has become a shared ideology throughout society. Industrialized societies no longer think in terms of time passed. Instead, time is spent. Yet time and money are not equivalent. Money can be saved and accumulated. Generally, time cannot be saved (Adam 1990: 114), although workers often think in terms of accumulating sick, vacation, and compensatory time as saving time, and employers devise operations to maximize productivity and minimize wasted time and labor – thus saving time. It has also been argued that the value of money grows as money accumulates, but time is most valuable when it is scarce, losing value under conditions of surplus. Time's value also varies by status, wealth, and authority (Adam 1990: 114).

Thompson (1967: 63–9) argued that the general diffusion of timepieces occurred at the very moment when the Industrial Revolution demanded greater synchronization of labor. As noted above, church clocks, public clocks, and sundials kept time, supplemented by human bell ringers and whistles whose sound would notify a community of the time. Whistles signaled starting and quitting times at mines. While the use of sundials persisted into the nineteenth century, by 1800 clocks and watches were manufactured and distributed widely, having become convenience items instead of the luxury items they had been decades earlier.

In the early period of manufacture, when craftwork prevailed in private houses or small workshops and processes had not been intricately subdivided into detail work, the necessity to synchronize labor was minimal and task-oriented time prevailed. Patterns of labor were somewhat irregular, particularly when individuals were in control of their own work time. Fluctuations between periods of intense labor and idleness were common. These irregular work rhythms were associated with different chants on different days, temptations to sleep late in the morning, and "religious" observance of Saint Monday and Saint Tuesday.[3] "Sunday was holy, Monday was holy, and Tuesday was often needed to recover from so much holiness" (Landes 1983: 229). The irregularity of the workday and -week were linked to the irregularity of the work year. Traditional holidays and fairs were periods of idleness, and custom had established so many "Holy-days" that few of those employed in manufacturing were regularly employed more than two thirds of the time (Thompson 1967: 76 n.70). In some places, Saint Monday persisted into the mid-nineteenth (Pahl 1984: 45) and even twentieth centuries (Thompson 1967: 74). Even today, in offices, for example, Monday morning and Friday afternoon may be slow periods when staff request time off.

Synchronization of time – and labor – was more than a response to the technical needs of manufacturing. Time measurement was also a means of labor discipline (Landes 1983: 229; Thompson 1967). The *Law Book of the Crowley Iron Works* (Thompson 1967: 81) illustrates the control of time as an exercise of power. Employees worked from 5 a.m. to 8 p.m. or 7 a.m. to 10 p.m., with 90 minutes for breaks for breakfast and dinner. Time was kept by the "monitor's clock"; it was not to be altered by anyone other than the clock-keeper; and the warden was ordered to keep it locked up so no one unauthorized could alter the time. The warden kept time and rang a bell to signify the beginning and end of work, breakfast, and dinner, according to the following schedule: 5 to 8 a.m. work; 8 to 8.30 a.m. breakfast; 8.30 a.m. to noon work; noon to 1 p.m. dinner; 1 to 8 p.m. work. The disciplinary code of the Wedgwood Potters (Thompson 1967: 82–3) distinguished between those who arrived on time and those who were late. Later arrivers were given a certain period of warning; if they persisted in being tardy, their pay would be docked equivalent to the amount of late time. Reverend Clayton's pamphlet dating from 1755, *Friendly Advice to the Poor*, is an example of an effort to inculcate time-thrift and discipline generally (Thompson 1967: 83).

The contest over time became most intense in the early textile mills and engineering workshops, where the new industrial time discipline had been most rigorously imposed. In those factories, masters had attempted to remove all knowledge of time from workers. Only the master and his son had a watch, and workers' watches were confiscated. According to court testimony (Thompson 1967: 85–6), employers and managers altered time to their own advantage to extract more labor from workers without adjusting pay. They moved the clock ahead during the dinner hour, reducing dinnertime and forcing workers to return to work sooner, and they moved the clock backward before the end of the workday to extend work time at the end of the day. Skeptics doubt such "fiddling," but acknowledge that many workers believed they were being cheated (Landes 1983: 230). To people who had been accustomed to working at their own pace in fields and cottage industry, the factory was a kind of jail, with the clock as the lock. Resistance to the new discipline was expressed in their inability or reluctance to show up on time. Employers levied the harshest fines on latecomers and absentees. For the vast majority of workers who had no timepiece, employers sent around wakers to tap on windows in the dark morning hours. Because the sound of the one o'clock bell was insufficient to bring his workers back to the machines after the noon break – the workers said they missed the single peal – one employer made the clock sound thirteen times (Landes 1983: 229).

The mechanical clock became a template for scientists and mechanics. Clocks required precisely fabricated screws and gears, and these requirements led to improvements in lathes and other machines used to make them. The origins of the mechanical assembly line can be traced to Henry Ford's understanding of timepieces. His assembly line emphasized clocklike regular movements – a workflow regularly timed to produce the desired output at a steady, even pace. Ford's assembly line became an archetype for manufacturing practice throughout the world (Bluedorn 2002: 11–13).

Rationalized clock-time discipline that emerged in the monasteries and diffused against resistance in a commodified form via industrial capitalism is taken for granted today as the "natural state" for the Western way of life and its organizations. It forms part of the "deep structure" from which management theory and practice have arisen, and takes new forms in an era of electronic instantaneity and interconnectivity (Whipp et al. 2002: 13, 19). But rigid time discipline may not be effective in virtual work environments (Whipp et al. 2002: 129). And the complexity of Western economies today, with their great variety of jobs and lifestyles, and global reach, has created a multitude of temporal experiences and timescapes (Adam 1998; Gergen 1991; Whipp et al. 2002: 175, 187).

Time-work Discipline in the Twenty-first Century

Today we live in a global, 24/7, technology-mediated, flexible economy that is giving rise to changing temporal structures, cultures, and experiences (Rubin 2007b). New rhythms, paces, routines, and schedules are transforming workers' time sense, yielding "layered-task time" (Rubin 2007a) as a possible successor to clock time in select occupations and organizations. In some organizations current practice has shifted from linear sequencing and routines to layering of tasks, and work effort is determined by completion of tasks rather than hourly segments. This is especially the case where technological and organizational innovations have accelerated development, production, and market cycles, breaking down boundaries between home and office and potentially extending the workday to 24 hours, seven days a week – or at least creating the feeling of work-all-the-time. Layered-task time encompasses the longer hours that characterize much contemporary work, particularly among salaried professional, managerial, and technical workers, who in the US are exempt from the overtime provisions of the Fair Labor Standards Act, and the multiplicity of tasks that workers attempt to complete simultaneously. As with clock time, there is still considerable pressure to maximize productivity, and time is still money, but now it is in terms of task completion. Increased pressure and technological capacity allow the tasks to become layered upon one another, not unlike the complex layering of household tasks, child care, and leisure undertaken by harried parents who, aided by machines, wash a load of dishes while they fold freshly laundered towels with an eye on the TV and help children with their homework (Negrey 1993).

Layered-task time includes several components (Rubin 2007a: 531–2). In addition to longer hours, it entails simultaneity, fragmentation, contamination, and constraint. Employees under layered-task time regimes work on multiple tasks simultaneously but discontinuously. The multiple tasks do not necessarily require the same kinds of skill or attention, and activities may interrupt and contradict one another (contamination). Layered tasks are constrained by irregular deadlines, employees' autonomy, and employees' positions within the organization. Under layered-task time, workers squeeze more tasks into any given time unit, and, although it is an empirical question, they exercise a certain measure of autonomy to make judgments regarding the most effective ways to multitask.

Flexible employment contracts (Barker and Christensen 1998; Belous 1989; Carre et al. 2000; Golden 2001; Houseman and Polivka 1999; Hudson 1999; Kalleberg 2000; Kalleberg et al. 2000; Kalleberg 2007; Negrey 1993; Presser 2003; Rubin 1996; Tilly 1996; and others), such as those associated with part-time, temporary, and contract employment, also contribute to a new time discipline. A "postmodern" time sense has emerged, characterized by hurry sickness, speed-up, concern for integrating work and family, and technologies that erase boundaries of time and space (Rubin 2007b), as well as job instability for some workers. Employees' experience of time on the job is related to organizational routines, schedules, pacing, allocation, sequencing, synchronizing, and punctuality, but there may be conflict between organizational demands and individual "temporal personalities," that is, monochronic or polychronic preferences (Bluedorn 2002; Rubin 2007b: 6, 8), family life, and the need for stable employment. The difference between organizational demands and individual needs and preferences creates "temporal mismatches" (Kalleberg 2007) such that many are overworked, underemployed, or working hours that are incompatible with personal preference. Yet organizations exist in a policy environment that influences industry and organizational practices. Organizations adhere to policy, complying with wage and hours laws and, where they exist, labor union contracts, but keeping part-time workers' hours below a threshold at which providing additional or any employment benefits would be required; operate on the margins of policy, "innovating" in the interstices of law where no policy exists; or outright violate policy, such as expecting workers to work off the clock, in violation of wage and hours laws. While many authors emphasize the newness of flexible employment contracts in recent decades, others argue that flexibility has always been a characteristic of employment in capitalist systems. In this view, "social scientists have 'discovered' what casual wage labourers (sic) and those outside paid employment – very largely women and youth – already knew, that not all 'work' is stable and secure" (Pollert 1988: 43; Pollert 1991). Increased vulnerability of labor, speed, or intensity of work today is occurring in a weakened union environment (Maume and Purcell 2007). While, arguably, flexibility has always been a characteristic of capitalist employment practices, for a time in the mid-twentieth century in the US labor unions gained sufficient strength to reduce instability and vulnerability in some sectors. Garment manufacturing is a good example, where labor unions were able to marginalize sweatshops and curb wage and hours violations until increased global competition in later decades has recently contributed to their resurgence (Ross 2004). Outside the US, unions have had similar effects, as will be seen in chapter 5.

Gendered Time

Commodification theory undergirds a social class analysis at its most fundamental level – the relation between employers and workers. The history of early capitalism permits a look at this essential relationship, but class relations today are more differentiated and complex, marked by variations in occupation, education, income, ethnicity, and gender – and, increasingly, work time. A bifurcated distribution of work time – long hours among professionals and managers and short hours among service workers (more on this in chapter 3) – parallels an increasingly bifurcated class structure. The shrinking manufacturing working class coincides with a shrinking percentage of the US workforce that works 40-hour weeks. Commodification theory offers a conceptual framework for understanding workers' lack of control of work time and, because work schedules tend to dominate daily life, time more generally. But commodification theory is limited by its focus on paid work. Time is also "structured through social relations of gender" (Sirianni and Negrey 2000: 59), in patterns of gender difference across and within paid work and unpaid work in the home. A feminist perspective that puts gender at the center of analysis is a necessary complement to commodification theory to more fully understand work time. Commodification theory by itself overlooks gender as a factor in (1) the differential valuing of paid work and unpaid work, and (2) paid work in the context of a gendered "rest of life" (Sirianni and Negrey 2000: 60).

Other theories have been developed to explain the distribution of time across paid work and other activities, but these theories often overlook gender as well. Becker (1965) exemplifies the neoclassical approach to time allocation, arguing that actors attempt to maximize the allocation of scarce time by making rational choices between paid work and other activities. Linder (1970), among the scholars who study complexity of options in modern society, argued that people try to economize on their time resources by obtaining an "equal yield" in all the various sectors of time use. One way to increase the yield is to accelerate consumption by increasing its goods intensity – and time devoted to paid work supports this consumption. The higher the value of goods consumed per unit of time, the higher the yield. This can be achieved by consuming more expensive versions of the same commodity, by consuming more goods simultaneously, or by consuming successively a number of commodities, each for a shorter period of time (Sirianni 1987: 175). Linder's theory is especially provocative today, in a period of heightened consciousness of global warming. The climate crisis brings into question the advisability of high rates of goods consumption.

Applying neoclassical time allocation theory to the household, Becker (1981: 18–19) argued that "at most one member of an efficient household could invest in both market and household capital and would allocate time to both sectors." He justified that this member is the woman – leaving the man free to pursue labor-market activities and human capital investments – by appealing to biological differences associated with bearing and rearing children and the gender wage gap in the labor market: biological differences give women an advantage relative to men in household production, at least in the initial stages, and gender-based wage differentials reinforce the pattern. Becker, however, ignores the various normative and institutional factors that account for the lower value of women's time in paid work, and his postulate of utility maximization in the distribution of household labor time holds up only under certain assumptions. For wives to make substantial contributions to paid work in response to household need, and yet for husbands not to make significant contributions to household labor time in response to such need, can be seen as utility maximizing only if wives, dead on their feet after a double day, are always more productive in household labor than their husbands (Berk 1985: 153). Further, this gender division of labor assumes it is nearly always the case that "the net household gain when the wife trades the 'next' household hour for a market hour exceeds the net gain to the household than when the husband trades the 'next' market hour for a household hour" (Berk 1985: 153). Such assumptions are upheld only if men always earn more in the "next" market hour than women and men are always less productive than women in doing household work. Thus, in addition to producing utilities, men and women divide up market time and household labor time in such a way that they are also "producing gender" (Berk 1985: 201ff) – which is just as much about producing relations of dominance and submission and reaffirming a gendered alignment of husband and wife as it is about maximizing utilities in the strict sense of that term. Hochschild's (1989) study, *The Second Shift*, in which she observed the division of housework and child care among 10 dual-earner couples, showed how women continue their traditional roles as primary caregivers even when employed, with a stressful "second shift" of unpaid work at home, and is just one of many that supports this notion (Sirianni and Negrey 2000: 64–5). There have been significant changes in women's and men's allocation to paid work and unpaid work in the home since Becker's theories were published, suggesting that utility maximization is not fixed but historically specific. As conditions change, decisions regarding rational action change. And because such decisions are infused with gender, the most prominent predictor of time use (Robinson and Godbey 1997: 17), gender relations change.

Feminist scholars advanced the notion of a public/private split dominated by an ideology that traditionally assigned women to the domestic sphere and its time regimen. Time in the home is not the rigid, repetitive clock time that emerged with the factory system; it is more task-oriented where seasonal and natural rhythms like day and night, babies and children (Everingham 2002), and the needs of the ailing and aging matter. Domestic time is subordinated to – and often clashes with – paid work time, and its status and structure are shaped profoundly by how paid work is structured. Domestic time is not measured; nor is it valued in the same way as paid work time. Pressures, however, from paid work routines and "time-deepening" behavior (Robinson and Godbey 1997: 39) of people driven to "do" more create a sense of speed-up and hurry sickness in our nanosecond culture (Gleick 1999) that can lead to a mechanistic temporal logic at home (Everingham 2002: 348).

Feminist theory and the macroeconomic history of human society contextualize work time in the largest sense and inform our understanding of changes in work-time practices and conventions, which will be explored throughout the book. At the middle range is the history of work time in specific places. The next chapter examines the history of work time in the US, from the colonial period to the establishment of the 40-hour legal standard.

2
Work-time Reduction in the US

It is common today to focus on worker struggles over pay, working conditions, and job duties, but an additional distinctive feature of capitalist society is the fight over work time. Capitalists seek to maximize labor productivity, including the amount of time workers work, for the wages they pay, whereas workers seek to minimize their work time (and maximize their pay) to have time for "what we will." As Western industrial societies developed and wages and living standards improved, work hours declined. The reduction of work hours was not "natural" or automatic, however; nor was it granted freely by employers. Generally, work-time reduction occurred in response to considerable pressure from workers motivated by concerns for political participation, leisure, and education; the health-and-safety consequences of long hours of work; protections for select groups of workers, especially women and children; and work sharing in times of high unemployment. Shorter hours and higher wages have been important goals of labor unions, and achieving either goal depended on sufficient union power. During some periods, hours took precedence over wages, but in recent decades protecting jobs and benefits has taken precedence over reducing hours.

Labor activism under crisis conditions was the main precursor to reducing work hours in the United States through the Great Depression, especially after 1900 (Steinberg 1982), although employers were typically reluctant to acquiesce.

Reducing hours was a greater threat to employers' *control* than raising pay, because they believed the latter could be more easily reversed (when prices fell, at least in the nineteenth century) (Cross 1988a: 11). Thus, workers' agitation for shorter hours was not always successful and often ambivalent. During economic downturns, when the incentive to share jobs was high, they lacked bargaining power. During booms, when labor markets were tight and bargaining power was enhanced, they preferred long hours to offset income lost during the previous recession (Cross 1988a: 11) and/or in anticipation of the next. The decades after World War II, however, were generally characterized by labor quiescence regarding work hours. This passivity has been attributed to a paradigm shift among Americans from a concern with working conditions, such as hours, to wages, benefits, full employment, and consumption (Hunnicutt 1988; Roediger and Foner 1989; Schor 1991; Woloch 1996). In recent decades, work hours emerged again as an issue, particularly among parents but also among part-time workers desiring more hours of employment and non-standard hours workers desiring more stable work schedules. The re-emergence of the issue, however, has to date not been a major source of coalition among workers within and without labor unions in the US. By contrast, work hours have been a significant political issue in a number of countries outside the US – a topic that will be explored more fully in chapter 5.

This chapter reviews the highlights of the 10- and eight-hour movements in the US and examines the conditions under which today's normative 40-hour five-day workweek emerged.[1] Likely unknown by many Americans, there was a federal legislative effort in the 1930s to reduce the workweek to 30 hours, which came amazingly close to being successful. Its culmination was the 1938 Fair Labor Standards Act (FLSA), which established the 40-hour five-day workweek. Subsequent efforts to reduce this legal standard have been unsuccessful, although shorter full-time hours have become the norm in select industries and occupations[2] and there have been isolated experiments with 30-hour workweeks. Two cases, one enduring five decades since the 1930s, at Kellogg's, in Battle Creek, Michigan, and one more recent and short-lived, at a small company in Indiana, Metro Plastics, are discussed at the end of this chapter.

The earliest efforts to reduce work time in the US developed in small artisan shops in a merchant capitalist economy, quite distinct from the English condition of mechanization and industrialization analyzed by Thompson (1967). In the US, reorganizations, subdivisions, and speed-ups of production spurred new attitudes about time, and these were colored by a republican ideology that placed a strong value on political participation (Roediger and Foner 1989: 1–2; Murphy 1988: 64; Rock 1988: 23–4), individual dignity (Cross 1988a: 9; Rock 1988: 30), and religious practice (Murphy 1988: 71). Reducing work hours was the prime demand in America's first industrial strike, its first citywide trade union councils, its first labor party, its first general strikes, its first organization uniting skilled and unskilled workers, its first strike by females, and its first attempts at regional and national labor organization. The length of workdays has been the American labor movement's central issue during its most dynamic periods of organization (Roediger and Foner 1989: vii) and begs the question, should the struggling contemporary labor movement make work time its central issue today? Often coincident with labor pressure, political reform campaigns to shorten the workday grew from early efforts to protect women and children; demands that governments set an example by establishing shorter hours for their employees; and calls for local, state, and federal laws limiting maximum hours of all workers. The historical decrease of hours in the US was gradual and piecemeal, often local and uneven (Roediger and Foner 1989: viii, x; Cross 1988a: 12; Murphy 1988: 59), and reflected American workers' increasing wages and improving standards of living. It is, however, a history of rather steady reduction in work hours until World War II. Since then, there have been no federal legislative successes to reduce work time – indeed, there has been little pressure for such change due at least in part to our preoccupation with consumption – but "market forms" of work-time reduction (Negrey 1993) have occurred in recent decades in the forms of part-time and temporary employment. Increasing proportions of Americans work short hours, as part-time workers, for example, or long hours, as professionals and managers (Jacobs and Gerson 1998).

Citizenship, Leisure, Education, and Health

The history of the 10-hour movement, which transcended most of the nineteenth century, reveals themes of political participation, leisure, education, and health within nascent political sovereignty and advancing industrialization. Workers wanted time for active citizenship, recreation and relaxation, and pursuits of the mind; and they wanted limits on the toll long hours of work could take on them physically and mentally.

Colonial America was heir to longstanding British concern over work hours by guilds and government. Regular work hours for laborers and craftsmen in colonial America generally extended from sunrise to sunset at least six days per week. Workdays of 14 hours in summer and 11 hours in winter were common, although custom made an average of just over 10 hours normative. A strong Puritan heritage and mercantilist strictures against idleness elevated steady labor to a significantly more exalted position than would be the norm in a pre-industrial society (Roediger and Foner 1989: 2–4). In 1663, for example, Massachusetts banned spending time "idly or unprofitably" (Mansfield 2011). Since most colonial artisans worked for themselves or looked forward to doing so, artisans controlled and were rewarded for their own labor (Roediger and Foner 1989: 4). Master craftsmen worked in their own shops or lodgings, worked their own hours, made goods to order, and were thus task oriented (Rock 1988: 22, 25–6). Puritanism and ambition were powerful forces, especially when combined, embodied in the legend of the historical figure of Benjamin Franklin (Rock 1988: 23), whose aphorisms have been passed down to schoolchildren throughout the generations.

The sunrise-to-sunset workday was punctuated by many breaks, variety, and conformity to natural work cycles and religious presentiments. There was little opposition to this routine. The only recorded action taken by workers in the

American colonies was in December 1724, by barbers in Boston, who reduced their workweek by refusing to shave or dress wigs on Sunday mornings. There were also colonial protests over working on Christmas Day. By 1725, most colonies had completed Sabbatarian legislation that banned Sunday labor (Roediger and Foner 1989: 5). These "blue laws" were common until recent decades when retailers began extending their business hours, and consumers' shopping time, into Sundays.

After Independence, the desire to participate in republican government grew; but opportunity was predicated upon available time (Roediger and Foner 1989: 7) and, among merchants, financial ambition (Rock 1988: 24). Building tradesmen in New York City in the 1780s undertook, it appears, the first sporadic disputes in US history concerning a day's work. Philadelphia carpenters mounted America's first strike for the 10-hour day in May 1791; this was a brief and unsuccessful effort to win work hours from 6 a.m. to 6 p.m., with two hours for meals (Roediger and Foner 1989: 7).

The initial protests over work hours in the nineteenth century were informal ones that resisted incursions on the customary schedule of the workday. Merchant capitalists often maintained the traditional sunrise-to-sunset workday and eliminated part of the time customarily allotted for meals, drink, and rest. Workers paid piece rates were often required to work more when wages fell and prices rose. The first major American strike involving both men and women was over breaks: in 1824, weavers in Pawtucket, Rhode Island, walked out in an attempt to forestall the employer's effort to add an hour to the workday by cutting time for meals. Similarly, factory workers in Paterson, New Jersey, demanded the 10-hour day when they went on strike over their employer's moving the dinner hour from noon to 1 p.m. The owners fired the strike leaders and acceded on the timing of lunch, but did not give in to the 10-hour demand (Roediger and Foner 1989: 9–11).

Increasingly, a key aspect of workers' complaints was the lack of time for education and leisure. Some 25 percent of labor offensives during the Jacksonian period were about work hours. The prevalence of child labor connected the issues of work hours and education. Actions occurred throughout New England and the Mid-Atlantic, including Baltimore, Boston, Lowell, New York City, Philadelphia, Paterson, and Pawtucket. In 1834, advocates in Massachusetts argued for legislation to establish a six-hour day for female and child laborers; advocates in Lowell argued that eight hours was enough for anyone to work; a year later, children agitated on their own behalf in Paterson. With advancing success from city to city, the number of strikes over the 10-hour demand declined in the last five years of the 1830s, and trade unionists turned their attention to higher wages. With the Depression of 1837, however, employers dismantled trade unions (their legal standing remained insecure for the next century) and rolled back the 10-hour system, although employers cut wages far more frequently than they augmented hours. With markets glutted and high rates of unemployment, it made little sense to add work hours (Roediger and Foner 1989: 19–37).

Reports from Philadelphia in the 1830s documented that youth commonly worked 14-hour days; immigrants from both England and Ireland maintained they worked longer and harder in the US than in Europe; and physicians testified to the ill effects of long hours on health. State action coexisted with efforts to make the federal government set an example by granting 10 hours to its manual employees. Some Philadelphia shipyards had granted 10 hours in 1834, and many shipwrights refused to continue to work the 12 hours required by the US Navy until the president ordered the Secretary of the Navy to grant 10 hours in the Philadelphia yards (Roediger and Foner 1989: 38–9).

The nation's first municipal ordinance setting 10 hours as the daily maximum, which applied only to city workers, was passed on June 4, 1835, in Philadelphia, in response to a walkout of public workers and receipt of petitions signed by "many thousand citizens" in support of the workers (Roediger and Foner 1989: 33). On March 31, 1840, President Martin Van Buren issued a broadly applicable executive order granting the 10-hour day to all government employees engaged in manual labor. This order capped more than a decade of intense activity surrounding the 10-hour issue (Roediger and Foner 1989: 40–1). The nation's first 10-hour law enacted at the state level was passed in New Hampshire seven years later. Local efforts had spread the 10-hour day prior to these national and state actions.

Protections for children and women were central to early work-time reduction efforts. America's first child labor law had been enacted in Massachusetts in 1836, forbidding employers from hiring a child under age 15 in any manufacturing corporation unless the child had studied under a qualified teacher for at least three months during the previous year. This was an important precedent for the state's legislation in 1842 limiting factory labor to 10 hours daily for youth under 12 (Roediger and Foner 1989: 37–8).

Women textile workers played a particularly distinctive role in the movement for the 10-hour day. During the late 1820s and 1830s, their workday averaged between 12 and 13 hours, according to investigations, travelers' accounts, and reminiscence. They probably found this routine confining, especially in summer, with little or no time for outdoor activities during daylight except on Sundays. Some factories also took extraordinary steps to shut out the outdoors; windows were nailed shut to regulate changes in humidity and prevent thread breakage. Family-type early mills, however, allowed for varied, self-paced work, so those conditions were not especially alienating. Records of the Hamilton Company Mills in Lowell suggest that many women resisted the factory discipline of mills by running away. Because at this time women's wage-working years were assumed to be temporary, formal protest tended to focus on wages rather than conditions and hours (Roediger and Foner 1989: 43–9; Sklar 1988).

A sharp increase in protest over work hours occurred in the 1840s, coinciding with production speed-ups in the form of longer hours, use of artificial lighting, tighter supervision, faster work pace, the "stretch-out" (a larger number of looms to tend per worker), and wage decline relative to increased productivity. Women shaped arguments for the 10-hour day around issues of health, intellect, and political participation. Statewide petition drives were their preferred action (see Sklar 1988 on the effort in Massachusetts). Efforts to win the 10-hour day in Massachusetts failed when the legislature ignored petitions it received in 1845 precisely because they were signed by women – they had defied a taboo on public speaking. Legislative success in New Hampshire in 1847, however, did not quell protest, as the law's inefficacy became clear. In addition to other loopholes, the law prescribed no penalties for employers who violated it. Legislation passed in Pennsylvania in 1848 contained similar loopholes (Roediger and Foner 1989: 49–61). The women's 10-hour movement disintegrated with the serious depression in the New England textile industry between 1848 and 1851. Employers threatened to move jobs if 10-hour schedules were enforced (Roediger and Foner 1989: 64).

US activism for 10 hours coincided with the same objective in England. The English movement was the first to unite labor broadly behind a specific objective. Although the Ten Hours Act of 1847 applied officially only to women and children, in practice it affected the regulation of all textile workers and was the culmination of popular struggle that began in 1818. It promised freedom from master and mill and time for political participation (Weaver 1988).

Workers' protests over hours in the US peaked in 1853. The most dramatic action occurred in Cincinnati, at the time the nation's third largest producer of manufactured goods. There, 17 crafts organized to seek shorter hours. Strikes also occurred in San Francisco, where the longshoremen won a nine-hour day, and at sites in Pennsylvania and Virginia. A number of subsequent strikes in various places were defensive efforts to resist the lengthening of hours. The movement was not confined to factory workers in the heavily industrialized areas of the northeast. After 1854, protests spread south and west to Richmond, Charleston, New Orleans, and Memphis, and involved clerks, artisans, day laborers, and farm workers, as well as factory workers (Roediger and Foner 1989: 67–70).

By 1855, legislatures in at least 14 states had considered the matter of shorter hours. New Jersey (1851), Rhode Island (1853), California (1853), and Connecticut (1855) emulated New Hampshire, Pennsylvania, and Maine by passing ineffectual 10-hour laws. Georgia reaffirmed that the workday for whites under age 21 should be from sunrise to sunset, with meals allowed at customary times. New York rejected a 10-hour law in 1853, but allowed 10 hours for public employees. In Massachusetts, debate and committee hearings on the

10-hour day became almost annual, and the state almost passed a 10-hour Bill in 1853. This proliferation of debate suggests 10 hours became a national issue. It did not. The reduction of hours in some places between 1852 and 1855 led to a decline in labor action on hours, and rising North–South tensions before the Civil War contributed to declining interest (Roediger and Foner 1989: 76–7).

Box 2.1:   Time for what we will

With declining work autonomy, industrial workers in Worcester, Massachusetts, sought autonomy in leisure and recreation. A "right to leisure" (Rosenzweig 1983: 39) played an important part in movements for the shorter workday there, in addition to the desire to reduce widespread unemployment.

By the late 1800s, 10 hours was the norm in Worcester factories. After Massachusetts passed a comprehensive liquor license law in 1875, permitting the legal operation of public drink places, leisure time and space moved from "kitchen barrooms" to public saloons (Rosenzweig 1983: 41). Saloons became sites of working-class community, organized by occupation, ethnicity, and/or neighborhood (Rosenzweig 1983: 53). As saloons declined in the face of public resistance, other leisure places emerged, especially movie theaters (Rosenzweig 1983: 191–2).

Vacations did not become common for blue-collar workers until the 1940s. Therefore, summer holidays such as the Fourth of July and Labor Day (the latter first celebrated in 1882) loomed larger, as did traditional ethnic holidays, although these often had to be adapted to work routines (Rosenzweig 1983: 69–70).

Crowded in tenements, Worcester's workers demanded public play space, especially parks and playgrounds. Worcester's 1886 comprehensive park plan was one of the first in the US endorsing parks as settings for "healthful recreation" (Rosenzweig 1983: 135). Work, however, remained the most fundamental constraint on recreation.

From Haymarket to Henry Ford

> We want to feel the sunshine;
> We want to smell the flowers;
> We're sure that God has willed it.
> And we mean to have eight hours.
> We're summoning our forces from
> shipyard, shop and mill;
> Eight hours for work, eight hours
> for rest, eight hours for what we will.
>
> Hymn of the Eight Hour Movement (1886)
> (Walsh and Zacharias-Walsh 1998: 8)

The 10- and eight-hour movements overlapped historically, but I separate them for analytic purposes because of
distinctive events and circumstances that shaped them. While
leisure and protection of children and women were enduring
concerns, job creation during periods of labor surplus and
time for consumption to fuel economic growth became new
rationales for work-time reduction. Calls for eight hours
occurred amid calls for 10, instances of eight-hour agitation
occurred earlier than the Civil War, and 10-hour successes
were achieved into the early twentieth century. But a distinctive eight-hour movement, lasting about 70 years until the
Great Depression, can be dated from the Civil War period,
when Short Time Committees, unaffiliated with organized
labor, sprang up in factory towns (Sklar 1988: 109). By 1866,
organizations promoting the eight-hour workday thrived
across the US, driven by concerns about the entry of some
500,000 men into the labor market upon demobilization after
the war, increasingly alienating labor associated with mechanization, and the productive potential of machinery (Green
2006; Roediger and Foner 1989: 81–3; Rosenzweig 1983).
Proponents of a new consumer society believed an increase
in leisure would create new wants and cause workers to seek
higher wages. Rising demand and ability to consume would
in turn encourage more production, creating economic
growth. Many anti-slavery theorists believed the inability of
slave labor to consume had been the chief barrier to economic
growth in the South (Green 2006: 26; Roediger and Foner
1989: 85; Rosenzweig 1983: 195).

Southern and border cities became new sites of activism after the abolition of slavery guaranteed that members of labor organizations could no longer be threatened with replacement by slave labor (Roediger and Foner 1989: 87). (With the entry of freed slaves into the labor market, racial occupational segregation limited direct competition for jobs by race.) In 1864, Louisville hosted the founding of the International Industrial Assembly of North America, whose delegates advocated a nationwide campaign to make eight hours a legal workday, but they never met again. Two years later, 60 delegates from unions and eight-hour leagues met in Baltimore to convene the National Labor Union, which made shorter-hours legislation the center of its early program. Baltimore was home to one of the most powerful local eight-hour movements in the nation. In 1866, the city passed the country's first thoroughgoing municipal ordinance giving city workers an eight-hour day (Roediger and Foner 1989: 87).

Detroit also adopted the eight-hour day for most city employees, and Evansville, Indiana, passed an eight-hour ordinance as well, both in 1866. Wisconsin passed an eight-hour law in 1867. By 1868, eight states had passed eight-hour laws, and during that same year Congress approved a statute making eight hours a legal day's work for employees of the federal government. In each instance, however, the laws lacked provisions for enforcement, contained loopholes, or became objects of conflicting interpretation. In no state did workers uniformly gain an eight-hour day, and only in New York City was there a general local change to that standard (Roediger and Foner 1989: 90–2, 101). Strikes by Massachusetts textile workers, Pennsylvania miners, and others seeking enforcement of laws applied pressure that kept the issue before Congress. The larger legal question had to do with the power of states to regulate the economy (Roediger and Foner 1989: 101–10).

Work hours remained long throughout the early 1880s. The most complete figures covering 552 establishments in 40 industries and 28 states date from 1883, and indicate that the average workday was still over 10 hours, including Saturdays. By that year, a 10-hour six-day week had become the norm in most of the surveyed industries, but glaring exceptions persisted. Street railway drivers and bakers in various locales worked more than 15 hours daily. Complaints concerning the shaving of time by employers arose regularly, especially in textile mills where, operatives complained, the manipulation of clocks often added 20 to 30 minutes to the agreed-upon workday. One Connecticut report showed that one child in three, one woman in five, and one man in eight working in cotton factories stayed more than 10 hours per shift (Roediger and Foner 1989: 123).

Arguably, the most significant mass action demanding eight hours, commonly referred to as "Haymarket," unfortunately turned violent, resulting in the death and injury of a number of police officers and protesters, and had a paradoxical effect that led to a loss of momentum for the eight-hour movement, divided Americans over the episode and subsequent trial, and raised doubts about the meaning of freedom and justice (Green 2006; Roediger and Foner 1989; Sklar 1988). May 1, 1886, had been designated by Samuel Gompers and the Federation of Organized Trade and Labor Unions (FOTLU, the predecessor to the American Federation of Labor) as the date on which the eight-hour system would take effect in all industries in the US. The FOTLU sought to enforce the eight-hour system with a mass strike on that date. The demand for eight hours had been raised during a depression, to "spread the work" and alleviate unemployment, and matured during a recovery, which made workers less fearful of losing jobs by striking. The trade union wing of the anarchist movement supported enthusiastically the idea of a mass strike on May 1. Thousands actually went on strike before May 1. One estimate sets the number of strikers on May 1 at 190,000, with an additional 150,000 who demonstrated or won a voluntary reduction in hours. An estimated 45,000 participated in New York; 32,000 in Cincinnati; 4,700 in Boston; 4,250 in Pittsburgh; 3,000 in Detroit; 2,000 in St Louis; 1,500 in Washington, DC; and 13,000 in a number of other cities combined. Mass actions continued for several days afterward in a number of places. Protesting raised drawbridges that prevented them from joining mass meetings in the city center, a group of immigrants, estimated at about 3,000 (Roediger and Foner 1989: 141), convened at Haymarket Square in Chicago on May 4 (Sklar 1988: 114). During the last speech of the day, after about two thirds of the audience had gone home, police issued an order to disperse and waded into the crowd, being met seconds later with a bomb that exploded in front of them. One officer died and many others were injured. An estimated 70 protesters were also injured, at least one fatally, when police fired at protesters in response to the bombing. Seven additional police officers died later from wounds received in the gunfire. The violence at Haymarket resulted in police dragnets that yielded hundreds of arrests in searches of homes and labor organizations, often without warrants (Green 2006; Roediger and Foner 1989: 141). Thirty-one indictments were handed down, eight cases selected for trial, and four protesters ultimately executed by hanging (on November 11, 1887, followed by a massive public funeral on November 13). Wildly divergent testimonies, and fabricated evidence (Green 2006: 298), were given at trial regarding events after the police order to disperse, particularly conflicting reports of the origin of the bomb, the identity of the bomber, and gunfire from the crowd in addition to police gunfire (Green 2006: 188–9). Antipathy toward anarchists, immigrants, and organized labor, and sympathy for stricken police officers framed a criminal conspiracy trial that divided Chicagoans, and Americans, by class and nationality, and raised doubts about the meaning of freedom and justice in America (Green 2006). In 1893, the three surviving Haymarket convicts were pardoned by the governor of Illinois, who feared the law had been bent to deprive immigrants of their civil liberties and that the Haymarket defendants had been tried for murder without proof of direct connection to the bomb thrower. They had been charged with murder for allegedly having knowledge of an assassination plot. The pardon itself was controversial, some calling it a disgrace and the governor a traitor (Green 2006: 291–2).[3]

In an incident the day after Haymarket, in Milwaukee on May 5, 1886, troops fired into a crowd that had formed after the mayor banned crowds on the streets and in public places in reaction to the violence in Chicago. Nine protesters were killed (resulting in no indictments for murder), nearly 50 protesters were indicted on riot and conspiracy charges, and some served short prison terms of less than one year. After Haymarket and Milwaukee, the eight-hour campaign lost momentum (Green 2006; Roediger and Foner 1989; Sklar

1988), having lost credibility among middle-class reformers who believed it had been tainted by foreign radicalism (Sklar 1988: 114), and the leadership of the anarcho-syndicalist movement in the US, the most radical faction of the eight-hour movement, was decimated. Work hours did decline in 1886 among those who went on strike, however, and in that sense the mass action was successful. Federal statistics show the average workweek of all those who went on strike over work time in 1886 decreased from just under 62 to less than 59 (Roediger and Foner 1989: 129–44).

The bloc of center and left trade unionists that had built the eight-hour campaign in the 1870s and 1880s split in the wake of Haymarket, and the organized labor movement itself shrunk temporarily with the decline of the Knights of Labor, a national organization that had emerged in 1878 that enlisted skilled and unskilled workers alike, as well as farmers, small business owners, immigrants, and women (Green 2006; Hodson and Sullivan 2008: 130; Roediger and Foner 1989: 145). The American Federation of Labor (AFL) gradually favored a narrow craft unionism, rejecting the mass strike as a tactic for gaining the eight-hour day and, especially after 1894, largely ignoring political action as means to reform working conditions. Eight-hour agitation became episodic, and women, whose labor-force participation was increasing, became the strongest proponents of shorter work hours (Roediger and Foner 1989: 145). Reformers' focus shifted to protective labor legislation for women and children, centered on limitation of hours; Consumers' Leagues in a dozen states and Washington, DC, helped to pass or extend short hours legislation for women and/or children between 1898 and 1922 (Roediger and Foner 1989: 173). One weakness of the labor protection campaign is that it built its argument on the assumption of women's biological disadvantages rather than their double oppression as wage-workers and homemakers (Roediger and Foner 1989: 174–5).

Scientific management ("Taylorism"), associated with time-and-motion study and efficiency, represented a turning point in thinking about work time. The time clock had come into common use in the 1890s, and long hours signified a failure to adopt efficient methods to raise productivity within a fixed time. Henry Ford argued that fewer work hours would

Box 2.2: Women and children first: the entering wedge

Women marched at the forefront of the first US campaigns for shorter hours because they constituted the majority of the nation's then-most mechanized occupation, textile operatives (Sklar 1988: 105). They viewed legislative strategies as complementary to trade union activity (Sklar 1988: 107). Although women couldn't vote until early in the twentieth century, they were members of families where men did vote. For example, in 1853, some Massachusetts corporations responded to political pressure and reduced factory hours to 11 for male machinists. Women's hours were unchanged, but, in 1853, when Boston businessmen wanted to influence the popular vote on a new state Constitution, women's hours were also reduced to 11 (Sklar 1988: 109). The first 10-hour law for American women workers was enacted in Massachusetts in 1874, although it was 1879 when the last attempts to repeal it were defeated (Sklar 1988: 112). The most notable struggle over women's hours after 1880 took place in Chicago in the mid-1890s, after the path-breaking eight-hour law for women and children employed in manufacturing in Illinois was found unconstitutional by the Illinois Supreme Court (Sklar 1988: 114).

Contests over women's hours endured until 1908 when, in the Muller *v.* Oregon case, the US Supreme Court unanimously upheld an Oregon law that set a 10-hour limit on the workday of women in factories and laundries (Sklar 1988: 121; Woloch 1996). This decision sanctioned classification of workers by sex, and female protective labor laws prevailed until the second wave of the women's movement around 1970 (Steinberg 1982; Woloch 1996). Representing the state of Oregon, lawyer Louis D. Brandeis argued that freedom of contract could be curbed by the state to protect the health and welfare of its people. Sexist in its emphasis by today's standards, but conventional in its own time, the "Brandeis brief" claimed that overwork was more deleterious to women's health than men's because of women's unique role in bearing children.

Progressive reformers had embraced protective legislation for employed women in an effort to eventually win maximum hours legislation for all workers. Protective laws for women

(Continued)

and children moved to the top of the agenda as reformers encountered roadblocks to maximum hours laws for men. Reformers believed protective laws for women would establish precedents, serving as an "entering wedge." Four conditions in particular (McCammon 1995) allowed a gendered movement to counter the economic interests of employers: the ability to organize and form coalitions with powerful political actors, use of a legitimating ideology, historically specific circumstances, and the nature of particular forms of legislation being demanded. Moreover, laws that covered women also pertained to men who worked in the same industries. In Massachusetts, for example, limits on women's hours in textile mills also reduced men's hours in the mills. The model for the entering-wedge strategy, adapted to the American federalist system, had been England's factory laws. Since the beginning of the nineteenth century, Parliament had passed laws to limit work hours in mills and factories, first those of young apprentices, then of all child workers, and then of women (Woloch 1996: vii, 3, 5–6, 9; Sklar 1988: 110). Organized labor in the US had also been an obstacle to maximum hours legislation. The labor movement had been a proponent of the eight-hour day until the late nineteenth century, but the American Federation of Labor (AFL) favored collective bargaining and organizing tactics to achieve maximum hours regulations for its constituents – men in skilled trades. Thus, the AFL gave nominal support to maximum hours laws for women and children but rejected such measures for men in general, fearing legal protection was weak because laws could be challenged in the courts (Woloch 1996: 10–11). The National Consumers' League and its affiliates, headed by Florence Kelley, who had drafted the Illinois maximum hours law of 1893, opposed the unions by arguing that leisure is a human right, workers deserve to share in the gains from improved productivity, and this right could be attained only through statute because collective bargaining and organizing tactics covered only those workers in well-organized trades (Woloch 1996: 22–4).

States jumped on the bandwagon after the Muller decision – 24 in the legislative sessions of 1911 and 1913 – and enacted or expanded female protective labor laws (Sklar 1988: 121). The downside of these laws, as feminists made clear some 60 years later, is that they permitted discrimination against women by limiting women's work hours and employment opportunities (Kessler-Harris 1982; Ratner 1980; Steinberg 1982; Woloch 1996). Hours laws in certain circumstances increased women's share of employment, but did not alter patterns of occupational gender segregation (McCammon 1996).

In 1913, Oregon passed a law that established a maximum 10-hour day for all industrial workers but allowed employees to work overtime for another three hours if their employers paid them time and a half. In Bunting v. Oregon, in 1917, it was argued that the toxicity of industrial work justified a shorter workday for men. In upholding the Oregon legislation, the US Supreme Court acknowledged the constitutionality of hours legislation for men (Sklar 1988: 124; Woloch 1996: 45). However, whereas Muller v. Oregon had led to more states enacting female protective labor legislation, Bunting had no such effect, probably for several reasons. Organized labor favored direct trade union action to achieve shorter hours for men, but men preferred long hours and overtime pay, and by 1917 reformers were shifting their focus from maximum hours to a minimum wage (Woloch 1996: 46).

generate increased consumption, and he used hours reduction as a tactic to disarm organized labor.

Evidence as late as 1912 shows that Taylorism did not reduce the workday, however, but the average workweek in all industries did decline by 4.9 hours between 1890 and 1914. The American Federation of Labor (AFL) was the nominal umbrella under which work-time reduction occurred in a piecemeal, craft-by-craft fashion with an emphasis on the practical aims of eliminating unemployment (Roediger and Foner 1989: 147–51). The period around World War I was particularly significant. From 1905 to 1920, the average workweek of non-agricultural workers plummeted from 57.2 to 50.6; in manufacturing from 54.5 to 48.1. Thus, by 1920, in manufacturing the eight-hour day, six-day week was becoming normative. In 1910, just 8 percent of American workers labored 48 hours or less per week; in 1919, 48.6 percent did so. The proportion of workers laboring over 54 hours weekly declined from 70 to 26 percent during the same decade. Trade unionists started to look forward to a six-hour workday (Roediger and Foner 1989: 177).

Henry Ford offered a wage of five dollars a day, which he considered a family wage, in addition to granting the eight-hour day to his employees in 1914, justified by his consumption theory, in the hope of disarming the Industrial Workers of the World (IWW), which had led a brief unsuccessful strike of 5,000 Studebaker workers seeking eight hours and had won the shorter day at three Detroit metal-wheel factories in 1913. Quits and truancies were high at Ford's factories, reflecting alienation engendered by rapid rationalization of production. Labor turnover declined 90 percent and absenteeism was at least halved as a result of Ford's 1914 reforms (Roediger and Foner 1989: 189–93).

The Ford hours reduction is interesting for its novelty in American business and labor history, but business generally opposed Ford's action. Aware of this, Woodrow Wilson declined when Ford encouraged him to include a national eight-hour law in his presidential platform in 1916 (Roediger and Foner 1989: 194). However, in 1916, Congress passed the Adamson Act, which provided an eight-hour day to some railroad workers, and the Keating Owen Child Labor Law, which made eight hours the maximum workday for children aged 14 to 16 working in industries engaged in interstate commerce. The War Labor Polices Board and the War Labor Board provided for the eight-hour day on war contracts. The federal reforms came largely in response to agitation or threatened agitation by labor (Roediger and Foner 1989: 194).

In 1919, nearly half (48.6 percent) of all US agricultural (sic) workers had attained the 48-hour week (eight hours/six days), and a clear majority of organized labor had done so (Roediger and Foner 1989: 212). The movement to reduce work hours did not stop with this success, however. Gompers had briefly called for a seven-hour day during World War I. An unprecedented strike wave in 1919 sought to generalize and transcend the eight-hour day (Roediger and Foner 1989: 212–13). In the coalfields, well organized at the time but plagued by unemployment, the United Mine Workers became the first major American union to fight for the six-hour day. Unions in the clothing trades and in printing sought the

44-hour week. Strikes in the largely unorganized steel and textile industries attempted to enlist workers with very long hours around the demand for a workweek of six eight-hour days coupled with union recognition (Roediger and Foner 1989: 213).

The 1919 steel strike was the pivotal hours conflict of the period after World War I. It was a watershed in the organization of mass production industries, and its defeat partially marked the decline of aggressive union organizing and set the stage for a new series of efforts to reduce the workday in steel. Nearly one production worker in three labored 12 hours daily at US Steel in 1919. Wages did not enable workers to rise above the poverty level despite long shifts. Skilled American-born workers worked fewer hours than the unskilled immigrant workers, but few totaled less than 60 hours weekly. Layoffs in early 1919 gave added force to shorter hours, share-the-work arguments. Union recognition headed the list of demands, but below this were calls for an eight-hour day at an "American" wage, one day's rest in seven, and an end to 24-hour shifts. The strike peaked in late September 1919 with about 365,000 strikers at plants in Chicago, Wheeling, Johnstown, Lackawanna, Cleveland, Youngstown, Pueblo, and elsewhere (Roediger and Foner 1989: 222–5).

US Steel used anti-immigrant and anti-radical propaganda to sway public opinion about the strike. When the strike officially ended on January 8, 1920, production had already returned to normal in all major steel centers, and the 12-hour shift was intact. After the defeat of the steel strike, most trade union action concerning the workday was defensive until the limited five-day week campaigns of the late 1920s. The exceptions were the achievement of the eight-hour day for police and firefighters in New York City (Roediger and Foner 1989: 225–7).

In Steinberg's (1982: 10) analysis of legislation, the major campaigns for the eight-hour day were concentrated in two periods: 1884–6 and 1888–91. Subsequently, increasing numbers of states adopted maximum hours laws and laws regulating night work. In an examination of a sample of 28 of the 48 states constituting the US by 1930 (the six with the largest populations in 1930 and half of the remaining states, divided by region and drawn via systematic sampling), 26 percent had adopted maximum hours laws by 1900, 76 percent by 1920, and 92 percent by 1960. Laws regulating night work were adopted more slowly; 14 percent of the states in Steinberg's sample had done so by 1900, 60 percent by 1920, 83 percent by 1960, and 92 percent by 1970. Employee coverage ranged from a low of 4 percent (maximum hours) and 1 percent (night work) in 1900 to peaks of 19 percent (maximum hours) in 1960 and 5 percent (night work) in 1940 (Steinberg 1982: 62). In the period from 1900 to 1930, few employees had legal rights to overtime pay as stipulated in state laws. In Steinberg's (1982: 89–90) view, most coverage during this time resulted from a special class of pre-1900 legislation. Between 1860 and 1910, several states, especially in the Northeast or North Central regions, enacted what came to be called normal day's work or legal day's work laws. Most employees were paid by the day rather than the hour in the nineteenth century, and workdays expanded or contracted as was necessary to the employer. Normal day's work laws established a fixed number of hours constituting a workday and required that additional compensation be paid for additional hours of work. They pertained to laborers in manufacturing and mechanical industries as well as a host of industries that employed mostly men, such as mining and railroads. Until 1940, coverage extended to a small minority – 12 percent – of employees. Federal regulations regarding hours and overtime became a factor after the enactment of the Fair Labor Standards Act in 1938.

The five-day workweek

The idea of cutting the workweek by cutting the days of labor had its earliest origins in Sabbatarianism and, later, in the Saturday half-holiday campaigns begun in the late nineteenth century. There was scattered achievement of the five-day week as early as 1908, but the goal remained a dream for the vast majority of American workers (Roediger and Foner 1989: 237). In the early twentieth century, followers of the Jewish faith opposed Sunday blue laws in an effort to reclaim Saturday as the historical Sabbath, which they had lost in the US in the nineteenth and early twentieth centuries. They had been forced by society and their jobs to observe Sunday as the religious holiday. Rabbi Bernard Drachman, president of the Jewish Sabbath Alliance, as early as 1910 advocated observation of both Saturday and Sunday as days of rest by Christians and Jews alike, thus offering a compromise in the form of the five-day workweek (Hunnicutt 1988: 72–3).

As late as 1928, the National Industrial Conference Board identified 270 companies as having the five-day week, employing a combined 218,000 workers. Of these, 80 percent worked at Ford Motor Company. Other estimates put the number of workers enjoying a five-day workweek at 400,000, with almost half employed at Ford. Ford had begun experimentation with the five-day week in 1922 and announced general elimination of Saturday work, with the exception of a few jobs, throughout his factories in October 1926. In public statements, Ford offered the same rationale as he had when he granted the five-dollar eight-hour day 12 years earlier: less work time meant more consumption time. The five-day week at Ford occurred during a deep slump in demand for cars, however; was combined with cuts in pay; and thus could be dismissed as mere cover for slowing down production (Roediger 1988: 142–3). Large corporations almost universally opposed the five-day week; only three other corporations employing 2,000 workers followed Ford's lead. Mercantile leaders objected that store closings shut out shoppers. Factories that kept hours of more than 40 per week spread over five days were happiest with the five-day system. Few unions secured the five-day week through bargaining, and the AFL's continuing commitment to voluntarism led to disdain for legislative reform (Roediger and Foner 1989: 239–41). The official "birth" of the 40-hour workweek, in the form of eight-hour days and five-day weeks, did not occur until late in the next decade, during the Great Depression, as federal legislation that revised an earlier Bill to establish a 30-hour week.

Work Sharing and Fair Labor

During the Great Depression, demands for work-time reduction turned on notions of sharing the available work. Federal legislation introduced in the Senate to establish a 30-hour workweek was eclipsed by industry codes adopted under the terms of the National Industrial Recovery Act and subsequently revised to establish the 40-hour week enacted under the Fair Labor Standards Act.

In 1929, on the eve of the Great Depression, only 19 percent of workers in manufacturing were scheduled for fewer than 48 hours per week; 26.5 percent were at 48; 31.3 percent were between 49 and 54; 15 percent between 55 and 59; and 7.4 percent worked a schedule of 60 hours or longer. By way of contrast, virtually all of the industrialized nations of Europe and Australia enjoyed the eight-hour day, while the Soviet Union had introduced seven hours (Cross 1988a: 14–15; Roediger and Foner 1989: 243).

In October 1929, fewer than 1 million Americans were out of work. Just three months later, after the October 1929 stock-market crash, employment had fallen precipitously with 4 million out of work; the figure reached 9 million in October 1931 and passed 10 million in December. The number of jobless passed 11 million in January 1932, crossed 12 million in March, and surpassed 13 million in June. In January 1933, there were more than 14 million persons out of work. The bottom of the Great Depression was reached in March 1933, three and a half years after the 1929 crash, when in excess of 15 million were unemployed (Roediger and Foner 1989: 243), or approximately one third of all workers (Piven and Cloward 1971: 49; Steinberg 1982: 109). Moreover, those who continued to work suffered major cuts in wages (Steinberg 1982: 109), and very large numbers of the employed were on short time (Roediger and Foner 1989: 243). Because the economy had become one of national rather than local markets and the states had been rendered insolvent after the 1929 crash (Patterson 1969: 24–6; Steinberg 1982: 110), the plane of debate over work hours shifted to the federal level.

Early in the Great Depression, the Communist Party and the newly formed Trade Union Unity League began to organize the jobless into Unemployed Councils. The councils issued a call for nationwide demonstrations in support of passage of an unemployment insurance bill; an end to evictions; improved relief in cash and in kind; state and federal aid; and a workweek composed of five seven-hour days, with a six-hour day for harmful and strenuous occupations, without reduction in pay (Roediger and Foner 1989: 244).

The demand for shorter hours dominated the AFL Convention in October 1930; most of the discussion centered around the five-day week. By summer 1932, work sharing was receiving such enthusiastic support among *employers* (emphasis mine) that the movement crystallized into a national enterprise, and a share-the-work committee was appointed by President Herbert Hoover. Most unions opposed the idea, believing share-the-work meant share-the-misery. The shrinking number of actual work hours over a larger number of people with no increase in hourly wages would simply decrease the earnings of the employed (Roediger and Foner 1989: 244–5).

The AFL Executive Council urged President Hoover to call a conference of labor and industrial leaders to explore the early adoption of the five-day week and six-hour day for the nation's wage earners to create job opportunities for the unemployed. At its convention in November 1932, the AFL advocated the 30-hour week *with no reduction in weekly wages* (emphasis mine) and instructed the executive council to take steps toward having proper legislation introduced in the incoming session of Congress (Roediger and Foner 1989: 246).

US Senator Hugo L. Black (D-Alabama) obliged a few weeks later, introducing a 30-hour Bill on December 21, 1932. Witnesses in favor of the legislation cited technological improvements as the chief cause of unemployment. Industrial unions and those with large numbers of semiskilled and unskilled workers favored inclusion of minimum wage provisions. Most labor groups and the Bill's sponsor viewed it as a plan to reduce unemployment, increase total wages, increase aggregate demand, and start the wheels of recovery (Roediger and Foner 1989: 246–8). While organized business groups objected to the legislation, fearing inflexibility, Northern and Southern textile interests were intrigued by the prospect of legislation that would enforce a reduction of spindle-running time throughout their industry (Vittoz 1987: 83–4).

The Senate Judiciary Committee reported the Bill favorably on March 30, 1933, and urged Senate adoption. Debate concerned chiefly the Bill's scope. Some senators wanted exemptions for dominant industries in their states. Ultimately the Bill passed by a vote of 53–30 on April 6, 1933, less than four months after the legislation was introduced. It went to the House of Representatives 11 days later. The House Labor Committee acted favorably and Representative William P. Connery, Jr (D-Massachusetts), chair of the committee, urged House passage. Most of industry, led by the National Association of Manufacturers, opposed the Bill. President Franklin D. Roosevelt also opposed the Bill as unworkable and unconstitutional, believing the proposed National Industrial Recovery Act (NIRA) would reduce hours more rapidly and boost wages. The House Rules Committee buried the Black-Connery 30-hour Bill as a result of administrative pressure (Roediger and Foner 1989: 248–9).

The NIRA, adopted in June 1933, gave unprecedented voice to workers in diverse industries to influence the conditions of work, and included maximum work hours as a cornerstone. The NIRA declared a national state of emergency and accorded employees the right to organize and bargain collectively with employers to establish maximum work hours, minimum wages, and other labor standards subject to approval by the president (Vittoz 1987: 91–2, 95). Many employers, especially in heavy industry, refused to negotiate with independent trade unions; and work stoppages over the matter of union recognition increased dramatically subsequent to the NIRA. The number of employee days lost because of strikes tripled between June and September, and the calendar year 1933, especially the last half, witnessed the largest number of work stoppages during any 12-month period since 1921 (Vittoz 1987: 138). By 1935, renewal of the NIRA was doubtful, and, ultimately, the US Supreme Court nullified it in its Schecter decision in May 1935.[4] Following the demise of the NRA codes, there was an immediate reversion in private industries to the lower wages and longer hours that had prevailed before the codes were established. A US Bureau of Labor Statistics study of 16 important industries found that in all 16 weekly hours increased substantially in the 12 months following the nullification of the NIRA. The Roosevelt administration voiced concern over the lengthening of the workweek in the wake of the NRA codes, and it was reported that Roosevelt regretted that he had not supported Black's 30-hour bill (Roediger and Foner 1989: 251–2).

Although no 30-hour law was enacted during the Roosevelt administration, legislation did reduce work hours for some workers: the Motor Carriers Act of 1935 set maximum hours of employees in interstate transportation for safety considerations; the Postal Act of 1935 fixed the hours of all postal employees except charwomen and part-time employees at 40 hours per week; the National Bituminous Coal Conservation Act of 1935 regulated hours for coal miners (who had previously obtained the 35-hour week along with a wage increase in a union agreement in 1934); the Maritime Hours Law of 1936, which replaced a nine-hour day with the eight-hour day; and the Sugar Act of 1937 that limited the workday of children between 14 and 16 years of age to eight hours in the beet-sugar industry unless the family of the child owned the crop (Roediger and Foner 1989: 250, 252–3).

The NIRA had also created the Works Progress Administration (WPA), and work hours on WPA projects had been limited to 30 when feasible. The NRA codes, however, which covered some 22 million workers, established 40-hour weeks on average, with some weeks as long as 48. The 40-hour week was a proviso in 85 percent of the codes, which covered 50 percent of all workers. Less than 40 hours a week was provided for in about 7 percent of the codes, covering 12 percent of all workers. More than 40 hours was allowed in the remaining codes, which applied to 38 percent of workers (Roediger and Foner 1989: 249–50). These norms influenced the standards, "'an echo' of past progress" (Grossman 1978: 29), that were written into the Fair Labor Standards Act of 1938. The legislation for the FLSA was a revision, initially written in February 1935, of the original Black-Connery 30-Hour Work-Week Bill that had died in the House in 1933 (Roediger and Foner 1989: 250). Not only did FLSA address work hours, but it also established standards for a minimum wage and child labor.

Fair Labor Standards Act

The Fair Labor Standards Act was signed into law on June 25, 1938, by FDR, to become effective on October 24, 1938. FLSA has been called the "cornerstone" of federal labor legislation (McGaughey 1981: 252) and has been assessed as "second only to the Social Security Act" in significance (Elder and Miller 1979: 11). The FLSA established 44 hours as the maximum workweek initially, stepped down to 40 two years later, in the industries that were covered by the law; time and a half for overtime beyond 40 hours; and a minimum wage. At the time, organized labor criticized the law for setting the initial level of maximum hours too high, not establishing a limit on daily hours, failing to provide specific and enforceable provision to hold wages steady when hours were reduced, vague language relating to maximum hours and overtime pay, and weak language concerning child labor. Employer groups were strongly critical; and the National Association of Manufacturers (NAM), for example, argued that it was a step in the direction of communism, bolshevism, fascism, and Nazism. Big business challenged the legislation in court on constitutional grounds, but it was upheld in two cases (Roediger and Foner 1989: 253–6).[5] Numerous exemptions limited initial application of the FLSA to about one fifth of the labor force (Grossman 1978: 22). By the late twentieth century, the law extended to about 60 percent of all wage and salary workers (Smith 1986: 7).

Concerned about absorbing World War II veterans and the labor-displacing effects of automation, motivations similar to those that inspired work-time reformers after the Civil War, auto workers, especially at the large United Automobile Workers (UAW) local at the Ford River Rouge plant in Detroit, considered reducing work hours to 30 with 40 hours pay. Walter Reuther, then president of the UAW, hesitated, in the Cold War environment, in part because of Communist Party support for the idea (Cutler 2004). He also believed workers wanted a higher standard of living with more material goods, an objective that couldn't be attained with fewer hours of work (Hunnicutt 1996: 148). His lack of support ultimately defeated the movement in the UAW. In the early 1960s, Presidents John F. Kennedy and Lyndon Johnson also made public statements in opposition to reduced work hours (the target was 35 by then), believing instead that the "War on Poverty" could be won through economic growth and the creation of new jobs (Cutler 2004).

The last time the federal government wrestled with the issue of generalized work-time reduction was in the late

1970s, during what was then the deepest recession since the Great Depression, after US Representative John Conyers (D-Michigan) introduced legislation to amend the FLSA by reducing the standard workweek to 35 hours, increasing premium pay for overtime, and eliminating mandatory overtime. Proponents argued that reduction of the workweek would decrease unemployment and offset the social costs of unemployment; combat technological unemployment; relieve stress on the job, thereby improving morale and productivity; decrease absenteeism; and improve the quality of life off the job. They believed it could also help conserve energy if work-time reduction decreased commuting and permitted buildings to be closed part of each week. By employing more people, income tax revenues would increase as would net consumption demand. Opponents, however, believed work-time reduction would increase labor costs and bring about a decline in productivity if unqualified persons were employed. It would be inflationary because increased labor costs would lead to an increase in prices, which, paradoxically, might exacerbate unemployment in the long run if employers tried to offset higher labor costs with increased mechanization. Further, a reduction of the workweek would increase multiple jobholding, and a legislated reduction, they believed, would interfere with the operation of the collective bargaining system (US Congress 1979; Negrey 1993: 119–20). Economists generally criticize efforts to reduce the workweek because such efforts assume the amount of work in a society is fixed. They argue that the amount of work can be increased if the economy expands (McGaughey 1981: 109; Negrey 1993: 120). The contest over reduction of the workweek reached a stalemate; Conyers's Bill never progressed beyond committee hearings (McGaughey 1981: 256; Negrey 1993: 120).[6]

Two 30-hour Experiments

The Great Depression gave birth to one famous experiment with 30-hour workweeks at Kellogg's in Battle Creek, Michigan, that endured until 1984. Initially, it was an effort to respond to labor surplus, but conditions had changed by the 1980s when, facing heightened competitive pressures, the company sought to reduce its payroll. Fearing for their jobs, workers caved to management pressure to increase work hours. But disputes over hours had existed at Kellogg's for decades, largely along gender lines, as men came to prefer longer hours and more pay and some women came to see short hours as discriminatory. The second, at a small plastics company in Indiana, more recent and short-lived, originated, by contrast, during labor shortage. In this case, too, gender played an important role in the construction of work time at a company that had difficulty recruiting and retaining workers.

Kellogg's

At the dawn of the Great Depression, Kellogg's, one of the first companies to institute the eight-hour day, five-day week (Hunnicutt 1996: 15), was the largest manufacturer of ready-to-eat cereals in the world, employing 1,500 workers. The company instituted the six-hour day on December 1, 1930.[7] Owner W. K. Kellogg and company President Lewis J. Brown argued the conversion of the existing three eight-hour shifts to six hours each would permit the addition of a fourth six-hour shift that would employ an additional 300 workers. They believed the solution to unemployment was shorter work periods and that mental satisfaction, what they dubbed "mental income," derived from satisfaction with a host of life activities, including activities outside work (Hunnicutt 1996: 13, 17). This was not unlike the concerns for health, leisure, participation, and education that had inspired work-time reduction efforts 100 years before.

Management sought to maintain workers' purchasing power by raising the minimum daily wage for male employees to $4.00 from about $3.50. In other cases, the loss of two hours work per day would be partially offset by raising the hourly wage, by 12.5 percent initially and another 12.5 percent a year later. Thus, the company and the workers would share the costs of shorter hours: workers accepted a modest pay cut in exchange for Kellogg's increasing hourly wages, total payroll, and number of employees (Hunnicutt 1996: 14). The night-shift bonus and half-hour lunch break were eliminated, and the overtime bonus was phased out and replaced with a production bonus, based on production and not work time. Removing the overtime bonus eliminated workers' incentive to slow down productivity to stretch out their work to gain premium pay during overtime (Hunnicutt 1996: 15–16).

In April 1931, Kellogg's made the six-hour day permanent (Hunnicutt 1996: 30), and throughout the Depression years the scheme worked as management hoped. The workers were sufficiently satisfied that when the National Council of Grain Producers represented the workers in 1937, one of the Battle Creek local's first demands was that the six-hour day become standard and that the few eight-hour workers (such as night watchmen) be permitted to switch to six hours if they wanted. Two thirds of the longer-hour workers subsequently voted to switch (Hunnicutt 1996: 1–2).

By the eve of US involvement in World War II, Kellogg's was under new management and the six-hour system was beginning to falter. The new managers did not share W.K. Kellogg's commitment to shorter hours. For a variety of practical reasons, the company had never scheduled six hours for a few employees in select departments; consequently, the company refused the union's request to standardize six hours throughout the plant. Management concerns about flexibility in the Container Department, in particular, to accommodate occasional periods of heavy production during the summer, permitted the division between the minority of long-hour "work-hogs" and the majority short-hour "rabbits" to surface. During the union's first strike, in 1941, a faction began to question publicly whether the six-hour system was worth the price; argued that weekly pay, insurance, and paid vacation were more important than short hours; and noted that workers at competitors' plants earned more per week because they worked more hours, albeit at lower hourly wages. At the strike's end, the union agreed to establish a joint union-management committee to study the possibility of abolishing the bonus system in favor of straight hourly wages and overtime, and, henceforth, management pursued a campaign against the six-hour day (Hunnicutt 1996: 89–95).

In response to FDR's executive order, mandating longer workweeks as a wartime measure to offset labor shortages, Kellogg's returned to three eight-hour shifts in 1943. At the end of the war, workers generally sought to return to six-hour shifts but with a pay increase to partially offset the loss of work time. The company's profit and cost concerns came into conflict with workers' desires for shorter hours and fears regarding competition for jobs from returning soldiers. The company opposed any pay increase above cost-of-living and contended that if employees wanted more pay they should work eight hours. The company also wanted to avoid adding a fourth daily shift and the associated expenses of more workers, new foremen and supervisors, and more benefits (Hunnicutt 1996: 2, 97–9). Kellogg's employees voted to return to six hours to absorb post-war labor surplus, but a gender split was evident in the vote: 87 percent of women and 71 percent of men voted for six hours. A few predominately male departments subsequently delayed the restoration of six hours, and management continued to press for eight-hour shifts (Hunnicutt 1996: 100–1). Nearly half the male workers were on eight hours, and six-hours came to be associated with women's work. The feminization of short hours masked the gender wage gap that had always existed at Kellogg's; women had been hired mainly for low-paid line jobs. The six-hour departments also became ghettoes of older and infirm employees (Hunnicutt 1996: 103–4). Whereas management during the Depression thought of unemployment as a local problem that the company could solve by shorter work hours, now management looked to the national government for solutions to unemployment (Hunnicutt 1996: 104).

A "work-based language of morals" (Hunnicutt 1996: 135) emerged in the 1950s among Kellogg's employees, especially men, which undermined the six-hour system. These workers justified their preference for eight hours by saying they had to work and distinguished themselves from the unemployed as hard workers with the "right attitude." By the 1970s, some of Kellogg's female employees had aligned with local women's rights groups and condemned six hours as a ploy to subjugate women. As a result of a lawsuit brought by some of the women, the company opened up the eight-hour departments to women (Hunnicutt 1996: 138).[8]

In the 1980s, Kellogg's had lost market share in an environment of heightened competition, as did many US companies, and sought to trim its payroll from 2,500 to 2,000 by cutting 25 percent of employees in each six-hour department over five years. The company threatened to relocate most of the jobs at the Battle Creek facility if six-hour workers, who numbered 530 in 1984, did not vote for eight hours. Ultimately, workers voted in December 1984 to give up the six-hour day in an effort to save their jobs (Hunnicutt 1996: 185, 187).

Metro Plastics

Headquartered in Noblesville, Indiana, outside Indianapolis, with production facilities in Noblesville and, until December 1997, Columbus, Indiana, Metro Plastics Technologies, Inc., put its production workers at the Columbus plant on 30-hour workweeks in July 1996, while retaining pay for 40 hours as a means by which to recruit and retain labor. Metro Plastics Technologies, Inc., had grown from a much smaller operation, Metro Molding, started in Indianapolis in 1975, that molded plastic pieces for name badges of the sort worn by service workers at most fast-food restaurants today. Metro's next product was "mood rings." The company molded the plastic stones that were in turn painted with a material that changed color with heat. A short-lived fad, Metro made more than 1 million of these before Christmas, 1975. The company grew steadily, thanks especially to new customers in consumer electronics, and moved to Noblesville in 1981. The second division, in Columbus, was added in 1986 when Metro acquired the molding division assets of Indiana Die Cast Tool. With this acquisition, Metro had molding machines with clamp tonnage ranging up to 750 tons, enabling the company to expand into larger products. In addition to manufacturing, assembly, decoration, and packaging, Metro offered services in industrial design, product design, development, and prototyping. As of summer 1997, when I visited the Columbus facility, Metro had 200 employees in production, maintenance, warehouse, clerical, design, and management. The Columbus plant closed in December 1997, due largely to the loss of business from Thomson Consumer Electronics when its Bloomington, Indiana, facility moved to Mexico. Columbus workers were offered the opportunity to transfer to Noblesville, where all of Metro's production was consolidated.

I toured the Columbus facility during the first shift in late June 1997. The plant was equipped with 11 machines, although not all were in operation when I was there, and approximately 10 workers were on the shop floor, about half women, engaged in various activities. Work was gender segregated. Men – molding technicians – programmed, monitored, and repaired the machines; women – press operators – collected the finished product from the machines, sorted quality pieces from scrap, and trimmed as necessary. The work appeared to be relatively easy, but tedious. Some machine operators stood while they sorted and collected finished products; others sat on tall stools. Products molded ranged from black 6-inch rings for installation of speakers in speaker cabinets, white air-vent covers to be affixed under doors of new refrigerators, and red short shovels that would be used for hazardous waste clean-up.

Metro struggled with labor recruitment and retention problems for about a year and a half before implementing its 30/40 scheme in July 1996. There were few applicants, and, upon hiring, workers would not show up at all or would leave on the first break on the first day, the plant manager told me. He reported having "some good employees" prior to 30/40, but he had to "work them to death" to keep customers happy. He described other workers as "bodies who didn't care," who would throw good parts into grinders, generating a high scrap rate. On the first day the company advertised the 30/40 scheme, 100 applied, and the plant manager claimed 250 to 300 applications were on file when I interviewed him in July 1997. Comparing the first six months after implementation of 30/40 (July–December 1996) to the first half of 1996, customer returns were reduced by 72 percent; scrap was reduced by 11 percent; internal rework was reduced by 29 percent the first month, 45 percent the second month, 56 percent the third, 79 percent the fourth, and 67 percent the fifth after implementation. Labor utilization increased to 93 percent, and machine utilization increased

22 percent. Absenteeism and tardiness were eliminated within three to four weeks of implementation of 30/40.

On eight-hour shifts before 30/40, workers would get lunch and two 15-minute breaks. On the six-hour shifts after 30/40, workers had no breaks and no lunch, although they were free to leave their machines to use the restroom and get snacks from the vending machines that they could bring back to their work stations. The base hourly rate of $6.60 was not increased under 30/40, but after 30 hours production workers received a 10-hour bonus. In this way the company discouraged absenteeism and tardiness. There was no overtime pay until workers worked more than 40 hours in a week. Thus, the effective hourly rate had increased one third to $8.80 under the 30/40 scheme and made Metro a more competitive employer in the local labor market.

The case of Metro Plastics is an interesting experiment in work-time reduction because it was implemented to combat difficulties associated with labor shortage. The extant literature on work-time reduction, such as the historical literature on the 10- and eight-hour movements and literature that debates the pros and cons of work-time reduction, assumes conditions of labor surplus. Metro also exploited the time squeeze, especially that experienced by women. The company had its greatest difficulty recruiting and retaining press operators – jobs filled by women. By implementing 30/40, Metro attracted experienced operators from local competitors and reduced labor turnover. Despite improvements in worker reliability and productivity, however, the plant could not survive the loss of business from the closing of Thomson.[9]

Conclusion

The history of work-time reduction, such as the US account here, is a history of class conflict over the hours of labor (their duration and timing), control of time (how much under the employer's control and how much for the rest of life), and the distribution of jobs under conditions of labor surplus and shortage. These inherent conflicts endure with new features specific to an expanding service and information economy;

the mass influx of women into the labor force; and the increase in the proportion of the workers in professional, managerial, and technical occupations.

Although work time in the US has not been reduced by legislative action in recent decades, work-time reduction has occurred in particular occupations and industries, especially in the forms of part-time and temporary employment. As will be seen in the next chapter, these as well as other non-standard employment arrangements have become commonplace, with implications for job stability, income security, and social justice. These portions of the labor market coexist with tendencies to long hours in other occupations and industries. The duration, timing, and control of work hours affect attention to family as expressed through the gender division of labor, as will be seen in chapters 4 and 5, and new forms of conflict emerge with new electronic forms of work, to be considered with other matters in pondering the future in chapter 6.

3
Current Trends

In 2009, American non-agricultural wage and salary workers worked an average of 38 hours per week, about the same as in 1980 and down slightly from 39.6 in 2000; the self-employed worked 35.6 hours, down steadily from 41.2 in 1980 (*Statistical Abstract* 2011, table 601). Seventy-two percent of Americans worked full time (35 hours or more), and 28 percent worked part time (less than 35 hours),[1] the latter averaging 22 hours (*Statistical Abstract* 2011, tables 602 and 612). This snapshot tells only part of a fascinating story, however, about long-term changes in annual and weekly work hours; the distribution of work time across occupations, men and women, and age groups; overtime; non-standard work; when Americans work (day, night, weekend); and their preferences. Generally, Americans work more hours annually than they did several decades ago, due primarily to increases in weeks worked, not hours per week, especially among women. But some do work longer hours (more than 50) per week, while others work short hours (less than 30) – revealing a bifurcated distribution of work time. Variations in weekly hours are related to type of occupation, gender, and age. Work schedules are more diverse as more people work at different hours of the day, night, and weekends. Mismatches between actual and preferred work hours abound; some Americans desire to work more hours, but many prefer to work less.

Unlike some European countries where the legal full-time workweek has been reduced to less than 40 hours, the historic reduction of work time in the United States stopped in the post-World War II period. Productivity gains after 1948 that could have been converted to more time off were instead converted to more income. In the 20 years after 1948, the productivity of American workers doubled, meaning the standard of living in 1948 could be produced in half the time decades later. Americans did not choose reduced hours, however, favoring consumption, and work to support consumption. Within a few decades, Americans owned and consumed more than twice as much as they did in 1948, with less free time (Schor 1991: 2).

Annual Hours

Annual hours worked per person declined slightly from the late 1960s to the early 1970s, falling below 1,700 hours, but have risen relatively steadily since then, approaching 1,900 hours in 2006 (Mishel et al. 2009, table 3.2, as cited by Schor 2010: 105). During the 1990s, a number of researchers investigated long-term changes in annual hours, especially after the publication of Schor's (1991) influential book, *The Overworked American*. Schor's analysis of full-time workers showed that an aggregate increase in annual hours was the result of almost 3.5 more weeks of work per year, what she called the extra month of work, not more hours per week. Women's increased labor-force participation, especially among married women with children, explained most of the increase in aggregate annual hours (from 1,406 to 1,711 among women and 2,054 to 2,152 among men). Multiple job-holding, overtime, and shrinking vacation time also contributed. The preponderance of evidence from these important studies, based on different data sets and samples as summarized in table 3.1, consistently shows an increase in women's annual work hours in the latter decades of the twentieth century. Some studies found increases in men's hours, too, although smaller than among women, and other studies found declines in men's hours. The contradictory

Table 3.1: Meta-analysis of studies of paid work hours

Study	Data source	Sample	Annual Men	Annual Women	Weekly Men	Weekly Women
Bluestone and Rose 1998	Panel Study of Income Dynamics (1967–1974) and Current Population Surveys (1974–1996)	PSID annual CPS monthly households	−200 (workers age 25–54)	+400 (workers age 25–54)		
Coleman and Pencavel 1993	Decennial censuses and Public-Use Microdata 1940–80, March Current Population Surveys 1980, 1988	Census households, CPS households, black and white male wage and salary workers	−6 (white) −151 (black)		−1.7 (white) −4.9 (black)	
Leete and Schor 1994	March Current Population Survey Supplements 1970, 1974, 1980, 1990	Corrected for rise in unemployment and underemployment	−139 (pop. 18+) −20 (labor force) +72 (fully employed)	+276 (pop. 18+) +208 (labor force) +287 (fully employed)	+0.5 (employed)	+0.9 (employed)

(Continued)

Table 3.1 Continued

Study	Data source	Sample	Annual Men	Annual Women	Weekly Men	Weekly Women
McGrattan and Rogerson 1998	Decennial censuses 1950–90 (Census of Population and Housing and Public-Use Microdata)	All households			−5 (total population)	+8 (total population)
Robinson and Godbey 1997	Americans' Use of Time Project 1965–1985 (Survey Research Center, University of Maryland)	Adults age 18–64			−7	−6
Rones et al. 1997	Current Population Surveys 1976–1993	60,000 households nationwide (monthly)	+100 (employed)	+233 (employed)	+1 (non-agricultural wage and salary workers age 25–54)	+2.5 (non-agricultural wage and salary workers age 25–54)
Schor 1991	National Income and Product Accounts (1948–68), March Current Population Surveys (1969–87)	All full-time and part-time employees in all domestic industries, corrected for rise in unemployment and underemployment	+98 (full-time)	+305 (full-time)		

trends among men are explained by methodological differences among the studies. Declines in hours among men are explained in part by deindustrialization and the shift to services in the last half of the twentieth century. Manufacturing jobs are disproportionately full time; low-wage retail and service jobs are disproportionately part time. Many men displaced from manufacturing, especially African-American men who were disproportionately concentrated in manufacturing jobs in the mid-twentieth century and disproportionately affected by deindustrialization (Wilson 1987; Hill and Negrey 1989), have had to take jobs in retail and services.

Weekly Hours

Although there is strong evidence that Americans on average work more hours annually than they did decades ago because of more weeks worked per year, there is controversy about change in the average workweek. Some key studies found an increase in average weekly hours; others found a decline. The different results seem to be because of different periods of study, different samples, and different ways of measuring work time.[2] Perhaps more importantly, a focus on average weekly hours masks growing bifurcation in the distribution of work time (Jacobs and Gerson 2004), arguably the most significant work-time trend in recent decades.

Similar to previous research, Jacobs and Gerson (1998, 2004) found that average weekly hours changed little, less than an hour or two, from 1960 to 2000. American men averaged 42 or 43 hours compared to women's 36 or 37 hours. However, the stable average, which declines during recessions, masks important shifts in variation around the average. The 40-hour workweek remains the modal pattern, with 40 percent of both men and women reporting this in 2000. In 1970, however, almost 50 percent of men and women reported working 40-hour weeks. This decline is offset by increases in the percentages working long (50 hours or more) and short (30 hours or less) weeks as shown in table 3.2.

Table 3.2: Percentage of men and women working long and short hours

	1970		2000	
	Men	*Women*	*Men*	*Women*
Long	20	5	25	10
Short	5	15	10	20

Source: Jacobs and Gerson 2004: 32–5.

Box 3.1:   Medical residents' long hours

In the last decade, concerns for patient safety led to scrutiny of medical residents' work hours. Regulations imposed in 2003 by the Accreditation Council of Graduate Medical Education limited US residents' hours to 80 per week averaged over four weeks, down from 100 hours previously, and shifts to 30 hours (admitting patients up to 24 hours) once or twice a week with a minimum rest period of 10 hours between day shifts. The Institute of Medicine, in 2008, recommended a maximum 16-hour admitting period; breaks of 10 hours after day shift, 12 hours after night shift, and 14 hours after extended duty shift of 30 hours; and at least one day off per week. Of a nationally representative sample of the American public, 89 percent support this or stricter limits (Blum et al. 2010; Moonesinghe et al. 2011, table 7).

In the UK, under the European Work Time Directive, residents' hours went from no restrictions to 72 (1996), then 56 (2004), then 48 (2009) hours per week, with shifts limited to 13 hours and 11-hour breaks between shifts (Blum et al. 2010; Moonesinghe et al. 2011, table 7).

Critics of residents' work-hours reduction cite concerns about costs of replacement providers, workforce sufficiency, disrupted continuity of care, and residents' training (Blum et al. 2010).

The increase in the percentages working long hours is explained by increase in the proportion of Americans in professional, managerial, and technical jobs; workers in such jobs are more likely to work 50 hours or more per week than workers in other kinds of occupations. The increase in the percentages working short hours is explained by an increase in the proportion of Americans in part-time and other non-standard short-hours arrangements. These occupational trends are characteristic of service economies and not exclusive to the US. Different national regulatory environments, however, affect patterns of work-time dispersion.

Overtime

A factor in long workweeks is the increasing number of American workers who are "exempt" from the overtime protections of the Fair Labor Standards Act because they are employed in professional, managerial, and technical occupations – an occupational category that has grown over the decades. Some employers prefer overtime to hiring because of the added expense of training and health insurance for new hires. Changes in the overtime rules in 2004 may have added to the number of workers exempt from overtime pay. The Fair Labor Standards Act of 1938 established the legal norm of the 40-hour workweek and overtime premium pay at time and a half for each hour worked beyond 40 in a week. But employers are not required to pay overtime to workers "employed in a bona fide executive, administrative, or professional capacity." Implementation initially focused on duties that distinguished white-collar employees from, for example, clerical workers, technicians, and foremen, and this "duties test" has remained the basis of overtime protection since (Eisenbrey 2004; Linder 2004).

Historically, average overtime has increased with recoveries and fallen with recessions, but overtime reached an unprecedented level during the expansion of the late 1990s. In 1999, almost 80 percent of American wage and salary workers were entitled to overtime protection under FLSA (Eisenbrey 2004), but exclusions rose from about 32 percent of the workforce in 1978 to 40 percent in the late 1990s (Hamermesh 2000), when 45 percent of workers reported having to work overtime on little or no notice (Heldrich Center for Workforce Development 1999). Manufacturing, in particular, became dependent on overtime, reaching an average 4.9 hours in the late 1990s, the highest level since the US Bureau of Labor Statistics (BLS) began gathering data on overtime in 1956 (Hetrick 2000: 30). Much of the increase in overtime in manufacturing was concentrated in motor vehicle manufacturing and iron and steel foundries (Hetrick 2000). Global competitive downward pressure on wages, weaker government enforcement of regulations, and declining union power have contributed to a resurgence of sweatshops in garment manufacturing, with uncompensated overtime and other labor code violations (Ross 2004).

An explosion of litigation occurred when companies such as Starbucks, Taco Bell, and Walmart were sued by workers who claimed they had been denied overtime pay. Business groups pressured President George W. Bush's administration to revise the rules (<www.cnnmoney.com> 2004).

In 2004, the US Department of Labor issued new rules regarding overtime pay, the first major overhaul of federal overtime law in more than 50 years. The federal government claimed the new rules would strengthen overtime rights for nearly 7 million workers, including more than 1 million low-wage workers who were denied overtime pay under the old rules. Critics, however, said the new rules would prevent 6 million workers from getting overtime pay (www.cnnmoney.com 2004). The controversy boiled down to interpretation of job tasks, or the "duties" test, because the "salary basis" and new "salary-level" tests are straightforward. Workers are exempt from overtime pay if they are paid a salary, not an hourly wage. This has long been the rule, and the new rules do not change this requirement, although it is possible employers convert employees from hourly to salary to avoid paying overtime (<www.cnnmoney.com>2004; Eisenbrey 2004). The 2004 rules raised the salary level under which employees are entitled to overtime pay from $155 a week (for professionals), in effect since 1975, to $455 a week ($11.38 per hour for a 40-hour week or $23,660 a year) for all employees – the lowest threshold in nearly 50 years when adjusted for inflation (Eisenbrey 2004; Linder 2004). This threshold is not indexed to inflation (Eisenbrey 2004), so fewer and fewer workers will qualify unless the federal government acts to raise it, as it has done irregularly in the past.

Also, the new rules exclude more workers from overtime through the revised "duties test" which aims to clarify the type of work that qualifies as executive, administrative, or professional, relying less on job titles and more on actual duties (<www.cnnmoney.com> 2004). Hourly workers who regularly perform a single executive, administrative, or professional task and earn more than $100,000 annually are now ineligible for overtime. For example, the new rules exempt employees who lead teams of other employees assigned to complete major projects for the employer even if the employee does not have direct supervisory authority over the other members of the team. Thus, team leaders, who were nonexempt and thus entitled to overtime pay under the old rules, are now unable to receive it. Similarly, work experience is now part of the definition of learned professional as a basis for exemption from overtime pay. Previously, learned professionals were those who had completed a prolonged course of intellectual instruction, culminating in a professional degree. The new rules, however, allow for substitution of knowledge gained from work experience for knowledge gained through a prolonged course of instruction. For example, workers who attended engineering school for one year with additional experience in on-the-job training, training in the armed forces, and other work experience could be exempted even though they never completed an engineering degree and did not have the status or receive pay comparable to that of a degreed engineer. New creative professional and learned professional exemptions potentially eliminate overtime pay for chefs and sous chefs who previously were non-exempt. Under the old rules, only the chef in charge of the kitchen, who manages the operation, supervises the kitchen staff, and plans the menu, was exempt as an executive. The new creative professional exemption applies to any chef "who has a primary duty of work requiring invention, imagination, originality or talent, such as that involved in regularly creating or designing unique dishes and menu items." The new learned professional exemption makes any cook, chef, or sous chef who has approximately the same skills as a graduate of a culinary arts school ineligible for overtime pay even without obtaining a professional degree. Computer professionals, under the old rules, were exempt if they did work that requires the consistent exercise of discretion and judgment and their primary duty was "the performance of work requiring theoretical and practical application of highly specialized knowledge in computer systems analysis, programming, and software engineering." These requirements were eliminated in the new rules, which makes the exemption applicable to less-skilled trainees, entry-level workers, and those who do not work independently or without supervision (Eisenbrey 2004).[3]

Non-standard Work

"Non-standard work" emphasizes the "otherness" of forms of employment, such as part-time, temporary, and contract, that contrast with standard employment. Standard work is usually full time, on a fixed schedule, at the employer's establishment, under the employer's control, and with the mutual expectation of continued employment (Kalleberg et al. 2000: 258). Workers receive benefits, training, and sometimes opportunities for career mobility (Carre at al. 2000: 1). Until the end of the Great Depression, most jobs were insecure and wages unstable; pensions and health insurance were almost unheard of. New Deal reforms stabilized the labor market and working conditions, and regular full-time jobs were the norm by the 1950s (Kalleberg et al. 2000: 257). Standard jobs with benefits became incentives for skilled, experienced workers (Carre et al. 2000: 3; Smith 1998). Employers continued to rely on a "peripheral" workforce to contain labor costs, but that segment of the labor market has grown in recent decades (Kalleberg et al. 2000: 257).

Increase in non-standard jobs over the last few decades, a trend also in service economies outside the US, represents a breakdown in the New Deal system of labor relations, or the "social contract" between capital and labor. This social contract integrated organized labor into normal business practice to gain labor peace (Bluestone and Harrison 1982; McCammon 1990, 1993, 1994; Rubin 1996), and productivity increases extended to organized labor in the form of higher wages and improved benefits generalized throughout the labor market. Although this social contract thrived under conditions of US economic hegemony after World War II, such conditions no longer exist. Since the 1980s, global markets have become more competitive, American business dominance is no longer assured, and US policy has come to favor capital over labor. Unions have been weakened (Goldfield 1987) as has their position at the vanguard of labor. Those alarmed by the dramatic growth of non-standard work are concerned for workers' insecurity (Kalleberg et al. 2000; Lambert 2008; Sweet and Meiksins 2008). Others, less concerned, interpret these changes as perhaps akin to the "creative destruction" (Schumpeter 1989) that occurs among businesses in a dynamic but healthy economy.

Non-standard work today is not without ambiguity (Hudson 1999; Carre et al. 2000). Early on, researchers emphasized the "contingent" nature of non-standard work, emphasizing impermanency (Barker and Christenson 1998; Freedman 1985; Serrin 1986), short duration (Hodson 2000: xvii), and lack of fit with the traditional full-time, permanent job with benefits (Callaghan and Hartmann 1991: 1). Some contingent jobs are of long duration, however, such as part-time retail workers who retain part-time status indefinitely; temporary faculty, hired on a course-by-course basis semester after semester for years; or Microsoft's "permatemps" (Grimsley 2000). Contingent jobs give employers flexibility in the use of labor. Contingent workers are "buffers" (Pitts 1998: 101), marginal to the organization that employs them (Wacker and Bills 2000: 232), and often marginal in the labor market, earning low wages with few if any fringe benefits (Parker 1994: 2). Contingent workers are more likely than all other workers to hold more than one job, and nearly three fifths prefer a permanent job (Hipple 1998; US Department of Labor 2005b).

The US BLS distinguishes contingent and alternative employment arrangements. Contingent work is that lacking a long-term contract or having variable hours (Polivka and Nardone 1989: 11). Alternative arrangements encompass independent contractors, on-call workers, workers paid by temporary help agencies, and workers paid by contract firms (Cohany et al. 1998). Applying these definitions, contingent work ranged from about 2 percent (narrow estimate) to 5 percent (broad estimate) of total employment in the late 1990s and 2005 (Cohany et al. 1998; US Department of Labor 2005b). Contingent workers tend to be part-time workers, but the vast majority of part-time workers are not in contingent arrangements (Hipple 1998; US Department of Labor 2005b). About 10 percent of all workers were in alternative arrangements in the late 1990s and 2005 (Cohany et al. 1998; US Department of Labor 2005b), with the plurality in independent contracting, followed by on-call, temporary help agency, and contract company workers.

Hudson's (1999) broad definition of non-standard jobs combined part-time work with independent contracting, temporary employment, on-call work, day labor, and self-employment, noting that non-standard work differs from regular full-time jobs in at least one of three ways: absence of an employer, as in self-employment and independent contracting; a distinction between the employer and the organization for whom the worker works, as in contract and temporary work; or the temporal instability of the job. Nearly 30 percent of American workers were in non-standard jobs in 1997, using this definition, consistent with Belous's (1989) estimate of 25 to 30 percent.

Non-standard work reflects both the strength and weakness of the statutory 40-hour norm in the US. If the 40-hour norm is too rigid for many of the jobs in our economy at the dawn of the twenty-first century, why not change it? If the 40-hour norm is too rigid for the lifestyles of many workers, why not change it? Or, politically, is it too difficult to change? Is it advantageous to retain the 40-hour legal norm despite the fact that increasing numbers of workers fall outside it in their actual employment routines, and, if so, advantageous for whom? These questions underlie the discussion of part-time, temporary, and contract employment that follows.

Part-time employment

The US Department of Labor BLS defines part-time employment as less than 35 hours of work per week, and distinguishes between voluntary and involuntary part-time employment. Voluntary part-time employment occurs when workers choose to work part-time because of family care, enrollment in school, or other personal reasons. Most voluntary part-time workers are women who want to accommodate family care. Feminists are critical of the notion of women's choice, however, because there are few satisfactory options. Women and men are more equally divided among involuntary part-time workers (US Department of Labor 2004: 232), who work part time because their hours have been cut due to slack economic conditions or because part-time jobs were the only jobs available to them when they preferred full-time work. In a panel study of part-time women workers (Caputo and Cianni 2001), the number of years of previous *un*employment increased the likelihood of involuntary part-time employment; marriage and private-sector employment decreased it. Among women, the researchers concluded, part-time employment may be a function of immediate circumstances and motivations than a patterned behavior or way of life.

Part-time employment has grown faster than full-time employment in recent decades (Deutermann and Brown 1978; Dupuy and Schweitzer 1995; Tilly 1996), accounting for 30 percent of all net employment growth in the US during the 1980s alone (Wise 1989). Voluntary part-time employment constitutes the vast majority of all part-time jobs, but involuntary part-time employment doubled from the 1960s to the 1990s (Dupuy and Schweitzer 1995). The rate of involuntary part-time employment tends to fluctuate with the unemployment rate; however, after each recession from the 1970s to the 1990s, the rate of involuntary part-time employment remained slightly higher than after the previous recession so that the rate overall has followed an upward trajectory (Tilly 1996: 121–2; US Department of Labor 2008b). During the expansion in the 1990s, when a decrease in involuntary part-time employment should have occurred based on past trends, involuntary part-time employment actually increased – the only time to date this had happened in the post-World War II period (Tilly 1996: 3). Overall, part-time employment grew throughout the 1980s and into the 1990s in industries that themselves exhibited growth, especially services and retail trade (Fallick 1999). In the Great Recession, involuntary part-time workers were about 5 percent of all workers, doubling from about 2.5 percent in

April 2006. As is typical in labor market downturns, the bulk of the increase in involuntary part-time employment was due to hours reductions because of slack demand. Such increases in involuntary part-time employment frequently occur before a rise in unemployment, because many employers tend to reduce workers' hours before layoffs. Conversely, during a recovery, some employers increase workers' hours before hiring new workers (US Department of Labor 2008b).

Part-time workers are concentrated in service, sales, and clerical occupations and are represented less by unions – 8 percent compared to 16 percent of full-time workers in 2002 (US Department of Commerce 2003: 431). Over half of those paid minimum and sub-minimum wages are part-time workers, and only about half of part-time workers are eligible for employer-provided health insurance compared to more than 80 percent of full-time workers. Sick leave and pension plans also are less available to part-time workers than full-time workers (Connolly 2000: 148–9). Health insurance is a quasi-fixed cost to employers, thus the cost per hour worked is greater for part-time than full-time employees (Lettau and Buchmueller 1999), and has a significant effect on the distribution of part-time workers across economic sectors. Part-time workers are a larger fraction of the workforce in industries with lower hourly wages and a lower probability of health-care coverage for part-time employees (Pitts 1998).

Employers' supply of part-time jobs is related to gender of the workforce. During the 1980s, part-time employment overall grew primarily in conjunction with the female composition and female entry rate of occupations (Cassirer 1995). Regardless of whether the part-time jobs are taken by workers voluntarily or involuntarily, employers desire a flexible labor force to cover long hours of the business day and week and to respond to the ebb and flow of consumer demand (Lambert 2008). The increase in the rate of involuntary part-time employment compared to the relative stability of the rate of voluntary part-time employment over the last few decades indicates that supply more than demand explains the growth of part-time employment in the US (Tilly 1996). This argument holds for the recent growth of other forms of non-standard employment, such as temporary, contract, and day labor, as well (Carre et al. 2000).

Box 3.2: Part-time employment in grocery stores

Labor dominates the costs of doing business in food retailing, and profit maximization requires labor cost reduction. Customary strategies to reduce labor costs have included self-scan checkouts, large displays that require less frequent restocking, rearrangement of storage areas for greater efficiency, and adjustment of employee responsibilities to peak business hours. The heavy reliance today on a flexible, part-time workforce perhaps is the supermarket industry's hallmark.

Because of high turnover, the US BLS ranked jobs for cashiers, nearly a quarter of whom are in supermarkets and other food stores, second among the top jobs expected to grow until 2016 (<www.bls.gov/oes,www.bls.gov/news.release/ecopro.t07. htm>). Yet these jobs are often part time and low paid. The median hourly earnings of all cashiers (including those outside grocery stores) were just $8.08 in 2006 ($8.20 in grocery stores; $17,930 and $19,060 annually respectively) (<www.bls.gov/ oes>), and nearly half of all cashiers were on part-time schedules (<www.bls.gov/oco/ocos116.htm>).

Supermarkets have employed a large percentage of part-time workers for a long time, about twice the proportion of total non-agricultural employment (Haugen 1986: 13). In grocery stores (SIC 541, NAICS 42445100), of which supermarkets are a subcategory, the rate of part-time employment, already at 35 percent in 1962, increased slightly to 37 percent in 1992 (Tilly 1991: 16, 1996: 25). In retail trade, part-time employment rose from 24 percent of the workforce in 1962 to 35 percent in 1993, much of this growth accounted for by an increase in eating and drinking establishments (Tilly 1991: 16, 1996: 25). In March 2007, the rate of part-time employment was 27 percent in retail trade and 34 percent in grocery stores.[4]

The reduction in workers' hours coincides with the expansion of business hours in supermarkets. Increasing numbers of stores are open during evening hours, on Sundays, and 24 hours a day. In 1959, stores were open on average 72 hours each week; by 1982, the weekly average had increased to 102 hours in chains and 89 hours in independents. Extended hours were a response to women's employment during traditional daytime hours and reflect grocers' desire to keep stores open for "family shopping" on nights and weekends, especially in

(Continued)

stores with a large percentage of non-food items. Walmart is the most familiar example of this supercenter format today (Strople 2006). Whereas workers' hours were confined to traditional hours of 9 a.m. to 6 p.m. Monday through Thursday, 8 a.m. to 6 p.m. Friday and Saturday, some three decades ago, today workers work most any day of the week and any hour of the day or night in what Presser (2003) has dubbed the 24/7 economy.

The expansion of business hours in grocery stores also may be an expression of the decline in power of butchers and meat cutters, the most skilled workers in the stores. Historically, stores closed at 6 p.m. because butchers and meat cutters refused to work past that hour. But technological changes in meat retailing (Walsh 1989, 1991, 1993) have contributed to a decline in the number of butchers and meat cutters in stores and their relative power to assert their will. Retail meat departments rely increasingly on pre-packaged items, particularly what is known in the trade as boxed beef. Standardized cuts are cut and packaged at central meatpacking facilities, thus removing the work of cutting and wrapping from stores. Grocers believe wage cost reduction more than offsets the additional cost of pre-packaged items. In some areas (St Louis and Chicago, especially), unions have placed restrictions on retailers' purchases of boxed beef. Still, the number of butchers and meat cutters employed in grocery stores has declined as a result of this technological innovation; most workers in meat departments today are essentially clerks who fill the meat cases. In stores where a few skilled meat cutters are still employed, they cut a narrow range of specialty items or fulfill a limited number of customer requests.

The elimination of large numbers of butchers and meat cutters in stores and the deskilling of meat-department employees probably facilitated the merger in 1979 of the Amalgamated Meat Cutters and Butcher Workmen of America with the Retail Clerks International Association, the union that represented cashiers and other non-meat employees, into the United Food and Commercial Workers Union (UFCW). This merger created a larger union as measured by membership, but its power in the face of corporate competitive pressures seems limited. It has not been successful in inhibiting the use of tiered wage agreements (Martin and Heetderks 1990); nor has it stemmed the tide of part-time jobs in the industry.

Temporary employment[5]

For-profit labor market intermediaries, such as temporary help supply (THS) companies, play an increasingly important role in the economy, and an increasing number of workers across a wide spectrum of industries and occupations are now employed on a temporary basis (Henson 1996; Parker 1994; Rogers 1995; Smith 1997, 1998). From 1972 through the late 1990s, employment in the American THS industry increased at an annual rate of over 11 percent, while total non-agricultural employment grew only 2 percent per year, accounting for 10 percent of net employment growth in the US during the 1990s (Estevão and Lach 2000; Houseman and Erickcek 2002; Kalleberg 2000). From the mid-1980s to the mid-1990s, personnel supply services, consisting of temporary help, employee leasing, and employment agencies, formed the number one growth industry, and Manpower, a leading THS company, became the largest US employer (Smith 1998). Almost 1.25 million THS workers accounted for 1 percent of total employment in 2005 (US Department of Labor 2005b). Historically, THS employment was associated with clerical jobs, but recently temporary manufacturing jobs have shown particularly strong growth (Blank 1998; Estevão and Lach 2000; Segal and Sullivan 1997).

Temporary employment is an integral feature of employers' personnel strategies (Kalleberg 2000), providing great flexibility to employers in responding to variable or cyclical demands in a changing business environment and lowering costs of recruitment, screening, training, and monitoring (Autor et al. 1999; Blank 1998; Houseman and Polivka 1999; von Hippel et al. 1997). More than half of temporary agencies offer some form of training (e.g., computer-based training) that also functions to recruit and screen better-quality workers, and the agencies offering skills training were more likely to place their workers in permanent positions than those that did not offer training (Autor et al. 1999). Many firms in turn use temporary workers to screen for full-time permanent positions before making a commitment (Houseman and Polivka 1999).

Some argue that temporary employees tend to be situated in disadvantaged parts of the labor market, in "bad jobs" with low pay and few benefits (Benner et al. 2001; Kalleberg et al. 2000), and limited help in building a career (Benner et al. 2001). Training alone is seen as insufficient in achieving upward career mobility or improving employment conditions. THS agencies gain workers' compliance by tacitly threatening to deny them assignments or giving them undesirable assignments and generally maintaining their disadvantaged, vulnerable status (Gottfried 1991; Henson 1996; McAllister 1998; Parker 1994; Rogers and Henson 1997; Smith 1998). This line of research implies that low-skilled, low-income workers hired by THS firms face serious obstacles in overcoming their disadvantaged economic status due to low wages, the lack of fringe benefits, and job insecurity.

Jobs in the THS industry vary, however, and workers seek employment through temporary agencies for a variety of reasons (Blank 1998; Polivka 1996): some appreciate the

---

Box 3.3:   Being a temp

"Most of the time it's up to you to call. At least that's what I've found. You have to call and say, 'Look, I'm available. What do you have for me?' And really bug them. I bug my agency all the time. They get tired of hearing me . . . If I don't bother them, they're not going to get me work. I've gotten to the point where I know I bother them, but I get work." (Jon)

"The way they got rid of us was just incredible. We got out at a quarter to five every day. And I get home and I get this call from my temporary counselor: 'You don't need to go back tomorrow.' You mean to tell me they couldn't tell me this before I left? When all the managers left with me on the same elevator? They knew before I left that they didn't want us anymore." (Bobby Jean)

"My file has been activated here at the Busy Temps office as well. I haven't gotten an assignment from them in Chicago. I'm probably going to register with one or two other places, because I need to support myself. And if places are just not getting me assignments, I know so many people who are, like, 'Yeah, you have to register with a whole bunch,' in order to work consistently enough to earn decent money." (Ginny)

(All quotes from Henson 1996: 65–6, 82–3)

flexibility of temporary employment that helps them mesh work and other obligations, without which they may not have access to the labor market; others seek temporary jobs to gain a diversity of experience before settling for one job, to get skills training, or to search for full-time permanent employment. This suggests that THS firms have the potential to aid low-skilled workers in overcoming their disadvantages by providing skills training and placing them in a job with the potential for career advancement.

The wages of temporary workers vary by occupation and are sometimes higher than those of regular employees (Blank 1998; Segal and Sullivan 1997). Yet it appears that high-skilled workers who command higher earnings benefit more from temporary arrangements than low-skilled workers. Temporary engineers and technicians often earn more than their counterparts in regular jobs (Carey and Hazelbaker 1986). Segal and Sullivan (1997) also found that white-collar temporary workers earn slightly more than other white-collar workers, while pink-collar or blue-collar temporary workers earn substantially less than their permanent counterparts. The disadvantaged earnings of many temporary workers are exacerbated by the fact that they are less likely to have access to health and pension plans.[6]

Although there are some variations in the nature of temporary jobs, the average length of employee assignment is estimated to be about three to five months, and the majority of temporary workers would prefer to have a more permanent, traditional work arrangement (NATSS 2001; Polivka 1996). Segal and Sullivan (1997) estimated from CPS data for the period 1983 to 1993 that a little over half of temporary workers became permanent employees one year later. The others became unemployed, exited the labor force, or remained temporary workers.

Contracting

Independent contracting is the largest of the four alternative arrangements (temporary help agency workers, contract company workers, on-call workers, and independent contractors) defined by the BLS, accounting for 6.7 percent of all workers, two thirds of workers in alternative arrangements in 1997 (Cohany 1998), and 7.4 percent of the employed in 2005 (US Department of Labor 2005b). Contract company employment is the smallest of the four at just 0.6 percent of all workers (Cohany 1998; US Department of Labor 2005b).

The current trend toward increased contracting out of services represents arguably the most significant change in the structure of work, with firms abandoning their commitment to secure employment relationships in favor of labor purchased on the open market (Benner 1996). In many cases, contracted employees perform jobs that were previously held by workers directly employed by these same employers or even alongside regular workers, such as Microsoft's "perma-temps" (Grimsley 2000).

Demographics of non-standard work

Non-standard work arrangements vary significantly in their gender and racial composition. More women than men (33.7 and 24.3 percent respectively) work in non-standard jobs, and women are concentrated in non-standard arrangements of poor quality. For example, regular part-time employees and temporary workers – work arrangements with the largest pay penalties and the lowest likelihood of providing health insurance and pensions – are disproportionately female. In contrast, independent contractors – the best-paid type of non-standard work, who are more likely to work in higher-status and professional occupations than their wage and salary counterparts – are disproportionately male (Cohany 1998; Hudson 1999; US Department of Labor 2005b).

Table 3.3 shows that men are a larger proportion of the full-time employed than women, and women comprise a particularly large proportion of voluntary part-time workers. Yet women are more than half of those working part time involuntarily, and the plurality of all involuntary part-time workers are prime-age (25 to 54) workers. This suggests weakness in the labor market when large percentages of prime-age workers who desire full-time jobs are working part time. Larger proportions of men than women are in contingent and alternative arrangements, except temporary help agency workers, and relatively high percentages of prime-age (25–54) men are

Table 3.3: Age and sex distribution of workers employed full time and part time (percent)

Age and sex	Full time	Involuntary part time	Voluntary part time
Men	58	47	31
16–24	5	14	14
25–54	43	27	8
55 +	10	6	9
Women	42	53	69
16–24	4	12	20
25–54	31	34	34
55+	7	7	15

Source: US Department of Labor. 2008a. *Employment and Earnings*, Table A-18, January.

contract workers (see table 3.4). Contingent and alternative arrangements can be labor market entry-and-exit transitions for young and older workers, respectively, but contract work occurs disproportionately among men at ages when they might normally have standard full-time jobs.

When race and ethnicity are added to the equation, the best types of non-standard work (i.e., independent contracting and self-employment for men) are disproportionately filled by white men, while the worst types of non-standard jobs (i.e., regular part-time and temporary work) are disproportionately filled by women and minority men. These racial-ethnic patterns are related to educational and occupational differences. Independent contractors tend to be more highly educated and, as noted above, often do professional jobs; many temporary jobs are in administrative support, manufacturing, and construction and require less education. And also as noted above, regular part-time jobs tend to be in retail trade and services, often taken by women meshing employment with family care. Like other groups, however, the majority of racial-ethnic minority groups have standard jobs (Hipple 1998; Hudson 1999; US Department of Labor 2005b).

Table 3.4: Age and sex distribution of workers in contingent and alternative arrangements (percent)

Age and sex	Contingent (broadest estimate)	Independent contractors	On-call workers	Temporary help agency workers	Workers provided by contract firms
Men	51.1	64.7	50.6	47.2	69.0
16–19	4.0	0.3	3.3	1.9	0.9
20–24	10.5	1.9	8.1	8.8	7.5
25–34	14.5	9.7	12.2	15.2	17.0
35–44	9.5	17.6	10.3	9.8	17.2
45–54	6.4	17.1	8.5	5.8	17.6
55–64	4.6	12.4	4.4	4.3	8.6
65 +	1.6	5.7	3.7	1.3	0.4
Women	48.9	35.3	49.4	52.8	31.0
16–19	4.3	0.5	2.1	0.7	0
20–24	8.4	1.6	6.3	7.8	3.3
25–34	10.8	5.0	9.6	14.6	8.2
35–44	8.8	9.0	13.0	10.9	7.0
45–54	8.9	10.0	8.5	10.6	5.3
55–64	4.8	6.3	6.5	6.8	5.4
65 +	2.8	2.8	3.4	1.4	1.9

Source: US Department of Labor 2005b. "Contingent and Alternative Employment Arrangements," *BLS News*, February.

The complex economy of non-standard work

Although there are exceptions, especially along the lines of gender, non-standard workers tend to be in jobs of lower quality than full-time workers and fall outside the scope of labor protections that many Americans now take for granted. The growth in non-standard jobs also has implications for the class structure of American society.

Non-standard workers, on average, are paid less, are less likely to receive health insurance or a pension, and have less job security than workers in regular full-time jobs (Ferber and Waldfogel 1998; Hipple and Stewart 1996a; Hipple and Stewart 1996b; Hudson 1999; Kalleberg et al. 2000). Of all non-standard workers, 60 percent earn less than workers with similar characteristics in regular full-time jobs (Hudson 1999). As such, non-standard work is often substandard work (Kalleberg et al. 2000). However, this hides a high degree of wage inequality among non-standard jobs when compared to regular full-time jobs (Hudson 1999). Some non-standard workers' wages are comparable to or even exceed the wages of standard workers with similar job and personal characteristics (Hudson 1999): contract company workers and male (though not female) independent contractors are paid more, on average, than their regular full-time counterparts with similar personal characteristics (Cohany 1998; US Department of Labor 2005b). This bifurcation suggests that there is a dual economy of non-standard work.

There are also differences in terms of job satisfaction. Some workers prefer their non-standard arrangement: independent contractors and self-employed workers "overwhelmingly" (90 percent) prefer their non-standard work arrangements; the majority of temporary and on-call workers, however, would rather have a regular full-time job (Hudson 1999; US Department of Labor 2005b). Workers who prefer non-standard jobs are more likely to work in those arrangements for reasons other than economic necessity. They are also likely to be employed in non-standard arrangements that have relatively better wages and benefits. Women working on-call are exceptions, however, in that these women, like most workers in low-quality non-standard jobs, prefer traditional employment; yet 41.6 percent of these women report they work on-call for flexibility and family reasons (Hudson 1999). This suggests that when some women "choose" to work in poor-quality non-standard arrangements, they would actually prefer to have regular full-time jobs if those jobs could be more accommodating of family care.

There are a number of reasons to be concerned about non-standard work, particularly employers' increasing use of contingent labor. A growing workforce employed in non-standard situations may contribute to downward mobility and a declining standard of living for a significant fraction of the population. Rothstein (1996) found that the typical contingent worker's current job was a step down from the previous job, whereas for full-time standard workers the current job was a step up. The flexible scheduling associated with many forms of non-standard work causes instability of hours and income for workers (Lambert 2008). Additionally, the institutions and laws that provide worker protections and a social safety net were conceived and established for the standard full-time worker who receives employer-provided benefits. Non-standard workers usually are not eligible for these protections. Occupational health-and-safety regulations, unemployment insurance, and pension regulations are often nullified by some of the alternative employment arrangements that have emerged (Benner 1996; Callaghan and Hartmann 1991: 13; Carnevale et al. 1998; Connolly 2000; duRivage et al. 1998). In addition, because part-time and temporary workers tend to be concentrated in particular occupations and industries (clerical, sales, service, and unskilled labor occupations in the retail trade and services industries), and employers likely do not want to invest in training such workers, employers do not structure career ladders for the workers who fill contingent positions. Thus, contingent workers' opportunities for increased earnings and advancement are curtailed (Benner 1996; Callaghan and Hartmann 1991: 12). Further, few part-time workers and virtually no temporary or contract employees are represented by labor unions, meaning major inequities may exist between contingent workers and their standard counterparts doing the same jobs. They may receive vastly different wages, benefits, and rights in a tiered internal labor market. Contingent workers also may be denied due process when problems arise, and they can be more easily dismissed (Benner 1996; Callaghan and Hartmann 1991: 14). Because contingent workers are less likely to have pensions and employer-provided health insurance and generally earn low wages, they are more likely to suffer economic hardship than other workers (Callaghan and Hartmann 1991: 15; Hudson 1999). They may also have difficulty acquiring regular, full-time employment (Ferber and Waldfogel 1998; Negrey et al. 2007).

Box 3.4:   Non-standard work and welfare reform

The welfare reform objectives of the federal Personal Responsibility and Work Opportunity Reconciliation Act (PRWORA) of 1996 are situated in the context of labor market change. PRWORA gave considerable autonomy to states to fashion Temporary Assistance for Needy Families (TANF) programs, placed a five-year lifetime limit on public cash assistance, and encouraged rapid employment. Many states adopted a "work-first" philosophy, thereby requiring welfare clients to relinquish cash assistance and obtain jobs quickly – often within two years – with limited opportunities for training or education.

Welfare recipients in the US tend to be single or divorced mothers who may or may not receive additional income in the form of child support payments from the fathers of their children. Welfare recipients typically move into jobs in services and retail trade, industries that are composed disproportionately of part-time jobs. Most research on welfare leavers indicates that they find unstable, low-wage jobs (Christopher 2004; Rangarajan et al. 1998; Rangarajan and Novak 1999; US Department of Health and Human Services 2000). In one pre-PRWORA study (Rangarajan and Novak 1999), 24 percent were in temporary jobs, and 18 percent obtained a job (any job) through THS establishments. This suggests that THS establishments probably continue to play an important role in moving public assistance recipients from welfare to work.

Results of a panel study of mobility from part-time to full-time employment among a sample of women leaving welfare

(*Continued*)

in Kentucky (Negrey et al. 2007: 61–2) showed that welfare leavers who exited part-time employment and acquired full-time employment within the three-year duration of the panel – 1998 to 2001 – were 28.7 times more likely to have work experience at intake and some college education (22.8 times more likely with work experience and a high-school diploma, and 17.5 times more likely with work experience and a GED (General Educational Development test qualification)) than those who did not make the transition from part-time to full-time employment. In 1998, 83 percent of the sample did not have a full-time job. While the percentage declined at each data point, by the end of the panel in 2001, 38 percent still had not acquired full-time employment (Negrey et al. 2007: 59). These findings suggest that mothers who are forced off welfare without prior work experience and adequate formal education are likely to be employed part time for a long time and perhaps indefinitely, making self-sufficiency elusive. It should be noted, however, that full-time employment is not a guarantee of self-sufficiency if the job's wages are low.

Non-standard Schedules

Trends are toward a non-standard day and week (Golden 2001: 50). Many workers work evenings, nights, weekends, and rotating schedules. Despite a decline in evening and night work between the early 1970s and the early 1990s, the proportion of workers working at the "fringes" of the traditional workday, 7 a.m. and 6 p.m., increased (Hamermesh 1999). The daytime standard workweek, 35 to 40 hours five days a week Monday through Friday, applies to just 29 percent of Americans today. Women are somewhat more likely than men to work standard daytime hours. If we include everyone who regularly works during the daytime, all five days from Monday to Friday, for any number of hours, the proportion of all employed Americans increases to a bare majority – 54 percent (Presser 2003: 15). The percentage of workers increases to 80 percent using an expanded definition of the day, 6 a.m. to 6 p.m. This overlaps the most common "alternate" shift, however, the evening shift, 2 p.m. to midnight (McMenamin 2007: 8–9).

Part-time workers are most likely to work non-standard hours on their principal job (Presser 2003; McMenamin 2007: 10). Men are slightly more likely than women – 40.3 to 38.9 percent – to work non-standard days, that is, other than a five-day week, Monday through Friday. Men are more likely to work weekends; women are more likely to work weekdays but fewer than five days a week. Weekend workers, both men and women, tend to work long (more than 40) or short (under 35) hours. Very few work weekends exclusively; almost all who do are part-time workers (Presser 2003: 18).

Ten occupations – cashiers; truck drivers; commodities sales workers in retail and personal services; waiters and waitresses; cooks; janitors and cleaners; sales supervisors and proprietors; registered nurses; food-serving and lodging managers; and nursing aides, orderlies, and attendants – account for about one third of all who work non-standard schedules. With the exception of truck drivers, all 10 are jobs that serve the local community. Many are low paid (Presser 2003: 21–2). Generally, there is no premium for working non-standard and weekend hours. Registered nurses are an exception; they do have higher earnings for weekend work, although the difference is not statistically significant (Presser 2003: 22).

Most who work non-standard schedules do so because they could not get any other job, the hours were mandated by the employer, or the nature of the job required non-standard hours. Less than 10 percent mentioned making better child-care arrangements as a reason for working non-standard hours (McMenamin 2007: 11, Presser 2003: 20), with a somewhat higher percentage among part-time than full-time workers saying this. Part-time workers in particular were also much more likely than full-time workers to say they worked a non-standard schedule because it allowed time for school (McMenamin 2007: 11).[7]

Disproportionately high percentages of workers in most of the jobs that were projected by the BLS to grow the most in absolute terms by the year 2010 (specifically, food preparation and serving workers, registered nurses, retail salespersons, cashiers, security guards, and waiters and waitresses) worked weekends and other than fixed-day schedules. Thus, the proportion of the total workforce that works non-standard schedules is likely to increase in the future as the very jobs that require such schedules grow. Many of these jobs are female-dominated, and a number employ large percentages of racial/ethnic minorities (Presser 2003: 43–6).

Hours Mismatches

Many Americans prefer to work fewer hours, according to a number of recent pre-Great Recession studies, although there are important differences by employment status, gender, and race (Bell 1998; Clarkberg 2000; Golden and Gebreselassie 2007; Jacobs and Gerson 2004; Reynolds 2003). Of these, 60 percent prefer fewer hours, generally five to 10 per week. Although women on average worked six hours less per week than men, the gap between actual and ideal hours was similar among both men and women. The percentage who felt their actual hours equaled their ideal hours declined from 1992 to 1997 from one third to one fifth (Jacobs and Gerson 2004: 63–5). This gap between actual and ideal hours goes a long way toward explaining the sense of overwork that many Americans feel, as explored in research by The Families and Work Institute which approached the problem of overwork differently in their 2001 and 2004 studies, focusing not on work hours but instead issues such as experiences of stress, depression, multitasking, job pressure, work "contact" outside normal work hours, and work during vacations (Galinsky et al. 2004). The preference for fewer hours declines, however, to under 10 percent, if income would decrease (Golden and Gebreselassie 2007; Jacobs and Gerson 2004: 74). Half prefer to work the same hours for the same pay (Jacobs and Gerson 2004: 74).[8] Because the Great Recession put downward pressure on hours and wages, it has likely contributed to a greater increase in the percentage preferring more hours than these studies reported.

It makes intuitive sense that many who work long weeks would prefer fewer hours and that many who work short weeks would prefer more hours. Both men and women working above 40 hours a week would prefer fewer hours in general, with the mismatch increasing as the number of hours worked per week increases. Those working 20 hours

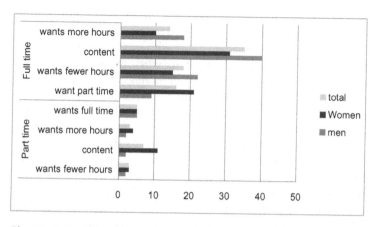

Figure 3.1 Mismatches in work hours and work status by gender (percent)
Data Source: ISSP 1997 (Reynolds 2003: 1184).

a week, of both sexes, desire more hours (Jacobs and Gerson 2004: 66).

Although most who work full time are content with their status, women employed full time are more likely than men to desire part time, and women employed part time are more likely than men to be content. Men employed full time are more likely than women to desire fewer hours or more hours, but they are considerably less likely to desire to change their employment status from full to part time (Reynolds 2003: 1184). Overall, 58 percent of American workers had some type of hours mismatch: 38 percent reported wanting to change the number of hours they work and approximately 20 percent wanted to change their work status (Reynolds 2003: 1184–5).

Work–life conflict may not always lead to a desire for different work hours. In the US, economic pressures appear to be more important. Reducing work hours may alleviate work–life conflict, but it may also create financial difficulties. Employees with few dependents or high incomes are most likely to desire to reduce work hours (Reynolds 2003: 1192). Those with frequent work–life conflict want to reduce their workload because they work substantially more hours than other employees (Reynolds and Aletraris 2007).

More African-Americans than whites are dissatisfied with their hours, because they want to work more hours. Forty-one percent of African-American males and 27 percent of white males who worked full time desired more hours at the same rate of pay. White females are more likely than African-American females (11.7 vs 7.8 percent among full-time workers) and male workers generally to desire fewer hours (Bell 1998: 486). While African-Americans and whites at higher income and higher educational levels were more likely to desire fewer hours than their lower-income, less-educated counterparts, African-Americans are still more likely than whites to desire more hours at all income and educational levels. This racial difference most likely is due to greater wage inequality among African-Americans than whites (Bell 1998; Golden and Gebreselassie 2007).

Paradoxically, workers with both schedule and location flexibility tend to experience overwork, suggesting that these types of flexibility do not necessarily alleviate overwork (Golden and Gebreselassie 2007: 26–7). Schedule and location flexibility, characteristic of select occupations that permit them, may contribute to a feeling of work-all-the-time by blurring the boundaries of paid work in time and space.

In sum, the large number of studies conducted before the Great Recession show that generally Americans work more hours annually than several decades ago. The increase in annual work hours is explained largely by an increase in the number of weeks worked per year, especially among women, rather than the number of hours worked per week. Some Americans work longer hours per week, many of whom would like to work less, and others work short hours, many of whom would like to work more. Increasingly, Americans work non-standard schedules. Work time has always been an important aspect of business strategy, and non-standard arrangements have become more commonplace as the service sector has expanded. Non-standard arrangements in the US create job insecurity and contribute to downward mobility, and non-standard workers fall outside the scope of standard labor protections. One non-standard arrangement, however, part-time employment, has become the default form of employment among many women in the US meshing employment and family care, as will be seen in chapter 4. Women outside the US often work part time, too, to accommodate family care, but the regulatory environment in many countries differs from that in the US, as will be seen in chapter 5.

4
Work–family, Work–life

We're employed as individuals, but we exist in families. Of American employees, 80 percent live with family members and have daily family responsibilities, almost half are parents with at least one child under age 18 who lives with them at least half of the time, and 20 percent of employed parents are single. Of married employees, 78 percent have spouses or partners who are also employed, and 35 percent of employees have significant elder care responsibilities (Bond et al. 2003). How work and family mesh affects our satisfaction with job, family, and life.

Women's employment, especially mothers', increased in the last half of the twentieth century, and, with it, potential stress and conflict in juggling paid work and family. Initially, researchers focused on areas of work–family conflict and spillover effects from one domain to the other.[1] While spillover effects can be negative (e.g., stress), they can also be sources of satisfaction and well-being (e.g., enhanced self-esteem) (Lewis 2003: 345; Warhurst et al. 2008). Emphasis has shifted away from conflict to work–family balance/integration/reconciliation (researchers favor different terms), and, especially in the US, the difficulties workers experience in also caring for children, and for ill, or aging, family members. Unlike most other countries (Heymann and Earle 2010), especially in Europe (Gornick and Meyers 2003, 2009), where paid leaves are available as matters of public policy, no such paid support exists in the US for working parents to take time off for family care. They adapt within the current structures of available child care, non-standard work, family-friendly benefits and paid sick days if their employer offers them, and unpaid leave per the federal 1993 Family and Medical Leave Act. Inadequate institutional support too often forces US workers to choose between job and family, leading US researchers to advocate paid leaves and more workplace flexibility.

Increasingly, however, especially in Europe where the lack of work–family supports is not an issue (although their practical effects are), attention is turning more holistically to work–life. Work–life debates are more gender neutral, recognize that workers without family care duties are not necessarily insulated from life stresses and work–family tensions, and embrace individuals' desires to simply "have a life" outside work (Kossek and Lambert 2005; Lewis 2003: 346). European work–life researchers are especially sensitive to the illusion of autonomy in workplace flexibility and knowledge work. For them, flexibility represents an unwelcome erosion of boundaries that permits work to encroach on personal and family life (Brannen 2005; Everingham 2002; Lewis 2003). I may exaggerate the continental distinction here, but it seems that in Europe, where work–family supports are well institutionalized, albeit imperfect and more or less gender egalitarian, the erosion of the work–life boundary with non-standard work contracts, intensification of professional work, and 24/7 demands of telework has become a more pressing concern.

Because there is copious research on work time, parenting, and the household gender division of labor in the US, that area forms the focus of this chapter. These themes will spill over to the next chapter as well, where I discuss work–family policies in European countries as part of a quick work-time world tour. I will return to the broad issue of work–life at the end of this chapter to reflect upon promising new areas of investigation.

From Family-based to Family Consumer Economy

A "subtle revolution" (Smith 1979) of American women's increasing labor-force participation after World War II has transformed workplaces and homes. Vestiges of the old gender system persist, however, contributing to unsatisfactory work–family integration and lingering gender inequities in occupational gender segregation and pay, and, more importantly for this book, hours of paid work, unpaid work, and free time. Women continue their traditional roles as primary caregivers even when employed, with a stressful "second shift" of unpaid work at home (Hochschild 1989). Increasingly, men assume more family responsibilities, and many women and men feel pressed for time. Individuals and families adapt as best they can within limited options, and organizational and public policy initiatives in recent years foster better work–family integration. But contradictions of the old and new remain.

Before industrialization, the home was the principal site of production in a family-based economy (Baca Zinn and Eitzen 1993; Boris and Lewis 2006; Cowan 1983; Gornick and Meyers 2003; Haraven 1990; Wharton 2006); farming and small handicrafts were the primary economic activities. Work occurred in and around the home and in home-based workshops. Men and women, while specializing in different tasks, worked alongside each other to meet the family's needs, and a concept of work as paid work was largely non-existent.

A family-wage economy (Baca Zinn and Eitzen 1993; Boris and Lewis 2006; Cowan 1983; Degler 1980; Gornick and Meyers 2003; Wharton 2006) emerged with industrialization, which changed the spatial location of work, the social definition of work, and gender relations. Paid work in factories was valued over unpaid work in the home. Fathers became the sole breadwinner in families that could afford it. In families permitting only male earners, fathers and work-age sons entered the paid workforce. Occasionally fathers, work-age sons, and work-age unmarried daughters were earners. And in yet other instances fathers became the primary breadwinner in families in which mothers also earned wages. In the US, these patterns varied by ethnicity. Immigrants of southern Italian heritage often opposed women's employment outside the home, whereas Irish, Polish, Swedish, and German women worked as domestics in middle-class homes. At no time during this period, however, did more than 10 or 15 percent of wives of any nationality work outside the home.

As unionism spread, many working-class men could afford to support a family on their own wages, similarly to more affluent middle-class men, and, by the mid-twentieth century, more women were stay-at-home mothers. Under a system of domesticity (Baca Zinn and Eitzen 1993: 57–8; Williams 2000) in which the majority of married women did not work outside the home, paid work was a domain almost exclusively of men that assumed the availability of full-time workers without family care responsibilities. This was the system inherited at the dawn of American women's increasing labor-force participation after World War II.

The expansion of the service economy and women's higher educational attainment created more employment opportunities for women as deindustrialization and union decline occurred in the US. As well-paid manufacturing jobs shrank as a percentage of total employment, and as non-union, low-wage service jobs increased, it became increasingly difficult to support a family on one income. During the closing decades of the twentieth century, families, having become more consumption-oriented, increasingly preferred two adult earners (Baca Zinn and Eitzen 1993; Boris and Lewis 2006; Gornick and Meyers 2003; Wharton 2006).

Women's Labor-force Participation

Labor-force participation is a measure that includes the employed and unemployed, that is, those without jobs who are actively seeking employment. (Persons not actively seeking employment are considered outside the labor force.) In 1900, nearly 85 percent of men were in the labor force compared to 18 percent of women and only 5 percent of married women (Blau et al. 2002). Women's labor-force participation in the US, especially among married women and mothers, increased since then and particularly since World War II. Trends have been steadily upward for virtually every female socioeconomic and demographic group. In 1940, 86 percent of married women were full-time homemakers, but, by 1994, 61 percent were in the labor force (Blau and Ehrenberg 1997: 1). Between 1940 and 1995, women workers increased from one fourth to nearly half of the labor force. Before World War II, labor-force participation was highest among working-class, poor, and minority women. Today, large numbers of middle-class and affluent women hold jobs. Through much of the twentieth century, each new birth cohort of women worked more than the one before, more as they aged, and more steadily during the child-rearing years, spending less time out of the labor force when they have children. While labor-force participation had declined between ages 20 to 29 among women born before the 1950s, this trend was reversed among women born in later years (Hartmann 2001: 130): today, women are less likely to exit the labor force to bear and raise children.

Women's labor-force participation continues to be lower than men's, but the rates are converging (table 4.1). Women's labor-force participation reversed direction in 2000 and is projected to continue to decline somewhat; men's rates have declined steadily since 1950 and are projected to continue to decline due to greater participation in education, job displacement, and early retirement. The increased labor-force participation of mothers is shown in table 4.2. Though fewer women than men are in the labor force, the distribution of the labor force by age has become nearly identical for both genders. The age category 25 to 34 is particularly important because that is when childbearing and care of young children tend to

Table 4.1:　Civilian labor-force participation rates (age 16+)

	M	F
1950	90.0[1]	35.0[2]
1970	79.7	43.3
1980	77.4	51.5
1990	76.4	57.5
2000	74.8	59.9
2005	73.3	59.3
2009	72.0	59.2
2018 (projected)	70.6	58.7

Sources: [1]Wharton 2006; [2]US Department of Labor 2006; US Department of Commerce, Bureau of the Census, 2011, *Statistical Abstract of the US* 2011, table 586.

Table 4.2: Women's labor-force participation by presence and age of children

	1970	1980	1990	2000	2005	2009
Single w/children	NA	52.0	55.2	73.9	72.9	72.0
<age 6	NA	44.1	48.7	70.5	68.5	67.8
age 6–17 only	NA	67.6	69.7	79.7	79.7	78.9
Married w/ children	39.7	54.1	66.3	70.6	68.1	69.8
<age 6	30.3	45.1	58.9	62.8	59.8	61.6
age 6–17 only	49.2	61.7	73.6	77.2	75.0	76.7

Source: US Department of Commerce, Bureau of the Census, 2011, *Statistical Abstract of the US* 2011, table 598.

occur. By 1996, 24.9 percent of the female civilian labor force was between the ages of 25 to 34 compared to 25.6 percent of males. In 1960, 17.8 percent of the female labor force was in this age group compared to 22.1 percent of males (US Bureau of the Census 1997: 400).

Women's employment hours

Consistent with studies cited in chapter 3, analysis of women's weekly work hours and patterns of full-time, year-round employment from 1978 to 1998 (Cohen and Bianchi 1999) showed that more women were employed outside the home, but the number of *weekly* hours of paid work was only slightly higher than in the 1970s. However, the average *annual* hours of paid work for all women increased from 900 to 1,239 during that time. Most of the increase in annual hours was the result of an increase in the proportion of all women who worked for pay, not an increase in weekly hours. Among employed women, average weekly hours of paid work increased from 34 to 36 hours from 1978 to 1998, and the average number of weeks of employment increased from 42 to 46. Among married women with children under six, the percentage employed outside the home increased 20 percent from 1978 to 1998, but average weekly hours increased less than three hours, from 31 to 33.7. Average weeks increased from 36 to 45.

Family Structure and Employment Hours

Because most people function in households with others, although the proportion of adults who live alone continues to increase, the household may be conceived as a labor unit in which the combined labor of workers becomes the total household labor or the combined labor of couples becomes couples' joint labor. Jacobs and Gerson (2004) argued for a focus on families (a subset of households because households can be inhabited by one person or unrelated persons) rather than individuals because dual-earner couples, especially those with children, and single-parent families are most likely to feel squeezed for time.

In 1970, the male breadwinner type was most common; however, by 2000, dual-earner couples had become a solid majority of married couples. A small change in work time occurred in male-breadwinner families; a larger change occurred among dual-earner couples, particularly in the percentage working long weeks (table 4.3). Growth in work time has been concentrated among couples with the most education, who occupy a disproportionate share of professional and managerial occupations.

As a unit, dual-income parents worked less per week than dual-earner couples without children. Individually, the arrival of children tends to push men toward stronger work participation while pulling women toward less involvement in paid work. Work hours of husbands increased slightly with the presence and increasing number of children, and married women with children worked fewer hours than married women without children (Jacobs and Gerson 2004: 49–51).

Housework, Child Care, and Free Time

Men's and women's total work time is almost equal, but women's paid work time is about two thirds of men's and

Table 4.3: Average work hours by family type, 1970–2000

	1970	*2000*
Married couples (age 18–64) (%)		
Dual earner	35.9	59.6
Husband only	51.4	26.0
Wife only	4.6	7.1
No earner	8.2	7.2
Average weekly hours		
Husband only	44.4	44.9
Dual earner (joint)	78.0	81.6
% Long weeks (100+)	8.7	14.5
Average hrs husband	–	+0.9
Average hrs wife	–	+2.7
Single parents		
Mother only (%)	9.9	21.9
Average weekly hours	38.5	38.5
% 40 hours	45.3	37.4
Father only (%)	1.2	2.4
Average weekly hours	38.8	36.8

Source: Jacobs and Gerson (2004: 43–52), from CPS data. Earner defined as employed at least one hour in the previous week.

women still do, on average, more unpaid work than paid work and more unpaid work than men (table 4.4).

Over three decades (1965–98), men's and women's time use converged (Sayer 2005) because men's paid work, still larger than women's, declined and women's increased. However, women still spend more time per day than men in unpaid work activities. But the ratio of women's to men's time in unpaid work declined in most housework and child-care activities, with substantial decreases in three core activities of cooking, cleaning, and daily child care. The dwindling gender difference in cooking and cleaning is due to increased minutes among men in conjunction with decreased minutes among women. In terms of child care, the declining ratio is due entirely to fathers' increased investment: mothers' minutes per day in daily child care were virtually the same in 1965 and 1998, while fathers' time increased by 24 minutes per

Table 4.4: Average hours per week of unpaid household work and paid work, 2003–2007 (age 15+)

	Men	Women
Paid	31.4	21.0
Unpaid	15.9	26.7
Total	47.3	47.7

Source: US Department of Commerce, Bureau of the Census, 2011, *Statistical Abstract of the US* 2011, table 638, from American Time Use Survey.

day on average (Sayer 2005: 291). Decreases in unpaid work among women have not offset their increase in paid work time as women's total work time rose over the three decades. In contrast, men's increased time in unpaid work activities has been offset by a slightly larger decrease in paid work time. Additionally, there are gender differences in multitasking; women multitask to squeeze more than 24 hours' worth of work out of a day (Sayer 2007).

Studies reviewed by Robinson and Godbey (1997) and Coltrane (2000, 2009) show that generally women still do twice as much routine housework as men. Women perform about two thirds of the total household labor in most American homes (Ishii-Kuntz and Coltrane 1992: 630; Robinson and Godbey 1997: 100). Women continue to feel responsible for family members' well-being and are more likely than men to adjust their work and home schedules and make other job tradeoffs to accommodate others (Coltrane 2000; Maume 2006). And mothers are much more likely than fathers to take time off from their jobs when a child is ill (Bond, Galinsky, and Swanberg 1998: 7). Married women are still expected to manage home and family; and, not surprisingly, employed wives enjoy less leisure and experience more stress than their husbands (Coltrane 2000: 1212). Research by Paden and Buehler (1995) has suggested that women cope primarily by planning and thinking positively about their situation, while men practice positive thinking and put off certain tasks until the pressure subsides, or temporarily withdraw from high-pressure situations. These coping mechanisms prevail over efforts to limit job responsibilities.

Men's involvement with child care and housework is greater among more educated groups, and in households where men have lower working hours and women have longer working hours, as well as where women have higher relative earnings. Couples still tend to see women's work schedules as the ones that need to bend to accommodate child care. Whereas the likelihood of which parent takes responsibility for child care is affected by multiple dimensions of the mother's employment schedule (such as hours per week, weekend work, and non-day shifts), only one aspect of the father's employment schedule – the time of day – affects his capacity to respond to child-care demands, suggesting that this is the only aspect of fathers' employment which is seen as available for taking into account when calculating child-care responsibilities. For this reason, fathers are most likely to take care of their youngest child in those situations where they work different hours from their partners (Brayfield 1995).

Some scholars are concerned about a caregiving gap (Harrington 1999; Heymann 2000; Thorne 2004), but recent research by Bianchi et al. (2006) shows no change in the amount of time mothers spend with their children today compared to a few decades ago, despite increases in their hours of paid employment. They found that parents today are spending as much and perhaps more time interacting with their children than parents in 1965, "the heyday of the stay-at-home mother" (Bianchi et al. 2006: 1). Parents are multitasking and incorporating children into their leisure activities. Although maternal time with children dipped between 1965 and 1975, the time today's mothers spend caring for their children is as high or higher than during the 1960s. Married fathers' time with children increased substantially after 1985 and is higher than it has ever been. While today's mothers are spending as much if not more time in active engagement with their children, they are spending less time doing housework. Fathers have picked up some of the slack, but standards have changed too. The tradition of Monday as laundry day and Tuesday as ironing day is long gone! Wrinkle-resistant fabrics require little if any ironing. Dishwashers allow other activities to be undertaken while the machine does the work. More convenience foods are available, making food preparation less time-consuming. Families eat at restaurants more often, or bring home carry-out items, and some pay others to clean the house or maintain the yard. Demographic changes are important as well. Today, mothers have fewer children, childbearing occurs later, it is possible to control when childbearing occurs, and it is more acceptable to forgo having children at all. While there are fewer children to care for, norms regarding parenting have changed, which some scholars have labeled intensive parenting, especially among more highly educated parents who not only spend more time with their children but also do more intellectually stimulating things with their children (Bianchi et al. 2006). And even if mothers' time with their children has not declined despite paid employment, finding and paying for substitute care can be a challenge, especially among low-income families. The gender specialization of women as primary caregivers in the family and men as primary breadwinners remains very strong in families with children, particularly young children, giving rise to a neo-traditional (Moen 2003) gender division of labor in which mothers and fathers both engage in paid work.

Women's employment hours have a strong effect on women's housework time (Coltrane 2000: 1220), but results are mixed when it comes to the effect of women's employment on men's housework. Some studies report that wives' employment status – that is, whether they are employed full time, part time, or not at all – has little effect on how much housework men do (Reskin and Padavic 1994: 151; Shelton 1992; Thompson and Walker 1989). Others find that men living with women who are employed longer hours do a greater share of domestic work. Men contribute more housework when women are involved in shift work or flexitime employment, especially if their employment hours do not overlap (Coltrane 2000: 1220; Presser 1994). Less paid work generally means more family work for men, although some studies find no relationship between men's employment hours and their housework (Coltrane 2000: 1220). Men who are better educated or have a young child at home do slightly more than other men (Coltrane 2000: 1221; Reskin and Padavic 1994: 151; Shelton 1992; Thompson and Walker

1989), and some studies have found that African-American and Hispanic men do more housework (Coltrane 2000: 1222–3; Reskin and Padavic 1994: 151; Shelton and John 1993). Women with more education do less housework, and wives who earn more enjoy more equal divisions of labor (Coltrane 2000: 1220). However, the transition to parenthood is associated with movement toward less sharing of family work between men and women, and being married means more housework for women and less for men (Coltrane 2000: 1222; Hartmann 1981).

Housework and child care are not only about available time; they are about "doing gender" (West and Zimmerman 1987). A study of housework in marital and non-marital households (South and Spitze 1994) gives insight into this process. The authors found that women spend more hours than men on housework in all marital statuses – never married, living in the parental home; never married, living independently; cohabiting; married; divorced; and widowed. The gender difference in housework hours widened dramatically in couple households compared to the never married and those living independently, reaching its zenith among married couples. Much of the difference in housework time in married couple households was *not* explained by the presence of children and reduced hours of wives' paid work. Social and economic differences, especially the presence of children and hours of paid work, accounted for about half of the gender gap in housework overall, but marital status differences in housework among women were generally greater than the corresponding differences among men.

Women's increased total work time has come at the expense of free time. Sayer (2005: 296) found that free time among both women and men increased from 1965 to 1975 and then declined from 1975 to 1998, with parents having less free time than men and women overall. The decline among women was sharper than among men, and among parents this suggests that mothers give up free time so they can allocate more time to paid work and child care. Sayer's results are consistent with those of the 2002 National Study of the Changing Workforce. In that study, time "allocated to self" declined from 1977 to 2002 among both employed mothers and fathers, from 2.1 hours to 1.3 hours among fathers and from 1.6 hours to 0.9 hours among mothers (Bond et al. 2003).

Work–family

Time management can be difficult for anyone – female or male, married or not – who is juggling employment and family care. Almost 60 percent of respondents in the 1997 National Study of the Changing Workforce reported conflict in balancing work, personal life, and family life. More women than men felt used up at the end of the workday, weren't able to get everything done at home, and felt burned out or stressed by work. Men and women were equally likely to feel their jobs left them insufficient time for themselves (Jacobs and Gerson 2004: 85). This compares to about one third in the 1970s (Pleck et al. 1980), suggesting that work–family conflict has increased among American workers as the proportion of dual-earner and single-parent households has increased over the same period.

Predictably, parents are more likely than those without children to report conflict in balancing work, personal life, and family life; interference between job and family; inability to get everything done at home; and insufficient time for self and family or other important people. Men with children were slightly more likely to experience interference between job and family than women with children. Although parents experience the most work–family conflict, about 50 percent of individuals without children under age 18 experience conflict in balancing work, personal life, and family life. Women without children under 18 are more likely than their male counterparts to say they are not able to get everything done at home because of their job (one third compared to one fourth) and to feel burned out or stressed by work (30 percent compared to just over 20 percent) (Jacobs and Gerson 2004: 91–2).

Young adults today anticipating family formation express gender egalitarian ideals that will likely be difficult to achieve in practice because of inadequate child care, lingering workplace rigidity, insufficient institutional support for employed parents, and conventional mothering ideologies that place care responsibilities disproportionately on women by default (Gerson 2010; MacDonald 2009).

Private Adaptations

American families must cobble together their own solutions to manage family care and employment in a market-system of care. Unlike most European countries, where unions are stronger and have a say in family-support systems, and national governments have established policies to support working parents, the US federal government has been reluctant to fashion public policies to support working families, especially a system of publicly supported child care (Gornick and Meyers 2003; Huston 2004). Regarding work time, the most common solutions involve reducing the employment of one parent, usually the mother; arranging "split-shift" or "tag-team" parenting; working non-standard hours; and using child care outside the home. Mothers' labor-force participation has increased in recent decades, even among mothers of young children, as noted above, but mothers of young children are still more likely to work fewer hours for pay, if they work for pay outside the home at all, than either women without children or men. The trends in voluntary part-time employment discussed in chapter 3 are additional evidence of this private solution. In split-shift or tag-team parenting, one parent is employed while the other cares for their children; the second parent goes to work after the first returns home. An estimated one fourth to one third of couples in which one parent works non-standard hours rely on split-shift or tag-team parenting to provide care for their young children, and the presence of a preschool-age child increases mothers' likelihood of working non-day hours by 46 percent. Child care is the main reason for working non-standard hours among 35 percent of mothers; for another 9 percent, care for another family member was their primary reason (Presser 1995, 2004). As for out-of-home care, more than three fourths of preschool-age children with employed mothers are now cared for in non-parental child-care settings; half of these children are in care for 35 or more hours a week

(Capizzano, Adams, and Sonenstein 2000; Gornick and Meyers 2003: 44). Some of this care is provided by relatives, but nearly half of preschool-age children are cared for in child-care centers or family child-care homes. The use of child care has increased steadily with maternal employment. Two thirds of children of employed mothers are in non-parental care before their first birthday, as are three fourths of two- and three-year-olds (Ehrle, Adams, and Tout 2001; Gornick and Meyers 2003: 44).

Socioeconomic factors

The consequences and meaning of private adaptations vary, depending on the structure and socioeconomic position of families. A parent's part-time or non-standard employment, particularly at low wages and without health insurance or retirement benefits, is readily absorbed in a family in which there is a second earner who is well paid with good benefits. Child care, while costly, may not be a financial drain in afflu-ent families. Among low-income families, however, such private adaptations ratify their precarious financial position. Part-time and non-standard jobs may have long-term nega-tive consequences not only for earnings and retirement, but also for upward mobility (Ferber and Waldfogel 1998; Negrey et al. 2007). And child-care costs are a major financial burden in families with limited incomes. Although some low-income families, like other families, can find free care with relatives or in split-shift or tag-team arrangements, many low-income families pay for care. The average cost ranges from 15 to 25 percent of their total income, according to different estimates (Gianarelli and Barsimantov 2000; Gornick and Meyers 2003; Huston 2004; Phillips and Bridgman 1995), compared to 6 percent among families with higher incomes (Gianarelli and Barsimantov 2000).

Mothers in low-income families are less likely to be employed compared to those in families with higher incomes, but when they are employed they work fewer hours (Huston 2004) that are often irregular and non-standard (Presser 2004). A disproportionate number of low-income families are headed by single mothers – half of poor families today, up from 25 percent in 1959; among African-Americans, three fourths of poor families today (author's calculations of US Census data), and 30 percent of families headed by single mothers earn wages at or below poverty level (Hawkins and Whiteman 2004: 255).

Replacement of the welfare entitlement program, Aid to Families with Dependent Children (AFDC), with Temporary Assistance for Needy Families (TANF) in 1996 has, by design, reduced cash assistance by placing time limits on receipt (in "work-first" states, job ready within two years; in all states, lifetime limit of five years), reduced the number of welfare recipients since its enactment, and increased employment among low-income single mothers (Haskins and Primus 2002; US Department of Health and Human Services 2001). As a result, more low-income parents need substitute care for their children. Yet the supply is deficient in low-income areas. Not only do low-income parents have limited ability to pay for care and transportation challenges getting to care centers, but the number of spaces available may be considerably less than the demand. Care for infants and toddlers is in shorter supply and more expensive than that for older children, and care is also difficult to find for children with special needs and at non-standard and irregular hours (Gornick and Meyers 2003; Huston 2004).

Child-care subsidies are the principal form of assistance provided to low-income families by federal and state governments, and the amount of money in subsidy programs has increased substantially over the last 10 years (Huston 2004). The need for care outpaces these subsidies, however, and fewer than 25 percent of the federally eligible children receive any subsidies (US Department of Health and Human Services 1999). Subsidy duration is brief, from just three to seven months, in one study of five states (Meyers et al. 2002). Although state-funded pre-kindergarten services for three- and four-year-olds operate in nearly 40 states, they serve only about 10 percent of children in this age range and typically operate on a part-day, part-year basis, with long waiting lists (Barnett et al. 2004; Gault and Lovell 2006; Huston 2004). As such, child-care problems are often a barrier to getting and maintaining employment among low-income women (Huston 2004).

Personal relationships

Private adaptations in the form of non-standard hours may have negative consequences for marital quality. In an analysis of data from the National Survey of Families and Households conducted in two waves from 1987 to 1988 and 1992 to 1994 (77 percent of respondents in wave one were re-interviewed in wave two), Presser (2003: 105–8) found that working non-day rather than day shifts was linked to a higher-quality marriage among single-earner couples, providing it was the husband who was the earner. If the single earner was the wife, working non-days was associated with poorer-quality marriage, particularly among single-earner couples with children. Among dual-earner couples, there was evidence of lower marital quality when either spouse worked a non-day schedule, depending upon the particular measure of marital quality and which spouse worked the non-standard schedule. Weekend employment, however, seemed to have no effect on marital quality among dual-earner couples, whether they had children or not. Non-standard schedules increased the likelihood of marital instability over a five-year period among all couples under certain conditions, especially night and rotating shifts, but gender and duration of marriage had intervening effects. Non-standard schedules did not affect marital instability when couples had no children, but when couples had children, non-standard schedules appeared to complicate family life, increasing the risk of separation and divorce. Late-hours employment, especially after midnight, posed the greater risk when compared to evening employment. Weekend employment showed no such risk.

Gender

Private adaptations, especially in the form of reduced and/or non-standard hours of maternal employment, arise from the conventional gender division of labor in which women are primary caregivers and men are primary breadwinners and, in turn, reinforce this conventional gender division of labor. Arguably, women start from a disadvantaged economic position, and most remain there while juggling employment and family care. The factors underlying women's disadvantaged position are complex, encompassing historical effects, occupational segregation, women's socialization, and women's education (e.g., Reskin and Padavic 1994). Recent research has focused on the marginalization of mothers, not because they are women but because of their caregiving responsibilities. This occurs because market work is based on an "ideal worker norm" (Williams 2000) that assumes employees work full time (currently standardized at 40 hours per week); and uninterruptedly, that is, free of the necessity to bear children and without caregiving responsibilities that might interfere with full-time work. Because mothers' lives are at variance from the ideal worker norm, they are disproportionately relegated to marginal jobs – often at low wages – but with work routines that mesh relatively well with caregiving. The marginalization of mothers in market work results in wage and other penalties (Correll et al. 2007), although the estimates of this wage penalty vary somewhat – 6 percent for mothers with one child and 13 percent for mothers with two or more children (Waldfogel 1997), or 7 percent per child (Budig and England 2001).

Gender differences in paid and unpaid work clearly reveal that "working time is gendered time" (Sirianni and Negrey 2000). As work is gendered (Collinson 1992; Cooper 2000; Davies 1990; Hartmann 1976; Lee 1998), organizations are gendered (Acker 1990, 1992; Kanter 1977) in that organizations take on the gendered character of the employees within. In the abstract, jobs and organizations appear gender-neutral, but gender is a "constitutive element" (Acker 1990) in the underlying assumptions and practices of work organizations, and is thus embedded in the social structure of these. In the gendered organization, jobs are embodied, with different tasks being assigned to women and men, and the tasks of women and men are evaluated and rewarded differently. Job, like organization, is an implicitly gendered concept.

Laws against gender discrimination in employment, promotion, and pay have challenged the traditional gender practices of organizations, creating opportunities for women in occupations previously closed to them. Because domestic life is gendered, women bring to the world of paid work their duties and responsibilities as mothers and caretakers. As a new fatherhood (Coltrane 2009; Cooper 2000) emerges, in which men are more engaged in family care than in the past, they increasingly bring domestic responsibilities to the world of paid work too. And because the demands of the two worlds often clash, organizations have been pressured to offer more flexible employment arrangements.

Workplace and Public Policy Initiatives

Employers have become more responsive to employees' needs, but it is still a challenge for workers to integrate work and family. In the last few decades, flexible work arrangements have emerged at workplaces to alleviate work–family conflict, and in 1993 the US federal government took a significant step by enacting the Family and Medical Leave Act. Generally, flexible work arrangements offer workers increased flexibility, but they are band-aid solutions to a much larger structural problem. Relatively few workers use them, and women do so more often than men – thus ratifying gender inequity (Negrey 1993; Rapoport et al. 2002). Flexibility is a matter of degree (Altman and Golden 2007). Flexible arrangements may deviate from the standard 40-hour norm, but they do not challenge the norm per se; and the inability to work a standard schedule is assumed to be an individual problem, not a societal problem. The FMLA is more broad-based, but, because it provides for only unpaid leave and pertains only to episodic circumstances, it is inadequate as well. Two studies (Blair-Loy 2003; Stone 2007) of professional women who left full-time careers found that leaving occurred because of family crises (Blair-Loy 2003) or they were shut out by long hours, extensive travel, and 24/7 demands of "all-or-nothing" workplaces (Stone 2007). Family-friendly policies offered little relief because of discrepancies between formal policies and informal practices, and they did not address the problem of long hours (Stone 2007). In recent years, public policy activism has turned to expanding paid sick leave as a means to better accommodate family care.

Flexible work arrangements

Several forms of flexible work arrangements have emerged at workplaces throughout the US. Conventional part-time employment is by far the most prevalent "option" because employers in growing sectors, such as services and retail trade, make it widely available to fulfill their own needs for flexible staffing. This market-based form of flexibility (Negrey 1993) does not necessarily mean workers can control their schedules because part-time work schedules can be variable and unpredictable (Golden 2001; Lambert 2008; Negrey 1993). Flextime, compressed workweeks, job sharing, and home-based work are other increasingly popular alternatives. Flextime involves varying daily start and end times by individual preference, usually around a core of required hours from 10 a.m. to 3 p.m. Compressed workweeks alter the workweek of five eight-hour days to four 10-hour days. In job-sharing arrangements two workers share one full-time job, and each works part-time hours. Job sharing, when available, is a strategy for dividing quality full-time jobs to create part-time opportunities (Negrey 1993). Past research (Hayghe 1988; Hewitt Associates 1991) showed that flextime was far more common than compressed workweeks, job sharing, and work-at-home arrangements. Child-care assistance is also a work-family benefit that some organizations offer their employees, most commonly dependent-care spending accounts and information and referral services – less expensive benefits than on- or near-site child care or direct employer subsidies to pay for care (Glass and Estes 1997).

Work-family benefits are not well institutionalized and may be temporary ad hoc arrangements. Less than 10 percent of employees are offered flexible schedule arrangements by a formal employee benefit program (Beers 2000; Strope 2003), thus flextime practices, while more common, tend to be informal. Rather than establish formal programs, organizations may implement flextime or other arrangements in response to specific requests by individual employees (Glass and Estes 1997; Negrey 1993), and employees may not utilize family-friendly options if they fear doing so will jeopardize job security, work assignments, and promotion opportunities (Glass and Estes 1997; Hochschild 1997; Jacobs and Gerson 2004). Indeed, 40 percent of employees, and 60 percent of women, feared that using flextime or taking time off for family reasons would negatively affect career opportunities (Bond, Galinsky, and Swanberg 1998; Heldrich Center 1999). However, increasing numbers of organizations are finding it advantageous to offer work–family benefits to enhance recruitment and retention (Barnett and Hall 2001; Lambert 1993). Such benefits make it easier for workers to adjust family life to conform to the workplace rather than making work requirements accommodate family life (Lambert 1993).

Firm size and the proportion of women employed therein, especially in leadership positions, appear to be important determinants of the number of family responsive policies offered (Gerstel and Clawson 2002; Goodstein 1994; Osterman 1995; Seyler et al. 1995), although the effects of female concentration disappeared when occupation was controlled (Osterman 1995) and firm size was positively related only to formal benefits, while informal leave and schedule policies were more likely to occur in small firms (Glass and Fujimoto 1995). Firms whose product markets target families or who have family-sensitive constituents were often more likely to be committed to family responsive workplace policies because they see implementation as good for their public image (Glass and Estes 1997). While flexible scheduling has increased over time, it has reached a plateau recently; and the demand for flexibility exceeds the supply in the labor market. Surveys report that 30 to 40 percent of workers actually have flexible schedules on a daily basis, but as many as 79 percent would like to have more flexible options and would use them if feasible and there were no negative repercussions to doing so (Altman and Golden 2007; Galinsky et al. 2005).

Studies of unions provide inconsistent results regarding availability of work-family benefits, but one important characteristic is likely union strength. Not only is it important that unions assign priority to family issues, but unions must also have the strength to achieve their goals. Some unions oppose flexible schedules; others advocate for them. Most unions make child care a low priority; others fight for some form of child care. Most importantly, unions are concerned that benefits be affordable. Although collectively bargained contracts are an important means to obtain family benefits, workers win their greatest advances when there is public policy on which to build. Unions build on the Family and Medical Leave Act, for example, in at least two ways. They negotiate to extend benefits, for example, paid leaves or longer leaves, and they help workers know their rights and how to enforce them (Gerstel and Clawson 2002).

Numerous studies (Bond et al. 2003; Glass and Estes 1997) have found evidence that family responsive policies, particularly schedule flexibility, decrease tardiness, absenteeism, and turnover; increase employees' job satisfaction; and enhance employees' health and well-being, contributing to decreased depression and anxiety and fewer somatic complaints. On-site child care enhances recruitment and retention. Yet Hochschild's (1997) popular book *The Time Bind* showed how factors in company culture militate against workers' use of family-friendly policies, despite their availability and eligibility. Thus, workplaces must not only create work–family programs but foster a workplace culture that takes them seriously and encourages their use, amounting to a paradigmatic shift to become "life friendly" (Gewirtz and Fried 2007). Public policy could be used to encourage this paradigm shift (Altman and Golden 2007).

Box 4.1: Work and life at IBM

During the past quarter-century, International Business Machines Corporation (IBM) has expanded its menu of work–family programs to create a work environment that recognizes the individual as a whole person and fosters success both on the job and in the home. This expansion was facilitated by a series of work and life issues surveys, initiated in 1986, through which employees' opinions inform policies and programs.

In the 1970s, IBM hired thousands of women to fill positions throughout the company. Very capable professionally, many had difficulty transitioning into motherhood while maintaining a full-time career. In response to these needs,

(Continued)

the first work–family programs at IBM were implemented, including child-care referral services; six weeks' paid disability plus 10.5 months of unpaid maternity leave, and flexible work hours to allow employees to start work up to 30 minutes before or after regular work hours.

Flextime was expanded from 30 to 60 minutes after the 1986 survey. At this time, IBM contracted to implement the first extensive national elder-care referral service, and the company's leave of absence program was expanded from one year to three years. IBM also subsidized construction of high-quality child-care facilities in exchange for guaranteed slots for its employees, and maternity benefits were extended to adoptive parents. A work-at-home pilot was also initiated; and to improve the corporate work–life culture, work–life training was developed for management, and seminars were created and offered to employees.

In the 1990s, employees wanted even more flexibility. A flexible work leave of absence program was implemented through which employees could combine up to three years of leave with part-time employment. Participants would receive full benefits with a proportional reduction in pay. Two years later the program limit was expanded to five years, and managers became eligible to use the program. Flextime was expanded; employees could begin or end their workday up to two hours before or after regularly scheduled hours, and they could apply this flexibility to their lunch hour as well. Work from home during regular business hours was piloted, and policies supporting permanent part-time professional employment were created. Regarding the latter, accompanying proportional reduction in pay were full benefits for three years after which the employee would pay to maintain full benefits.

In 1998, a flexibility project office was established at the corporate level and charged with implementing flexibility initiatives that could be replicated worldwide. An "80/20" rule was established: 80 percent of the strategies should generally apply to all geographies and business units and 20 percent could be customized to fit individual business and country needs. Subsequently, after the 1998 Europe and Latin America Work and Life Issues Survey and the 2001 and 2004 Global Work and Life Issues Surveys, each area of the world would develop its own work–life strategy. The 1998 survey was conducted in 22 countries in Latin America and Europe, the 2001 survey was administered globally in 49 countries and in 20 languages, and the 2004 survey was carried out in 79 countries (Hill et al. 2006).

The distribution of flexible schedules among workers is quite uneven (Golden 2001; McMenamin 2007), appears to be associated with bifurcation of the workweek (Golden 2001), and is a dimension of ongoing destandardization of work time, much driven by employers, not employees (Golden 2001; Tilly 1991). Thus, workers with less market power experience a form of flexibility that may benefit employers more than themselves (Negrey 1993).

A special supplement to the CPS conducted in May 2004 on Work Schedules and Work at Home showed that nearly one third of all wage and salary workers (full time and part time) had flexible schedules on their primary jobs, meaning they could vary their starting and quitting times. This proportion increased from 1985 to 1997, but has remained fairly steady since. The proportions of employed men and women able to vary their work hours have been about equal, as have the proportions of both employed mothers and fathers. Industry is one of the main determinants of the prevalence of flexible schedules. Relatively fewer workers in manufacturing (25 percent) had such schedules, whereas nearly 40 percent of workers in finance or professional and business services had them. Despite the fact that the proportion of workers with flexible schedules has remained fairly steady in recent years, there were declines in particular industries such as retail trade; finance and insurance; educational services; arts, entertainment, and recreation; and accommodation (McMenamin 2007: 3–4).

Flexible schedules also vary by occupation, with the lowest percentages among production workers (13.8) and teachers (16.6), and the highest among managers (46.7) and a number of other professionals. Men were more likely than women to have access to flexible schedules, except among workers with less than a college degree among whom women were more likely than men to have a flexible schedule. Access was higher for those in highly skilled occupations with lower unemployment rates, suggesting that workers with market power also have power to create flexibility in their work schedules. White and Asian workers, who are disproportionately employed in professional and managerial occupations, were more likely to have flexible schedules compared to other racial-ethnic groups. College graduates were generally more likely than workers with less education to have flexible schedules, again showing the effect of occupation (McMenamin 2007: 4–5, 7). Access to daily flexibility was less likely for non-whites, women, unmarried persons, those with relatively less education, and public-sector employees (Golden 2001).

Part-time workers constituted a disproportionate share of workers with flexible schedules. Whereas about 19 percent of all wage and salary workers usually worked part-time, nearly a quarter of all workers with flexible schedules worked part time. Among part-time workers, 38.6 percent had flexible schedules compared to 27.5 percent of those who normally worked full time (McMenamin 2007: 8).

Family and Medical Leave Act

The other major innovation in work–family policy in the US was the enactment of the Family and Medical Leave Act of 1993. The FMLA requires businesses with 50 or more employees within a 75-mile radius of the workplace to provide eligible workers with up to 12 weeks a year of unpaid leave for pregnancy and maternity disability; care of newborns; placement of adopted or foster children; care for immediate family members who are seriously ill, including children, spouse, or a parent; or care for one's own serious illness. Eligible employees must have worked for their employer for one year or at least 1,250 hours within the year, and companies are permitted to exempt the top 10 percent of salaried employees (Fried 1998: 2, 31). Employers must also continue to provide health-care coverage during leaves, restore employees to their jobs or equivalent positions when they return, post notices of the law's requirements, and keep records regarding their compliance with its provisions. Because this leave is unpaid, many cannot afford to take it (Cantor et al. 2001; Gault and Lovell 2006). Also, the terms of eligibility limit coverage to approximately 55 percent of all workers in the US (Commission on Family and Medical Leave 1996; Sandberg and Cornfield 2000: 180). Although the majority of employers readily adopted and implemented the law, there have been a number of cases of employer non-compliance, most stemming from complaints that employers did not reinstate employees to the same or equivalent positions (Fried 1998: 149).

Organizations and states may go beyond the terms of FMLA if they so choose. Few private employers have done so, however. Employees in only 7 percent of all establishments can get paid family leave (Lovell 2008). Five states – California, Hawaii, New Jersey, New York, and Rhode Island – use temporary disability insurance for paid maternity leave. Maximum durations range from 26 to 52 weeks; average durations range from five to 13 weeks; maximum weekly benefits range from $170 to $487; average weekly benefits range from $142 to $273. Several states extend the FMLA to include smaller employers, increase duration, or both (Gornick and Meyers 2003: 127). California, the first state to do so, enacted paid parental leave in 2002 and launched the program in 2004 (Gault and Lovell 2006: 1155; Gornick and Meyers 2003: 127). Building on the state disability insurance program, it is funded through an employee payroll deduction capped at $63.53 per worker per year in 2005. The program covers leaves of up to six weeks to care for an infant or seriously ill family member and, under the previously enacted SDI program, up to 52 weeks of leave for an employee to recover from his or her own serious illness. Employees can receive up to 55 percent of their weekly wages up to a maximum of $728 (Gault and Lovell 2006: 1155; Milkman and Applebaum 2004). Interest in paid family leave has since diffused to other states, particularly New Jersey, Massachusetts, and Washington (Shellenbarger 2008; Gault and Lovell 2006: 1155).

Some labor unions have also made efforts to expand FMLA via their contracts with employers. These efforts have included longer leaves; paid leaves; continuation of all benefits, not just health insurance; and return to work on a reduced schedule. The American Federation of State, County and Municipal Employees (AFSCME) Local 11 and the State of Ohio, for example, agreed to four weeks of paid leave at 70 percent wage replacement and up to six months of unpaid leave (Fried 1998: 174).

Early estimates were that only 16.8 percent of those eligible to use leaves under the terms of FMLA actually did so (Commission on Family and Medical Leave 1996; Fried

1998: 157). Among those covered by the federal FMLA, women are more likely than men to take the leave. In 2000, 58 percent of leave takers were women and 42 percent were men. Leave takers were also more likely to be married and have children. Leaves tended to be longer when they were for maternity; disability; a worker's own health; and care of a newborn, new adopted child, or new foster child. Leaves tended to be shorter for care of an ill child, spouse, or parent (Cantor et al. 2001). FMLA is an individual, non-transferable entitlement; one parent cannot transfer his or her leave to the other parent (Gornick and Meyers 2003: 137). This structure is an incentive for both parents to take leave; however, because men often earn more than women, wages lost may be greater if fathers take leave. Paid leaves, even at partial wage replacement, would alter this dynamic.

In a study of leave takers drawn from a national sample of workers conducted for the Commission on Family and Medical Leave soon after FMLA was implemented, Sandberg and Cornfield (2000) identified a gendered pattern in leave takers' reasons for returning to work. Women were more likely to terminate their leaves in response to pressures from work (they could not afford to stay away longer, they had used up their leave time, they felt pressured by co-workers and bosses to return to work, they had too much work to do to stay away longer); men were more likely to terminate their leaves because they "wanted to." Working for an FMLA-covered employer and having a fully paid leave (an optional benefit that may be provided by employers as FMLA requires unpaid leaves only) reduced the constraints of work on women's reasons for returning to work. Having a fully paid leave increased the likelihood that women would return to work because they wanted to.

In addition to affordability, the existence of a male-defined workplace culture and an "overtime culture" can discourage use of FMLA. When work performance is evaluated based on face time and responsiveness to deadline pressures, in an organizational culture in which successful, high-ranking, typically male, employees are not primary caregivers and do not take leaves, workers may not request leaves when they are eligible for them or take shorter leaves than that to which they are legally entitled because pressure to conform to workplace norms is so great (Fried 1998).

While FMLA's enactment was momentous for American workers, it is modest compared to similar legislation in a number of other nations, as will be seen in the next chapter. Its passage lagged behind theirs as well. Prior to passage of the FMLA, only a quarter to a third of US employer policies matched current FMLA requirements in the protection they offered (Commission on Family and Medical Leave 1996; Fried 1998: 26), and the US was the only country of 118 surveyed by the International Labour Organization (ILO) that had no national laws mandating parental leave. Most other major industrialized countries mandate paid maternity leave, offer more than 12 weeks, and do not exclude small businesses.[2]

Although the enactment of new public policy in the form of the FMLA indicates recognition of a social problem, the law is intended to respond only to episodic circumstances of parenting and illness. President Barack Obama supports extending FMLA to employers with 25 workers and covering more purposes, including children's school needs and the care of a wider range of family members, and he proposed giving states $1.5 billion to start paid family leave programs (Shellenbarger 2008), but federal spending cuts will prevent legislative action for the foreseeable future. The daily challenge of integrating work with the rest of life is a chronic problem that FMLA does not address. Paid family leave does not address this problem either.

Paid sick leave

Traditional paid sick leave can be another tool for parents juggling employment and care, but paid sick leave is not universal. Employees in 59 percent of all establishments get paid sick days, and the benefit is more common in larger than smaller workplaces. In 80 percent of establishments, employees get some kind of paid leave, typically paid vacation (Lovell 2008). Nearly 50 percent of workers outside the federal government and military lack paid sick leave. Women are more likely than men to be in jobs lacking paid sick leave, and such jobs are more prevalent in food service, low-wage, and non-union jobs (Lovell 2004). Low-wage workers are more likely to be single parents and to experience obstacles to work, such as chronic poor health, disabilities, and unstable housing (Gault and Lovell 2006: 1153). Legislation introduced in 2004 by the late Senator Edward Kennedy (D-Massachusetts) and Congresswoman Rosa DeLauro (D-Connecticut) and reintroduced in 2005, called the Healthy Families Act (H. R. 1902, 2005; S. 1085, 2005), would require US employers with 15 or more employees to provide workers a minimum of seven days of paid sick leave annually to care for their own or family members' illnesses (Gault and Lovell 2006: 1155–6). President Barack Obama supports this legislation, although employers object, claiming it is rigid and not needed. On June 4, 2011, Connecticut became the first state to pass a paid sick days law, and support for similar legislation is growing in other states, such as Massachusetts, Georgia, and California (Dobuzinskis 2011). San Francisco is one of the few cities in the US in which all employers are mandated by law to provide paid sick days (Williams 2011), and Philadelphia, Seattle, and Denver are pursuing similar legislation (Dobuzinskis 2011).

Work–life

A holistic frame of work–life includes work–family issues and permits questions to emerge about the intersection of employment and other facets of life and the experiences of non-caregivers. As such, work–life research can take in the intersection of work and leisure, work and community engagement, and a host of other lifestyle matters. Especially promising is the investigation of different modes in which workers maintain boundaries between work and non-work time, for example, Nippert-Eng's (1996) integration-segmentation divide, discussed in box 4.2. Close examination is needed to determine where boundaries lie, their permeability, and the degree to which workers can control them (Lambert and Kossek 2005; Warhurst et al. 2008). The crux may lie in the difference between jobs that pay a salary versus an hourly wage. Although hourly workers may face numerous difficulties (mandatory overtime on short notice, employer abuses of unpaid overtime, variable hours, unpredictable schedules, work at undesirable times, too few hours, schedules that conflict with those of others important in one's life, and difficulties accommodating family needs, none of which are small matters), the difference between on- and off-the-clock is binary and the work–life boundary relatively firm. Among those paid a salary, whose labor is purchased by the year, boundary management may be more challenging. Work time may grow and work become more intensified when there are no firm daily, weekly, or monthly limits and all time is subject to the annual contract; when organizations are short-staffed due to cost pressures; when individual recognition and career mobility are competitive. Electronic technologies, which make work ever-present, exacerbate this problem, especially when parties to communication draw different boundaries around work time. The domain of online college courses is a good example, wherein students take them for their temporal and spatial convenience, may use weekend evenings as non-exam class time, and seek urgent consultation time from an instructor who defines weekend evenings as personal time. Work–family policies do not address boundary clashes of this sort.

As this chapter has shown, work–life integration is a challenge for many American workers, especially parents and those with elder-care responsibilities. They make private adaptations by bending work schedules to the extent they can, relying on other family members and friends, and purchasing care from care providers. Family-friendly organizations are usually characterized by an informal patchwork of flexible work arrangements, although these are often inadequate or workers participate reluctantly for fear of negative reprisal. The most common form of flexible arrangement, part-time employment, tends to be the default option of working parents, especially mothers. This arrangement exists within a contemporary labor market undergoing destandardization, as discussed in chapter 3, which often benefits employers more than workers. The Family and Medical Leave Act mandates unpaid leaves for eligible workers, but usage is

Box 4.2: Managing the work–life boundary: calendars

The number and type of calendars someone uses is one of the most telling indicators of where she or he falls along the integration–segmentation continuum . . . calendar maintenance shows how we help maintain a given relationship between the contents of home and work, including the selves we locate there . . .

The more we segment . . . the more we use calendars that are realm-specific both in their locations *and* their contents. These dedicated calendars rarely include references to other-realm activities . . .

Occasionally, these more segmenting discrete calendars include other-realm events that trespass on the time normally reserved for a given realm. Overnight business travel is listed on home calendars, for instance, as it usurps what is normally "home time." Likewise, daytime family events like lunch with a spouse, a child's concert, or a repair or delivery appointment requiring someone at home are listed on dedicated work calendars . . .

. . . an element of practicality helps promote more integrating and segmenting approaches to calendars. The more we segment, the more blocks of time are mapped out and dedicated to one realm or another. The more we integrate, the less time is cordoned off and reserved for realm-specific concerns . . . the more we integrate, the more we need to have all aspects of our schedules available simultaneously. (Excerpted from Nippert-Eng 1996: 43–4)

less than optimal because workers can't always afford to take them. The existence of paid leaves in other countries fosters better work–family integration, but even outside the US women are more likely than men to be employed part time to accommodate family care and workers may face other work–life challenges. In Europe, in particular, work–family policies exist in a larger work-time regulatory environment that limits work hours in other ways unheard of in the US. Arguably, the limits set for European work hours and paid family leave can be interpreted as benefits of high productivity extended to workers as a sort of social wage, but less developed countries with longer work hours and lower productivity offer paid leave too. The next chapter is an overview of work time outside the US as a brief exploration of global patterns.

5

Work Time Outside the US

How does work time in the United States compare to that in other industrialized countries? How does it compare to work time in less developed countries? Analysis of annual work hours in industrialized nations, especially the US and its nearest counterparts in terms of productivity and standard of living, Western Europe and Japan, reveals that this standard of living is achieved in Western Europe with fewer aggregate work hours than in the US and Japan. Non-standard work shows similar patterns to the US in that women are more likely than men to work part time, but in Western Europe part-time employment occurs in a work–family policy environment quite different from that in the US. Investigation of transition and developing countries reveals long work hours, due in part to lower productivity, reminiscent of early industrialization in the West. In a similar way to topics covered previously, the literature on work time around the world is vast. Although this single chapter cannot do justice to that literature's breadth and depth, it offers a broad survey of major issues and trends.

Work Hours in Industrialized Nations

Although there is much variation in work hours among the industrialized countries, generally, work hours in industrialized countries are lower than in less developed countries due to higher productivity and income. Non-standard work also exists in the OECD countries, although the nature and extent vary. Part-time employment is the dominant form of non-standard work in many nations and is the focus here. Factors contributing to increases in non-standard work are similar in the US and elsewhere, especially the growth of the service sector and increases in women's labor-force participation, but reducing the cost of employer-provided health insurance and pensions often is not an impetus outside the US. In many industrialized countries, universal systems of health care and public pension systems obviate cost pressures on employers. Although broad similarities exist among the industrialized countries, especially regarding long-term reduction in work hours and recent increases in non-standard work, differences in policies and practices have yielded specific national work-time regimes.

Annual hours

About 900 hours separate the countries that work the most (Korea) and the least (the Netherlands). Generally, work hours in European countries are shorter than in other industrialized countries (table 5.1). In all but five cases (Luxembourg, Spain, Slovenia, Hungary, Greece), work hours declined from 2007 (mostly before the onset of the Great Recession in the US in December 2007) to 2009, in the wake of the recession, showing the effects of slower economic growth globally and the 2008 financial crisis.

Why do work hours differ so much across the industrialized countries? We will explore the complex answers to this question throughout this chapter, but, overall, differences in productivity; work-time regulations; and labor utilization, especially women's labor-force participation, are key factors. National differences in work hours reflect to some degree differences in the general level of economic development. For example, hours per worker are highest where productivity is lower, as in transition and developing countries. However, there is no automatic link between hours and productivity. Work hours per capita have fallen since the 1970s in 14 of

Table 5.1: Average annual working time 2007 and 2009 (hours per worker, rounded to nearest whole number)

Country	Hours 2007	Hours 2009	Country	Hours 2007	Hours 2009
Netherlands	1390	1378	Portugal	1727	1719
Norway	1419	1407	Canada	1736	1699
Germany	1431	1390	Slovak Republic	1753	1693
Luxembourg	1515	1601	New Zealand	1763	1729
France	1556	1554	OECD[1]	1769	1739
Belgium	1560	1550	Japan	1785	1714
Denmark	1571	1563	United States	1798	1768
Sweden	1615	1610	Iceland	1807	1716
Austria	1630	1621	Italy	1816	1773
Ireland	1631	1549	Mexico	1871	1857
Spain	1637	1654	Israel	1945	1943[2]
Switzerland	1643	1640[2]	Poland	1976	1966
Slovenia	1655	1687[2]	Czech Republic	1986	1942
United Kingdom	1673	1646	Hungary	1986	1989
Finland	1706	1652	Estonia	1999	1969[2]
Australia	1713	1690	Greece	2116	2119
			Korea	2316	2256[2]

[1] Excluding Estonia, Israel, Slovenia.
[2] 2008.
Source: Employment and Labour Markets: Key Tables from OECD (<www.oecd-ilibrary.org/employment/average-annual-working-time_20752342-table8>, retrieved August 16, 2011), no data reported for Chile and Turkey.

19 OECD countries for which data are available, albeit just 1.5 percent on average, with the entire decline occurring during the 1970s. The fall was quite sharp in France (24 percent), Finland, Germany, Japan, and Spain (more than 15 percent). In Japan, the fall represents a trend from what had been very high working hours toward more typical levels

for a high-income country, a seeming consequence of the dramatic convergence of Japanese productivity levels toward those in North America and Western Europe. Yet this interpretation does not apply to the US, Canada, and New Zealand, where per capita hours *rose* during the same period by 20 percent in the US and more than 15 percent in Canada and New Zealand (OECD 2004).

In the US and Europe, where productivity is comparable, there are substantial differences in work hours. Chief among these differences are the fact that the typical European worker enjoys significantly more paid holidays and vacation each year, and the European workweek tends to be shorter. Some European countries also have a higher incidence of part-time employment, which is included in the total hours measure reported by the OECD. Cultural differences are another important factor that can help to explain these variations. Europeans, by contrast to Americans, tend to be more willing to sacrifice some potential earnings to have more leisure time. Additionally, higher taxes on earnings in Europe may tip the balance toward a preference for shorter workweeks and more vacation time because a higher share of the potential earnings that would result from working more would be paid in taxes (OECD 2004). Bowles and Park (2005) found that longer work hours are associated with greater inequality in the 10 countries whose long-term trends they investigated (Belgium, Canada, France, Italy, the Netherlands, Norway, Sweden, the UK, the US, and (West) Germany). While it has been argued that shorter hours create more jobs, this is not always the case. Indeed, among OECD countries there is some tendency for employment rates to be higher in countries where hours per worker are lower, but the US has generally combined high hours with high employment rates. Some European countries have suffered persistently high unemployment rates and/or low labor-force participation rates despite shorter work hours. Hours per worker do not consider labor utilization (which may be tapped by calculating work hours per capita), so work hours may be high where labor utilization is low, as in Greece and Mexico, due in part to lower women's labor-force participation, or, conversely, work hours may be relatively low where labor utilization is high, as in Switzerland (OECD 2004).

Part-time employment

The incidence of part-time employment in 2007 ranged from a low of 2.6 percent in the Slovak Republic to a high of 35.9 percent in the Netherlands, with European rates above the OECD average (table 5.2). The US was below the OECD average, at 12.6 percent; however, there is a discrepancy between the OECD and US Department of Labor definitions of part time. OECD defines it as less than 30 hours per week in the main job; the US Department of Labor definition is less than 35 hours per week. Thus, the OECD counts fewer Americans as part-time workers and more as full-time workers (30 hours and above). Japan had a much higher incidence of part-time employment at 18.9 percent. Part-time employment grew from 2007 to 2009, during a period of slow economic growth globally, except in France and Norway, where it was unchanged, and Poland and Portugal, where it declined (slightly in the latter).

Part-time employment has grown rapidly in the past 25 years in OECD countries among both men and women, due largely to increases in the labor-force participation of women and expansion of the service sector. In most OECD countries women account for close to 75 percent of part-time workers. Most women currently working part time do so voluntarily, within the constraints of the household division of labor and available child care. In most countries, transitions out of part-time employment to full time are comparatively rare. It is common only in the few countries in which the right to make temporary transitions from full time to part time is supported by law, as in Sweden and the Netherlands (Lemaitre et al. 1997; Evans et al. 2001; Stier et al. 2001).

Japan: Because Japan's definition of part-time employment is distinctive, it warrants singular discussion. Survey source definitions vary, but generally there is a relatively high incidence of part-time employment in Japan. Seemingly paradoxical, part-time employment in Japan does not always turn on the number of hours worked per week. Most part-time workers do work shorter hours, but a sizable minority works the same number of hours as regular full-time workers. This

Table 5.2: Part-time employment as % of total employment 2007 and 2009 (incidence, less than 30 hours per week)

Country	% 2007	% 2009	Country	% 2007	% 2009	Country	% 2007	% 2009
Slovak Republic	2.6	3.0	Spain	10.7	11.9	Denmark	17.3	18.9
Hungary	2.8	3.6	Finland	11.7	12.2	Belgium	18.1	18.2
Czech Republic	3.5	3.9	US	12.6	14.1	Canada	18.2	19.1
Estonia	6.8	8.4	Luxembourg	13.1	16.4	Japan	18.9	203.
Greece	7.7	8.4	France	13.3	13.3	Ireland	20.0	23.7
Slovenia	7.8	8.3	Sweden	14.4	14.6	Norway	20.4	20.4
Chile	8.0	10.5	Israel	14.6	NA	Germany	22.0	21.9
Turkey	8.1	11.1	Mexico	15.1[1]	NA	New Zealand	22.0	22.5
Korea	8.9	9.9	Italy	15.2	15.8	UK	22.9	23.9
Portugal	9.9	9.6	OECD[2]	15.2	16.2	Australia	23.7	24.7
Poland	10.1	8.7	Iceland	15.9	17.5	Switzerland	25.4	26.2
			Austria	17.3	18.5	Netherlands	35.9	36.7

[1] 2004.

[2] Excluding Estonia, Israel, and Slovenia.

Source: Employment and Labour Markets: Key Tables from OECD (<www.oecd-ilibrary.org/employment/part-time-employment_20752342-table7>, retrieved August 16, 2011.

is because the employer classifies the worker's position as part time, even if that worker works full-time hours. These part-time, or "non-regular," workers are subject to different personnel practices from regular full-time workers, who typically are given commitments of lifetime employment and whose wages and promotions are determined to a large degree by seniority (*nenko*). Lifetime employment and *nenko*-based wages and promotions rarely apply to part-time workers. Flexible employment practices in the manufacturing sector are structured by the use of full-time and part-time workers, a system that has been transplanted to some degree to the US (Dohse et al. 1985; Florida and Kenney 1991; Graham 1993). Despite different definitions, data from various Japanese sources reveal similar trends. The percentage of Japanese employees who are part time has increased dramatically, while the percentage of temporary workers has remained fairly constant. Temporary help agencies were prohibited in 1947 because Japanese officials believed that, before World War II, they had exploited workers. These agencies were legalized in 1985 but subjected to considerable regulation. As a result, the share of temporary help workers in paid employment is fairly small, although growing rapidly.

Overall, non-regular workers in Japan are disproportionately female. Almost all part-time and more than two thirds of temporary workers are women, many of whom return to the labor force when their children reach school age. Part-time employment is especially prominent in wholesale and retail trade, services, and manufacturing; temporary employment tends to be in seasonal industries of agriculture, fishing, and construction. The use of part-time and temporary employment is common, regardless of firm size, particularly in trade and services. Rates decline substantially with firm size in manufacturing, but increase with firm size in wholesale and retail trade.

Why is non-regular employment so common in Japan? In part, demand-side factors and public policies explain the high incidence of non-regular employment. Because Japanese women typically have greater household and child-care responsibilities than men, they often seek shorter hours or temporary assignments. Regular full-time workers in large companies often are expected to accept geographic transfers;

their wives often prefer flexible employment to accommodate such moves. Additionally, tax breaks exist for married women to work part time or in temporary jobs. They retain their dependent status and are eligible for some health insurance coverage under their spouse's plan and are entitled to receive some pension from the government. Moreover, the household head receives a dependent deduction from his taxable income and typically receives a family allowance from his employer. Thus, certain aspects of Japanese industrial relations and tax law provide incentives for many women to seek non-regular positions.

Secondly, on the supply side, the above-mentioned *nenko* system of reward is another important reason for the high incidence of non-regular work. In a similar way to non-standard work in other countries, Japanese companies hire non-regular workers to reduce labor costs and increase employment flexibility. Although the wages of non-regular and regular workers may not differ substantially for those with little or no tenure, wages for non-regular workers, who are not covered by the *nenko* system, do not increase with tenure, or at least do not increase at the same rate as regular workers. Additionally, Japanese employers are not subject to unemployment insurance, pension, and health insurance payroll taxes on many non-regular workers. Medium and large Japanese companies typically offer implicit guarantees of lifetime employment to regular workers, and Japanese courts have given these core workers strong protection against layoff. Part-time workers do not have the same degree of protection. Thus, non-regular workers may be a buffer during recessions because their contracts are easily terminated. This is a matter of growing concern, since the aging of the Japanese workforce also has put pressure on Japanese companies to lower labor costs. Japan is one of the countries most affected by the issues of a "graying" population; the percentage of the population age 65 and over is projected to reach 40 percent in 2050 from 23 percent in 2009 and only 5 percent in 1950. Japan has a somewhat higher percentage of aging population today compared to the US, but it will far outpace the US by 2030. Among European countries, Germany has a similar current and projected (to 2030) age distribution, slightly behind Japan in percentage age 65 and over. India, Brazil, and China, by contrast, have higher percentages of young people (below age 15), roughly twice the Japanese percentage (<www.stat.go.jp/english/data/handbook/c02cont.htm#ch2_2>, retrieved September 5, 2011). As the Japanese population has aged and economic growth has slowed, Japanese companies have become saddled with large numbers of well-paid, middle-age and older workers in the *nenko* system. One way companies have sought to increase labor flexibility and reduce labor costs, short of dismantling traditional industrial relations practices of lifetime employment and *nenko*, has been to hire a greater number of non-regular workers, who are more easily dismissed, whose pay is not tied to seniority, and who generally are not eligible for promotion (Houseman and Osawa 1995).

Work Hours Regulations in Europe

Since the 1990s, a supranational edifice of European Union work-time directives pertaining to weekly hours, vacation, parental leave, leave for family reasons, and part-time work has guided national legislation and practices (summarized in table 5.3[1]). EU directives provide a supranational framework within which member countries implement requirements through legislation, collective bargaining, or a combination of the two (Gornick and Meyers 2003: 157–60). In broad terms, this has led to a general picture of shorter workweeks, fewer work hours annually, paid and longer leaves for workers to attend to family matters, and more vacation time – quite different from the situation in the US.

By comparison to European countries, work hours regulations in the US are weak or non-existent. Several federal and state laws operate in conjunction with collective bargaining agreements, the latter pertaining to the small percentage of American workers represented by labor unions today. Two federal laws are particularly important: the Fair Labor Standards Act (FLSA) of 1938 and its subsequent amendments, and the Employee Retirement Income Security Act (ERISA) of 1974. Some states supplement federal laws regarding overtime and days off (Gornick and Meyers 2003: 147–8).

Table 5.3: EU Directives on working time

1993 Directive on working time	48 hours per week maximum, including overtime; employers cannot require longer hours, but countries may opt out; not less than four weeks paid vacation per year (up from three weeks previously)
1996 Directive on parental leave and leave for family reasons	establish minimum requirements for parental leave and unforeseeable absence from work to reconcile professional and family responsibilities and promote equal opportunities and treatment for women and men; enact measures providing men and women with at least three months paid or unpaid parental leave (distinct from maternity leave) following the birth or adoption of a child until a given age up to eight years; worker protections against dismissal for applying or taking parental leave, right to return to same or similar job, maintain previously acquired rights
1997 Directive on part-time work	requires members to prohibit employers from treating part-time workers less favorably than comparable full-time workers in pay, social security and occupational benefits, training and promotion opportunities, and bargaining rights; urges members to eliminate obstacles to part-time work and instructs employers to give consideration to workers' requests to transfer between part-time and full-time work as personal and family needs change

Source: Compiled from Gornick and Meyers (2003).

FLSA covers federal, state, and local governments and private enterprises engaged in interstate commerce. As discussed in chapter 2, it established the 40-hour workweek as the US standard, and employers are required to pay time-and-a-half for overtime beyond 40 hours in a seven-day week. It also places limits on work time for workers under age 18. Although the number and categories of workers covered by FLSA expanded over the years, it has never been the case that all workers were covered by the law; and recently a large and growing share of workers are not covered by the FLSA's overtime provisions. More than a quarter of full-time workers are "exempt" because their job duties classify them as executives, managers, or professionals who are paid salaries instead of hourly wages and salaries that are above the legal minimum defined by the law.[2] Unlike laws in European countries that define maximum weekly work hours, FLSA does not establish such a ceiling. Nor does it prohibit mandatory overtime. Thus, American workers who refuse overtime have no protection from job loss, demotion, or other repercussions. About a third of overtime workers in the US work compulsory overtime. Nearly all states have overtime laws that conform to the FLSA; a few provide additional protections. Alaska and Nevada, for example, require that overtime be paid after eight daily hours under most circumstances; and some states limit work time in specific activities and sectors for reasons of public or patient safety, as in transportation or health care. Seven states require that employees receive one day off out of every seven (Gornick and Meyers 2003: 148–9, 152–3).

FLSA does not include regulations pertaining to compensation and benefits for part-time, other reduced-hour, and non-standard work. ERISA, in combination with the US Tax Code, in fact, gives employers the right to offer different benefits to part-time and full-time workers. This legislation permits employers to exclude part-time workers from health insurance and pension plans (Gornick and Meyers 2003: 149–50).

Unlike European countries, there is no legislation in the US that requires that employees who work non-standard shifts be compensated with premium pay or compensatory time off. Also unlike European countries, the US lacks a national vacation policy. Vacation time is left to the discretion of employers; and Americans' vacation time, on average, is considerably less than that of Europeans. On average, in medium and large establishments, full-time workers in the US have 9.6 days of paid vacation after one year, 11.5 days after three years, 13.8 days after five years, and 16.8 days after 10 years compared to the legal minimum of 20 days in the least generous European countries – Belgium, Germany, the Netherlands, and the UK (Gornick and Meyers 2003: 155, 180–2).

As we have seen, it is assumed that paid work time has become progressively shorter in the industrialized countries following technological advances, but in reality there has been no clear linear trend (Figart and Golden 1998). Work time has varied considerably across countries and within countries by industry, occupation, gender, race, family type, and historical period (Figart and Golden 1998). In contrast to the twin trends of overwork and underemployment in the US, annual and weekly hours in Western Europe have declined in recent decades as a result of statutory and collectively bargained restrictions on standard and overtime hours in the EU. The trend toward shorter hours in Europe has slowed since the 1980s, however, as employers and governments have pursued greater flexibility, resulting in greater diversity and destandardization of work patterns, as in the US (e.g., Fagan 2001; Figart and Golden 1998; Golden and Figart 2000; Green 2004; Hinrichs et al. 1991).

Unions are another important factor in work-time regulation in Europe. Unions have much more influence on work time in European countries and Canada than in the US, partly because they cover more workers and have more power than in the US, and many European unions have made work time a high priority. Historically, they have been concerned with lowering unemployment through work-time reform; more recently, objectives include protection of family time and promotion of gender equality (Alesina, Glaeser, and Sacerdote 2005; Gornick and Meyers 2003: 157, 162–3).

Union coverage is generally much higher in Europe and Canada than in the US. In Canada and the UK, 36 and 47 percent of workers respectively are covered by collective bargaining agreements; in the Nordic and continental countries, union coverage ranges from about 70 to more than 90 percent of workers (Gornick and Meyers 2003: 157), with the exception of France where just 8 percent of workers are unionized (Bennhold 2008). By contrast, less than 13 percent of the US labor force belonged to a union in 2005, down from a high of 35.5 percent of employment at the time of World War II. In absolute terms, union membership peaked in the US in 1978 at 22.75 million (Hodson and Sullivan 2008: 143–4). In Denmark, Germany, and the UK, collective bargaining is the dominant mechanism for regulating work hours; in France, labor law is the primary mechanism; and in the remaining Nordic and continental countries studied by Gornick and Meyers (2003: 157–60), the institutional context of work hours is composed of a strong statutory framework supplemented by collective bargaining agreements.

The seminal work of Gornick and Meyers (2003) provides comprehensive comparison of work hours regulations in 10 European countries – the Nordic countries of Denmark, Finland, Norway, and Sweden; the continental countries of Belgium, France, Germany, Luxembourg, and the Netherlands; and the UK – to Canada and the US. Regulations pertaining to weekly work hours, vacations, non-standard hours, and part-time employment are discussed below in turn.

Weekly hours

As of approximately 2000, all across Europe, "normal" full-time weekly work hours, those above which overtime premiums become payable, are set at levels below the 40-hour legal norm in the US and Canada – 35 hours in France and 37 to 39 in the UK, the Nordic countries, and the continental countries. Currently, only the UK has opted out of the EU overtime-inclusive maximum of 48 hours. In selected cases, maximum weekly hours established by statute are well below the EU 48-hour maximum: specifically, 39 hours in Belgium and 40 hours in Finland, Norway, and Sweden (Gornick and Meyers 2003: 157, 161, 310). Movements to reduce work time even further remain active all across Europe, with a goal of a normal workweek of 35 hours in some cases (Gornick and Meyers 2003: 162–3).

Box 5.1:   France's 35-hour workweek

In France, the workweek was reduced from 40 to 39 in 1982. In 1998, a law known as Aubry I established financial incentives for companies to reduce all or some employees' work hours by at least 10 percent before January 1, 2000, in exchange for the right to reduce social security contributions for five years. Companies were required to preserve employment for two years or create jobs at a rate of 6 percent. In 2000, Aubry II was enacted. It set annual work hours at 1,600 and allowed variation in weekly hours in line with business fluctuations. Financial incentives were replaced by long-term subsidies in exchange for reduced social security contributions for low- to medium-pay levels, and companies were no longer subject to conditions of job preservation or creation. Access to long-term subsidies depends on negotiating an agreement accepted by a majority of employees in the company, establishment, or sector (Charpentier et al. 2006: 183).

By annualizing hours and permitting variability in weekly hours, Aubry II ended the decades-long tradition of standard workweeks. It contributed to greater segmentation of the French labor force, affecting workers in both insecure and core jobs, different categories of employees within the same company, and workers of different ages and personal situations (Charpentier et al. 2006: 207).

The Aubry laws established the norm of the 35-hour workweek in France, but variability of weekly hours means workweeks may not be 35 hours in practice. Some companies have negotiated Reduced Work Time (RWT) days, in effect compensatory time for long workweeks, which employees may use with ease or difficulty depending on the particular circumstances of their company, for example, market pressures or being short-staffed. At some companies, RWT days are increasingly regulated by management (Charpentier et al. 2006). Variability of hours is especially evident in French service industries that require contact with the public and where the rates of part-time and "unsocial" employment are high (Gadrey et al. 2006), similar to non-standard work and non-standard schedules in the US.

French trade unions, with two thirds popular support, successfully advocated reducing the workweek to 35 hours from 39 with no loss of pay to counter an historically high 12.5

(*Continued*)

percent unemployment rate. In its early stages of implementation and with amendment, however, the law seemed to have done little to genuinely reduce work time but permitted employers to make work time more flexible, sometimes longer, and unpredictable. Critics claimed the result was an increase in the size and scope of France's contingent workforce (Apter 1997; Arens and Thull 1999; Ford 1998; Thull and Arens 2000; Vinocur 1999). Declines in productivity growth have created pressure to increase work hours not only in France (Frost 2005), where President Nicolas Sarkozy advocated repealing the 35-hour law and lengthening the workweek, but Germany as well, where weekly hours in some sectors had also been reduced. In some instances, the workweek has been extended beyond the 40-hour limit, such as in the German state of Bavaria where the workweek currently stands at 42 hours, and short hours have been increased, as in the case of Siemens in Germany when the union signed a contract to lengthen the workweek from 35 to 40 hours at no increase in pay. In Britain, more than a fifth of the labor force works longer than the EU's mandated maximum of 48 hours a week (Landler 2004).

Crompton (2006: 132) found that work–life conflict is high in France relative to five comparison countries (Britain, Finland, Norway, Portugal, US). The French household division of labor is more traditional than in the aforementioned countries except Portugal (Crompton 2006: 149) and is a significant predictor of work–life conflict (Crompton 2006: 162). The high level of work–life conflict may seem paradoxical given the extensive state supports for child care and the shorter working hours in France. It appears, therefore, that the gender division of labor itself might be a contentious issue (Crompton 2006: 149) and in flux. Attitudes about the gender division of labor in France tend to be conventional, and state-supported child care has reinforced these attitudes by directing programs at mothers. Although French women's hours of household work have decreased considerably and men's have increased somewhat, French men have not been "forced" into domesticity to the same degree as British and American men, to enable their partner's employment, because of the wide availability of state-supported child care. State supports in the Nordic countries, by contrast, have facilitated comparatively more male domestic engagement because they have been purposely designed to encourage gender equity (Crompton 2006: 150–2).

Vacations

Some countries have raised the minimum from the EU-mandated 20 days – to 21 in Norway; 24 in Finland for workers with less than one year of service; 25 in Denmark, Sweden, France, and Luxembourg; and 30 days in Finland for workers with more than one year of service. Collective bargaining agreements provide an average of 23 days in Norway; 25 days in Finland, Sweden, Belgium, and France; 27 days in Luxembourg; 29 days in Germany; and 31.5 and 32 days in the Netherlands and Denmark respectively. In Denmark, employees with children under age 14 receive 33 days (Gornick and Meyers 2003: 179–80).

In Canada, two weeks (10 days) vacation annually is legally mandated; since 1997, employees have had a right to a third week, although employers are required to pay for only the first two. Most collective bargaining agreements secure 15 days after one to five years, 20 days after six to 10 years, and 25 days after 17 to 20 years. In the UK, 20 days vacation annually are mandated by law, and collective bargaining agreements provide an average of 24.5 days (Gornick and Meyers 2003: 180).

Non-standard hours

In defiance of capitalist principles, a number of European countries studied by Gornick and Meyers (2003: 172–7) reduce the demand for workers during non-standard hours by limiting the opening or production hours of enterprises, thereby reducing work hours during evenings, nights, and weekends. Among the Nordic countries, Denmark, Finland, and Norway restrict such hours by law, prohibiting shop-opening after 8 p.m. Monday through Friday and after 2 p.m. Saturday, and all day on Sundays in Denmark; after 9 p.m. Monday through Friday, after 6 p.m. Saturday, and on many Sundays in Finland; and by prohibiting night work between 9 p.m. and 6 a.m. and Sunday work in Norway, although there are numerous exceptions. While legal regulation of shop-opening hours has been abolished in Sweden, collective bargaining regulates work during "inconvenient" hours outside normal business hours of generally 9 a.m. to 8 p.m. In all of these cases, employees who work nights or Sundays receive premium compensation, as much as 200 percent of the normal wage.

Legal mandates regulate work during non-standard hours in the continental countries as well. For example, in Belgium, work between 8 p.m. and 6 a.m. is prohibited, with several exceptions. Night workers are entitled to financial compensation, and Sunday workers are entitled to compensatory time during the following week. Regulations limiting women's night work, similar to protective legislation that had existed in the US, were lifted in 1998, "freeing" women to work at night with entitlement to financial compensation equal to that of men. In France, shops are restricted to 13 hours per day, six days per week. Retail establishments are closed on Sundays, although small food shops may remain open until 1 p.m. Collective bargaining agreements require compensatory time, bonus pay, or a combination of the two for night work, and bonus pay for Sunday work. In 2001, all bans regarding night work for women were lifted. In Germany, Sunday work is prohibited, although there are many exceptions.[3] Gender variation of the sort seen earlier in this book – either to maintain women's role as homemaker and responsible for the family, or those related to perceived biological imperatives – clearly still persists. Pregnant and breastfeeding women may not work at night, with some exceptions (an echo of the biological reasons for gender variation in work time which, as we saw in chapter 2, held that for the sake of women's health they should not work as many hours as men), and women may not work between 10 p.m. and 6 a.m. if they have dependent children under age 14 living with them and there is no secure child care. Night workers get bonus pay via collectively bargained agreements. In Luxembourg, work on Sundays is prohibited, with several exceptions, and pregnant women cannot work between 10 p.m. and 6 a.m. Sunday workers can receive compensatory time and bonuses in pay. In the Netherlands, work between 10 p.m. and 6 a.m. is prohibited, with some exceptions. Sunday work is also restricted. Night workers, by law, receive compensatory time.

In Canada, federal and provincial law mandate a 24-hour rest period during the week, preferably on Sunday. Generally, shops are closed on Sunday, with the exception of cross-border shopping. Collective bargaining agreements may stipulate higher pay for night and weekend work. The UK has no laws regulating work during non-standard hours, but collective bargaining agreements often require that night workers receive premium pay.

In Italy, not among the 10 countries compared systematically throughout Gornick and Meyers's (2003) study, gender-neutral legislation disallows compulsory, but not voluntary, night work among some groups of parents. Since 1999, Italian employers are not permitted to require male or female workers to work night shifts if they have a child under the age of three, if they are the single parent of a child under 12, or they are caring for a disabled person. As Gornick and Meyers (2003: 173) note, the consequences of this law are not yet evident. Indeed, they can have negative effects by leading to discrimination against groups that have traditionally been excluded from the labor market, which is a sobering issue facing campaigners for greater equity in access to work for all groups. While the law is intended to promote gender equality and recognizes the caring work of both parents, it could lead employers, due to cost concerns or inflexibility, to discriminate against parents in hiring.

Part-time employment

Because employers tend to discriminate against part-time workers as a cost-saving strategy and part-time jobs tend to be marginal when compared to full time, in 1997 the EU adopted the Directive on part-time work to eliminate discrimination against part-time workers and improve the quality of part-time work. To foster better work–family integration, the Directive also facilitates the development of voluntary part-time work and contributes to the flexible organization of work time in a manner that takes into account the needs of employers and workers (Gornick and Meyers 2003: 163–4). All 10 of the European countries studied by Gornick and Meyers have implemented the Directive through a combination of legislation and collective bargaining. The Netherlands, as will be discussed below, is particularly interesting because it went far beyond the basic Directive in enacting work-and-care legislation to normalize part-time work.

UK law, for example, grants part-time workers the same rights as full-time workers in the areas of pay, holidays, training, parental leave and benefits, access to pension schemes, and a right to equal treatment (Gornick and Meyers 2003: 164). Prior to the Directive, Sweden had already set the standard on the right to part-time work. Since 1978, Swedish parents have had the right to work six hours a day at prorated pay until their children reach the age of eight. Since the adoption of the EU Directive, other countries have instituted varied types of policies. Belgium grants employees the right to work 80 percent of full time for five years. France enacted a right to part-time work exclusively for caregivers. In Finland, there is a work-sharing scheme of sorts under which employees can reduce working time by 40 to 60 percent for one year subject to employment agreement, and an unemployed person must be hired for the same position. During the 1990s, Finnish municipalities experimented with "six-plus-six" work-time arrangements, scheduling two six-hour shifts as a way to shorten employees' work hours and simultaneously lengthen service to the public. Other countries, such as Germany and the Netherlands, extended part-time employment rights to employees in companies with 15 or 10 employees or more respectively. Rights to work part time operate in tandem with complementary family leave polices in some European countries (Gornick and Meyers 2003: 164–70).

The Netherlands designed what may be the most comprehensive state effort to increase part-time employment of high quality. The 2001 Work and Care Act includes several measures to improve part-time work for Dutch women and men. The law permits workers to increase or decrease their work hours, unless employers demonstrate "specific conflicting business interests," and prohibits all forms of differential treatment based on work hours. These provisions were integrated with a series of reforms to strengthen family leave legislation, child-care provisions, and after-school programs. The stated intention of the 2001 Work and Care Act is to enable couples to hold "one and a half jobs" between them

– each holding a "three-quarter time job" – thus achieving both time for care and gender equality (Gornick and Meyers 2003: 165–71). However, the laudatory goal of gender equality is not always achieved because Dutch women's part-time employment continues to outpace men's. This important issue is discussed in box 5.2.

Box 5.2:   The Netherlands

According to the International Labour Organization (ILO) (2006), the Netherlands has made the greatest gains in fostering healthy work–life balance through the "normalization" of part-time work, yet the Dutch system continues to exhibit gender inequity.

Both the Dutch government and social partners supported families choosing part-time work and shorter hours as a way to achieve work–family balance. Policies were put in place to create standards in part-time workers' rights, earnings, and equality. Growth in part-time work in the Netherlands lagged behind other European countries until the 1980s when it began to grow along with an increase in Dutch women's labor-force participation. At first, women chose part-time work because of a lack of daycare options; employers, however, embraced part-time work's flexibility and cost savings. In the mid-1990s, legislation extended minimum wage and pension laws to part-time workers. Although part-time workers have been afforded equal treatment since then and today such jobs are found throughout the labor market, part-time jobs are disproportionately held by women, who remain responsible for the majority of domestic responsibilities. Nearly 60 percent of all jobs held by women are part time, the highest in the EU, and there reportedly is only a small gap between Dutch women's preferred and actual work time (ILO 2006: 31; Yerkes and Visser 2006).

In the Netherlands, average annual work hours per job (excluding overtime) for all workers decreased 39 percent between 1950 and 2001. This decline occurred because of the reduction of the full-time workweek and a rapid growth in part-time jobs (Fouarge and Baaijens 2006: 155). In no other EU country is part-time employment as widespread as it is in the Netherlands, and part-time work is seen as a means to

(Continued)

combine employment and caring activities. In this context, the Adjustment of Work Hours Act was passed in 2000, giving employees the right to request an upward or downward adjustment of work hours in their current job. Employers are expected to honor such requests unless conflicting business interests prevent them from doing so. The law covers both the private and public sectors, but organizations of fewer than 10 employees are excluded (Fouarge and Baaijens 2006: 159).

In 2002, 16 percent of Dutch employees preferred fewer and 6 percent preferred more hours. Of men, 15 percent wanted fewer and 10 percent wanted more compared to 18 and 13 percent of women respectively. Workers with higher levels of education in particular wanted fewer hours (Fouarge and Baaijens 2006: 164–5), similar to well-educated workers elsewhere in long-hours jobs. In an analysis of panel data from 1986 to 2002, Fouarge and Baaijens (2006) found that 15 to 27 percent of employees who preferred fewer hours and 22 to 35 percent of those who preferred more hours had adjusted their hours accordingly two years later (Fouarge and Baaijens 2006: 173), most often by changing jobs – either with the same or a different employer (Fouarge and Baaijens 2006: 168). Thus, it was easier for Dutch workers to realize an upward adjustment of hours. Male employees' hours were more stable than women's, thus women's pattern showed more flexibility (Fouarge and Baaijens 2006: 174). The authors found no significant effect of the Adjustment to Work Hours Act of 2000, which was intended to facilitate changes in hours in the same job, but it may be premature to draw a firm conclusion.

Women's Part-time Employment in Europe

As we have seen, the EU Directive on part-time work, combined with an array of family-supportive policies (to be discussed below), is the foundation of a domestic division of labor between fathers and mothers such that mothers often are employed outside the home part time. The relationship between women's labor-force participation and part-time employment is not direct, however, and there is variation among European countries (Rubery et al. 1998; Warren

2010). Women's increasing labor-force participation proceeds in different ways and at different rates across countries, as do rates of women's part-time employment (Drew and Emerek 1998: 90).

Comparing 12 countries (Drew and Emerek 1998: 91–2), women's labor-force participation ("activity rate" is the phrase used by European researchers) ranged from about 40 percent to almost 70 percent in 1983, with the lowest rates in Greece, Italy, and Luxembourg, and the highest rate in Denmark. Denmark was an outlier of sorts, with an activity rate more than 10 percentage points higher than the nearest countries, the UK and France, at just over 55 percent each. By the mid-1990s, activity rates had increased in most countries, although the range remained the same, from about 40 to 70 percent. Rates of women's part-time employment ranged from 10 to 45 percent in 1983, with the lowest rates in Italy and Greece and the highest rates in the UK and Denmark (no data for the Netherlands). In 2000, women's part-time employment ranged from lows of 5 and 7 percent respectively in Finland and Portugal and highs of 29 and 36 percent in the UK and Ireland respectively (46 percent in the Netherlands), with two broad types: a carer type, which British women exemplify, in which women mesh employment with family duties; and a transitional type, exemplified by Danish women, who work part time when entering and exiting the labor force (Warren 2010: 374–5). There was considerable variation among countries long term, with a slight upward trend in most, relative stability in a few, and in Denmark the rate of women's part-time employment declined. Where women's part-time employment declined or remained flat, the increased amount of women's labor-force participation represented an increase in women's full-time employment (Drew and Emerek 1998: 91–2). The Netherlands is an exceptional case, with unusually high rates of women's part-time employment, no doubt because of changes in work-time regulations there as discussed in box 5.2. Women's part-time employment in the Netherlands contributes to a mean of 30 weekly hours for all employed women compared at the high end to means of 36 in Denmark and the UK, 37 in Spain, 38 in Finland and Greece, and 39 in Portugal (Warren 2010: 374).

In Northern Europe, women's part-time employment grew rapidly in the period following World War II and stabilized in the late 1970s and beyond. The expansion of part-time employment among women in Southern Europe began later, in the 1970s, and reached comparatively low levels by the mid-1990s (Blossfeld and Hakim 1997; Drew and Emerek 1998; McRae 1998: 101). This is still the case, although France, Denmark, and Finland also have comparatively low rates of women's part-time employment (Warren 2010: 374), most likely due to the shorter workweek overall in France as discussed in box 5.1, and efforts in Denmark and Finland to better integrate working parents, especially women, into employment, as will be discussed below.

The growth of part-time employment among women and more generally in European countries is one factor in a larger set of political economic forces and labor market changes similar to those in the US creating more part-time and flexible work arrangements. The major impetus for labor market change has been the shift from agricultural- and/or manufacturing-based economies to service-based economies, in which service-sector occupations now predominate. Working conditions are no longer bound by 24-hour production cycles, usually in eight-hour shifts, as on assembly lines. With the growth of the service sector, there has been increasing demand for irregular, extended hours that may vary throughout the week (Drew and Emerek 1998: 89; Green 2004; Rubery et al. 1998). Some part-time employment is the result of workers' desire for reduced hours, as in the US. And some part-time employment is the result of employers' demand for a flexible labor supply, also as in the US, which can result in involuntary part-time employment (McRae 1998; Rubery et al. 1998).[4]

"Atypical" (the term preferred by European scholars that encompasses part-time, temporary, weekend, shift, and home working; readers will also encounter the term "unsocial" in reference to night and weekend work) forms of work are gendered in that women are more likely to be part-time workers than men and they tend to face poorer working conditions than female full-timers and men (Corral and Isusi 2004; Warren 2010). The proportion of European women working in temporary jobs is also higher than among men, although the absolute number of women working in temporary jobs is smaller. Men are more likely than women to work weekends and shifts; home working is more evenly distributed between the two genders. This is yet more evidence of gender disparity, as atypical work often maximizes men's earnings because they are paid overtime or bonuses, but it tends to reduce women's net earnings (Drew and Emerek 1998: 94; Rubery et al. 1998). This divergence in pay is a product of the different types of jobs men and women hold. European labor markets are characterized by gender segregation not unlike that in the US (Charles and Grusky 2004; Drew and Emerek 1998: 98; McRae 1998). Although working fewer hours contributes to women's satisfaction, except when short hours are involuntary, long full-time hours have the strongest (negative) effect on European women's temporal well-being. Work in low-level occupations – both part and full time – predictably undermine women's economic well-being (Warren 2010).

Family Policies

Public policies in Europe are more supportive of working parents, particularly employed mothers, than in the US because leaves are paid and often of longer duration. There is considerable variation among European countries, however, with particularly generous leave policies in Nordic[5] countries. The continental[6] countries' and Canadian leave policies are more modest, and the UK trends are close to the US. Policies to reconcile work and family are uneven and implemented within pre-existing policy and cultural environments within each country. Work–family policies also interact with the labor market and gender gaps in jobs and pay and, while seeming to promote gender equity on the surface, may increase gender inequalities (Cousins and Tang 2004). On balance, European countries are among the most generous worldwide, especially in the length of time allowed for paid maternal leave. We'll take a brief look at leaves in three areas (maternity, parental, and for family reasons) in Europe and Canada, but it is important to note that less developed countries offer paid maternity leaves too, leaving the US as one among few countries worldwide that do not offer at least some paid leave to new mothers (Heymann and Earle 2010: 110).

Maternity leave

Maternity leave policies in Nordic and continental European countries and Canada grant nearly all employed mothers job security and wage replacement around the time of childbirth or adoption. All of the countries have national statutory programs (Gornick and Meyers 2003: 121–7). Rates of coverage, eligibility, and women's usage are generally high (Kamerman 2000). Conditions are somewhat stricter in Canada, where only three-quarters of women who were employed before childbirth actually receive benefits (Gornick and Meyers 2003: 122).

The Nordic countries provide the most generous paid leave benefits for mothers when total weeks of full wage replacement available to mothers through both maternity and parental leave are considered. Mothers in these countries can receive about 30 to 42 weeks of leave with full pay, typically up to an earnings cap. In Norway and Sweden, maternity and parental leave are blended into a single program that grants couples an allocation of about a year to be shared between them; wage replacement is high for the whole period, at 80 to 100 percent. Finland and Denmark offer 18 weeks of maternity pay (at about two thirds of pay, on average), followed by separate parental leave options that couples may allocate to the mother if they choose. In Denmark, collectively bargained agreements compel many employers to "top up" public benefits so that, in practice, most workers receive their full pay.

More modest but still substantial public leave benefits are available to mothers in the five continental countries, which grant employed mothers the equivalent of 12 to 16 weeks of full pay. Maternity benefits are generally paid at high rates of 80 to 100 percent of wages for about three to four months. Some countries set caps on maximum covered earnings. Mothers' total leave rights and benefits lag behind those granted in the Nordic countries largely because the parental leave options are more limited in the continental countries.

Canadian mothers have access to paid leave benefits nearly as generous as those offered in Finland. The duration of paid leave in Canada is long by European standards, at up to 50 weeks of paid leave, but less economic security is provided – wages are replaced at a rate of 55 percent. Benefits are capped in Canada at a substantially lower level than in the European countries; replacement rates decline as earnings rise above the average. In the UK, statutory maternity pay is available for six weeks at 90 percent of wages plus 12 weeks at a flat rate, but eligibility for this benefit is strict. The maternity allowance is more broadly available for 18 weeks paid at 90 percent of wages or a flat rate, whichever is less. In 2003, both types of maternity leave benefits were extended from 18 to 26 weeks.

Parental leave

Maternity leave benefits are supplemented by parental leaves that provide both mothers and fathers paid leave during children's preschool years. Again, Nordic countries provide the most generous parental leave rights and benefits (Gornick and Meyers 2003: 124–30). Most employed parents have the right to take leave from one to three years and, through social insurance funds, receive about two thirds or more of their wages during most or all of their leave periods (subject to caps for high earners). Parental leave policies in the Nordic countries are flexible: Denmark and Sweden allow parents to take their allotted paid leaves in increments until the child is eight years old; Norway and Sweden allow parents to combine prorated leaves with part-time employment; and Finland and Norway permit parents to use a portion of their leave benefits to purchase private child care instead.

Four of the five continental countries also grant most employed parents paid parental leave, but once again it can be seen that provisions are less generous than in the Nordic countries. France and Germany pay portions of three-year leaves, but wage-replacement rates are much lower than in the Nordic countries. Parents can receive modest flat-rate benefits in Belgium, France, Germany, and Luxembourg; and in the Netherlands parental leave is unpaid.

The 1996 EU Directive on parental leave and leave for family reasons has been a factor in standardizing and expanding parental leave programs across these countries (Gornick and Meyers 2003: 310). Most were already in line when the Directive was enacted, a few had to make marginal changes, and some (particularly Belgium, the Netherlands, and the UK) passed substantial new legislation. Among the 10 European countries investigated by Gornick and Meyers (2003), the least generous parental leaves are in the UK where each parent is entitled to 13 weeks of unpaid full-time leave per child until the child is five years old. No more than four weeks can be taken in any given year (Gornick and Meyers 2003: 126–7). In Canada, parents may share 35 weeks of paid parental leave. The combined maternity leave (15 weeks) and parental leave cannot exceed 50 weeks. The benefit rate is the same as for maternity, at 55 percent of earnings up to an earnings cap. Parents can also receive some parental pay if they continue to work. These benefits are available until the child's first birthday.

Leave for family reasons

Leaves for family reasons grant both mothers and fathers time off throughout their children's lives to attend to routine and unexpected needs. Policies regarding the care of sick children are an example. Nordic countries have the most generous provisions for the care of sick children, particularly seriously ill children (Gornick and Meyers 2003: 130–3). In Denmark, parents with seriously ill children may claim up to 52 weeks of leave with about two thirds wage replacement. Swedish and Finnish parents may take 24 and 12 weeks, respectively, also with high levels of wage replacement. In Norway, sick-child benefits are paid for an unlimited length of time for the most seriously ill children and for shorter durations – typically 10 days – for children with routine illnesses. Legal entitlements in these countries are long, but in practice benefits are drawn for much shorter periods of time. In Sweden, for example, sick-child benefits are used on average for about seven days a year with just over 40 percent of days claimed by fathers.

The continental countries offer less extensive leaves for family reasons. Sick-child leaves generally provide wage replacement at a rate of 100 percent in Belgium, France, Germany, and Luxembourg, but typically for no more than 10 days a year.

Parents in some Canadian provinces are entitled to "emergency leave," such as in Ontario, where workers in companies with at least 50 employees may take up to 10 days per year. In the UK, parents are entitled to unpaid "time off for dependents," including sickness or a break down in child-care arrangements; each parent may take a "reasonable" number of days, usually limited to one or two per year.

Parental leaves are among the labor protections (with paid sick leave, overtime limits and premiums, paid annual leave, and weekly day off) that Heymann and Earle (2010) consider basic decent working conditions. These decent working conditions are available worldwide – to one degree or another – making it all the more troubling that they are not matters of federal policy in the US. Why aren't they? In the US, such policies are often believed to harm economic growth and development, but when one looks at international data to assess this assertion, they do not support such claims. Highly competitive countries[7] and low unemployment countries[8] generally offer these protections (Heymann and Earle 2010), apparently without damaging their economy or labor market. US beliefs appear to have little factual backing, leaving one to conclude that US myths simply justify US exceptionalism in offering few if any such protections. In fact, the US and Korea are the only low unemployment countries that do not guarantee paid annual leave and a weekly day of rest.

Financing

The cost of leave benefits is relatively modest when distributed across taxpayers (Gornick and Meyers 2003: 139–43). Nordic countries spend the most, from $594 to $808 on average for each employed woman. More moderate levels of spending in the UK, continental countries, and Canada, ranging from $67 to $465, reflect in part lower wage-replacement rates. (The US, of course, spends nothing, except in states with Temporary Disability Insurance programs that support paid maternity leave.) The paid leave programs account for a small percentage of GDP: 0.5 to 0.7 in the Nordic countries; 0.07, 0.35, and 0.39 in the continental countries of the Netherlands, France, and Germany respectively; and 0.13 in Canada. When costs are considered on a per capita basis, even the generous Nordic countries spend just three or four dollars a day for each employed woman.

Financing mechanisms vary, but paid leave programs in Europe typically are organized through social insurance schemes. Benefits are funded by employee and employer contributions, often supplemented by general tax revenues. Social insurance distributes costs of caregiving such that they are shared across employees' working years, among parents and non-parents, between those who take leaves and those who do not, and across enterprises. This means that employers are less likely to resist providing paid leaves when costs are distributed essentially society-wide, and when employers who wish to offer paid leaves are not competing against businesses that do not offer them. And public paid-leave benefits reduce the inequities among families who would otherwise divide into the haves and have-nots: those who have access to employer-provided leave and can afford to take it, those who have access but cannot afford to take it, and those without access. (Occupation-based inequities persist in the European and Canadian paid leave schemes, however, in that wage replacement is pegged to wages.)

Implications for gender equity

As we have seen, leave policies promote gender equality by securing fathers' rights and benefits and encouraging fathers' usage. If parental leave, for example, is used mostly or exclusively by women, mothers and children benefit from extensive periods of maternal caregiving, but these arrangements weaken women's labor-force attachment and exacerbate gender inequalities at home and in the workplace. Gornick and Meyers (2003: 133–9) concluded that none of the countries they studied achieved the goal of gender equality in the usage of leave. Mothers' take-up of parental leave is high, but recent estimates suggest that fathers take less than 10 percent of total days of paid parental leave in most European countries. Despite falling short of gender equality, steps are being taken in some countries to increase fathers' use of parental leave. High wage-replacement rates are one incentive. Because men often earn more than women, in the absence of full wage replacement it often makes economic sense for couples to decide that the mother should withdraw from the labor market. To undermine this logic, countries must offer high wage replacement with a high cap on earnings. Non-transferable rights, such that fathers must use their benefit or couples forfeit it, is another strategy. In the Nordic countries, total parental leave times are lengthened if fathers take their quota – two weeks in Denmark and four weeks in Norway and Sweden. In Norway and Sweden, fathers' parental leaves are supported by high wage-replacement rates, and in Denmark fathers who take parental leave are entitled to additional child-care leave. Finland does not stipulate "use or lose" fathers' parental leave time but grants fathers a comparatively generous 18 days of paternity leave. Public education campaigns have also been developed in the Nordic countries to encourage fathers' usage of parental leave.

Parental leaves in the continental countries have lower wage-replacement rates that can be disincentives to fathers' usage, although fathers' entitlements are individualized and non-transferable in Belgium, Luxembourg, and the Netherlands. These parental leave benefits are in addition to generous (100 percent wage replacement) but short (two days in the cases of Luxembourg and the Netherlands, three to four days in Belgium) paternity leaves. France and Germany offer no paid paternity leave, and there are no incentives for fathers to take parental leave. Canada and the UK do not offer paid paternity leave either; and while there are no incentives in Canada for fathers to take parental leave, there is an individualized non-transferable entitlement in the UK but without wage replacement. Thus, in the continental countries, Canada, and the UK, parental leave policies generally reinforce the gender status quo by providing support, to varying degrees (see the discussions of maternity leave and parental leave above), to mothers but not fathers.

Despite the relatively gender egalitarian design of Swedish policies, Swedish mothers and fathers experience more work–family conflict than their counterparts in the Netherlands and the UK, where policies are less gender egalitarian in design. In the Netherlands and the UK, women work shorter hours and have fewer difficulties balancing work and family care, but they have lower pay and less financial independence. Swedish women participate in paid work on a more even footing with men and gain more financial independence, but still experience work–family imbalance (Cousins and Tang 2004).

European Couples' Work-hour Strategies

Adapting Moen's (2003) notion of couples' work-hour strategies to the European setting, Crompton (2006: 172) identified five types of work arrangements: high commitment, in which both partners work more than 40 hours a week; dual moderates, in which both partners work full time but neither works more than 35 to 40 hours a week; neotraditionalists, in which the man works 40 hours a week and the woman works shorter hours, typically part time; alternate commitments, referring to couples who both work less than 40 hours a week but one works less than 35 hours per week; and traditionalists, in which the man works full time and the woman does not work outside the home. Applied to five EU countries, dual moderates are the majority in Finland and pluralities in France, Portugal, and Norway. In Britain and the US, neotraditionalists and traditionalists are the plurality respectively.

Variations in couples' work-hour strategies across countries are revealing, and reflect not only differences in couples' preferences (understood as both personal preferences and expressions of gender norms), but also social-class variation and different national work-time regimes (including the presence or absence and nature of family-supportive policies). For instance, high-commitment couples are likely to be composed disproportionately of couples in which both partners work at "greedy" professional or managerial jobs. But national work-time regulations may enhance or moderate this social-class effect. For example, in Finland, where work hours are the shortest of the six countries in table 5.4 and family-supportive programs are relatively generous, over half of the respondents reported living in dual moderate households and the proportion of neotraditional households is low. In Portugal, the percentage of neotraditional households is also low, in this case reflecting the relative lack of availability of part-time jobs there. In Britain, there is a high percentage of neotraditionalists because of wide availability of part-time jobs and the propensity of women to fill them. Of couples in the US, 32 percent are traditionalists, presumably in part because of the lack of family-supportive policies to help parents mesh employment with child care.

Household division of labor

Weekly household work hours in the same five EU countries ranged on average from 11.7 among women in Norway, to 26.4 among women in Portugal and 5.2 among men in Norway, to 7.7 among men in Britain, excluding child care. The figures compare to 12.7 average hours among women and 8.4 average hours among men in the US (Crompton 2006: 146). These variations reflect differences in national gender norms as well as income levels that support, or not, the purchase of labor-saving appliances and substitute services. Portugal, with the most traditional gender division of household labor among these five EU countries, is also the poorest. In all of the countries, total hours of household work are lower when both partners work outside the home and higher in traditional households, where the man works full time and the woman does not work outside the home. In all of the countries, women who work full time outside the home reported fewer hours of household work than women who work part time outside the home, and hours of household work are greatest among married women not in paid employment (Crompton 2006: 147). Similar to trends in the US, women's hours of household work have declined considerably since the 1960s and men's have increased a small amount,

Table 5.4: Couples' work arrangements by country

Type of work arrangement	Britain	Finland	France	Norway	Portugal	US
High commitment	12 %	7 %	6 %	7 %	17 %	16 %
Dual moderates	16	55	36	32	34	14
Neotraditionalists	32	13	22	25	12	18
Alternate commitments	19	20	22	28	10	20
Traditionalists	20	6	14	7	28	32
N	817	401	643	839	412	299

Source: Crompton (2006: 172).

yet women still spend about twice as many hours as men on household work (Bianchi et al. 2006; Crompton 2006: 141; Gershuny et al. 1994; Sullivan and Gershuny 2001).

Work–life conflict

A discussion of work–life conflict in Europe first necessitates a closer look at employment hours. Figures 5.1 and 5.2 show that the majority of employed men and women in all six countries work full time and that women are much more likely than men to work part time. Some full-time workers, especially men, work long hours, 45 or more a week on average. Among these countries, women in the US are most likely to work long hours. Men and women in Finland are much less likely to report working long hours than their counterparts in the other countries.

Data from the Luxembourg Income Study show that for men, the average workweek in most of nine industrialized countries hovered around 40 per week, with only the Netherlands having a particularly short workweek. The US is at the higher end of the sample countries, but it does not stand out markedly from the others in terms of average length of the paid workweek. Regarding very long hours, however, the

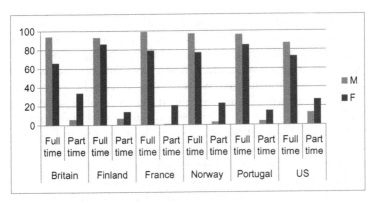

Figure 5.1 Employment status by sex
Data Source: Crompton (2006: 131).

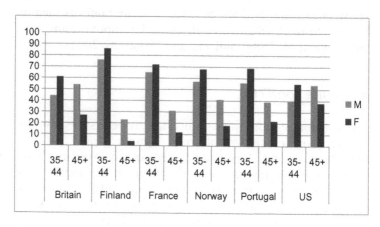

Figure 5.2 Full-time workers by average weekly hours
Data Source: Crompton (2006: 131).

US is distinctive. For men, the US and Australia have the highest proportions, working 50 or more hours per week. American women, like American men, have among the longest workweeks in the nine countries. The proportion of women working part time is also among the lowest, and the proportion working 50 hours or more per week is among the highest. The Netherlands again has the shortest workweek (Jacobs and Gerson 1998).

Work–life conflict is a substantial area of study in the sociology of work that draws on many important issues (e.g., work and family, psychosocial well-being of workers, boundary management, etc.). When work–life conflict is analyzed in relationship to work hours, it can be seen that questions of work time are still at the core of this debate, with much to offer. As might be expected, work–life conflict is highest among those who work long hours and lowest among those who work less than 20 hours a week on average. Of six countries, work–life conflict is highest in the US and Portugal, followed closely by Britain and France. Significantly lower levels of work–life conflict were found in Norway and Finland, with the lowest in Finland (Crompton 2006: 132–3).

Work Hours in Transition and Developing Countries

The International Labour Organization (ILO) Database of Working Time Laws permits an analysis of weekly normal hours in 21 industrialized countries and 80 transition and developing countries. Lee et al.'s (2007) study, with a central focus on transition and developing countries, is the first of its kind, and an examination of weekly normal hours begins to provide a broad picture of work hours globally.

In 2005, the 40-hour workweek was the most prevalent national standard. Almost half of the countries had enacted a limit of 40 hours or less, and among the others about half had laws of 41 to 46 hours and about half had laws of 48 hours. In the decade after 1995, no country had increased its statutory workweek, but 16 had reduced the normal workweek (Algeria, the Bahamas, Belgium, Bulgaria, Chad, Chile, the Czech Republic, Egypt, Italy, Mongolia, Morocco, the Netherlands, the Republic of Korea, Portugal, Rwanda, and Slovenia) (Lee et al. 2007: 12).

Despite an overall shift to shorter workweeks in the decade from 1995 to 2005, the 48-hour week remained the legal standard in a large number of countries. All of the industrialized countries that have a regulation regarding normal hours mandate a basic 40-hour workweek or less, with the exception of Switzerland specific to particular occupational categories. The 40-hour limit also exists in the 10 Central and Eastern European countries in the database. Almost half of the African countries had adopted a 40-hour or shorter standard, but three have limits above 46 hours. Most countries in Latin America have a 48-hour standard, and those Latin American countries with standards below 48 are in the intermediate category of 41 to 46 hours, with the exception of Ecuador with a 40-hour standard. Among the Asian countries, six have a 48-hour standard. The others have 40-hour workweeks, with the exception of Singapore, with 44 hours. There is no weekly statutory standard in India and Pakistan (Lee et al. 2007: 17). Table 5.5 displays details of weekly normal hours limits for a wide range of countries, showing the dominance of 40-hour norms, especially in industrialized

Table 5.5: Weekly normal hours limits (2005)

	No universal statutory limit	35–39 hours	40 hours	41–46 hours	48 hours	More than 48 hours
Industrialized countries	Australia, Denmark, Germany, Ireland, United Kingdom (48 hour limit on total hours)	Belgium, France	Austria, Canada, Finland, Italy, Japan, Luxembourg, Netherlands, New Zealand, Norway, Portugal, Spain, Sweden, United States	Switzerland (workers in industrial enterprises, offices, technical posts and sales staff in large commercial enterprises)		Switzerland (all other workers)
Africa	Nigeria, Seychelles	Chad	Algeria, Benin, Burkina Faso, Cameroon, Congo, Cote d'Ivoire, Djibouti, Gabon, Madagascar, Mali, Mauritania, Niger, Rwanda, Senegal, Togo	Angola, Burundi, Cape Verde, Democratic Republic of the Congo, Guinea-Bissau, Morocco, Namibia, South Africa, United Republic of Tanzania	Mozambique, Tunisia	Kenya

Table 5.5 Continued

	No universal statutory limit	35–39 hours	40 hours	41–46 hours	48 hours	More than 48 hours
Asia	India, Pakistan		China, Indonesia, Republic of Korea, Mongolia	Singapore	Cambodia, Lao People's Democratic Republic, Malaysia, Philippines, Thailand, Viet Nam	
Caribbean	Jamaica, Grenada		Bahamas	Cuba, Dominican Republic	Haiti	
Central and Eastern Europe			Bulgaria, Czech Republic, Estonia, Latvia, Lithuania, the former Yugoslav Republic of Macedonia, Romania, Russian Federation, Slovakia, Slovenia			

(Continued)

Table 5.5 Continued

	No universal statutory limit	35–39 hours	40 hours	41–46 hours	48 hours	More than 48 hours
Latin America			Ecuador	Belize, Brazil, Chile, El Salvador, Honduras, Uruguay (commerce), Venezuela	Argentina, Bolivia, Columbia, Costa Rica, Guatemala, Mexico, Nicaragua, Panama, Paraguay, Peru, Uruguay (industry)	
Middle East			Egypt		Jordan, Lebanon	

Source: Lee et al. (2007: 16) from ILO Database of Working Time Laws (<www.ilo.org/travdatabase>). Copyright © International Labour Organization 2007.

countries, select African and Asian countries, and the transition economies of Central and Eastern Europe, and a tendency to longer hours in less developed countries, especially in Asia and Latin America.

Laws, as national standards and representative in some sense of cultural ideals at a particular historical moment, are not necessarily the best indicator of actual practice, however. As has been discussed previously, level of economic development, productivity, industrial structure (manufacturing vs service), and occupational structure affect work hours, as do business cycle and sectoral shifts; the relative distribution of full-time, part-time, and non-standard work; and cultural traditions of work and leisure. Similarly, the differential power of labor unions and the market power of workers with valued skills vs the lesser power of the unskilled also affect work hours. A nation's age distribution, when workers enter and exit the labor force, and whether and how much women work and the occupations to which they have access are also factors. Individual preferences for occupation, full-time, part-time, or other non-standard work influence work hours too, although individuals often "settle" when they can't fulfill their preferences.

The US and Japan make for interesting comparative cases since they share a 40-hour norm; but, whereas Japanese workers used to work more hours than US workers, now their positions are reversed. Workers in the US and Japan have among the highest average annual hours on the job, as noted above in table 5.1, and considerably more than their European counterparts (200 hours or more in some cases). For much of the twentieth century, annual and weekly hours in Japan were higher than those in other industrialized countries, more characteristic of a developing nation. A 40-hour workweek was declared in 1977. Hours in Japan have gradually declined since 1980, in part due to government and trade union efforts and expansion of non-regular work, as discussed above. Although non-standard work has also grown in the US, as discussed in chapter 3, labor unions and government have not pursued work-time reduction. On an annual basis, also as shown above in table 5.1, US workers now average a long week more on the job annually than Japanese workers, down from two weeks more in the 1990s (Golden and Figart 2000: 1, 5). Both countries have seen a decline in annual hours as a result of the Great Recession, Japan more than the US (70 hours compared to 30 respectively).

Generally speaking, countries with higher average incomes as measured by gross national income (GNI) per capita have shorter weekly work hours. Differences in industrial structures make it hard to compare countries, however, so only manufacturing employment is considered here. Average weekly hours in manufacturing in the 44 countries and territories for which data are available in the ILO database ranged from 35 to 45 hours in the decade from 1995 to 2004, but a significant number of developing countries had longer weekly hours, often exceeding 48 (e.g., Costa Rica, El Salvador, Peru, Philippines, Thailand, and Turkey). Most high-income countries had short hours relative to the other countries in the database, with the exception of some Asian countries such as Singapore and the Republic of Korea, where the average manufacturing workweek is more than 48 hours. Average work hours in manufacturing were stable over the decade in many countries, most of which are industrialized, but they increased in a notable minority of countries and territories such as Costa Rica, Hong Kong (China), and Peru. A focus on average income, however, masks differences between low- and high-income countries. When low- and high-income countries are analyzed separately, it appears that economic growth is an important factor in the reduction of work hours until a certain point beyond which the impact of growth on hours becomes unclear and other factors apparently play a role (Lee at al 2007: 27, 32). These other factors can be the sorts of items discussed throughout this chapter and book: industrial structure, occupational structure, cultural preferences for work vs leisure, work-time regulations and relative distribution of full-time and non-standard work that produce distinctive work-time regimes, the extent and nature of women's labor-force participation, family leaves, and demographics such as age distribution, and individual preferences.

As discussed in chapter 3 regarding the bifurcation of work hours in the US, averages can mask important features of the overall distribution of work hours. Thus, it is necessary to examine national trends in long and short hours. The EU

Working Time Directive of 1993 established a maximum of 48 hours, including overtime, and the ILO Hours of Work (Industry) Convention, 1919 (No. 1), originally intended to limit work hours and restrain overtime, stipulates 48 hours as normal working hours (Lee et al. 2007: 45); thus, the ILO uses 48 hours as the threshold for long hours. Comparing 55 industrialized, transition, and developing countries for which data are available, there is considerable variation in the proportion of total employment that falls in the long-hours category. At one extreme, countries such as the Russian Federation (threshold of 50 hours), the Republic of Moldova, Norway, and the Netherlands have low percentages of long-hours employment (3.2, 4.9, 5.3, and 7.0 percent respectively), and strong regulation of work hours. At the other extreme, more than 40 percent of all employees work more than 48 hours in countries such as Ethiopia, Indonesia (threshold of 45 hours), the Republic of Korea, Pakistan, and Thailand, where statutory work hours regulation is at its weakest (Lee et al. 2007: 38–44). Long working hours are common in Asian developing countries where economic growth and productivity gains have not translated into shorter working hours (Lee et al. 2007: 45). Worldwide, it is estimated that about 22 percent of all workers are working more than 48 hours per week (Lee et al. 2007: 53).

Men and the self-employed are more likely to work long hours by comparison to women and employees, although rates vary by country. Among 18 industrialized countries, long-hours working as a proportion of total male employment (including the self-employed) ranged from 5.5 percent in Luxembourg to 54 percent in the Republic of Korea in 2004. In 16 transition countries, it ranged from 4.5 percent in the Russian Federation to 40 percent in Armenia. And among the developing countries in Asia, Africa, and the Americas, it ranged from 18.3 percent in Madagascar to 55.1 percent in Indonesia (Lee et al. 2007: 70–1). Average hours of work are particularly long in certain industries in the service sector, particularly wholesale and retail trade; hotels and restaurants; and transport, storage, and communications. Shift work, especially in the form of night and weekend work, is also quite common in the service sector across all regions of the world. By contrast, government and education have relatively short hours. Self-employment represents at least three fifths of informal employment in developing countries. The self-employed in industrialized countries tend to work very long hours (49 hours or more per week); in developing countries, however, work hours of the self-employed are diverse with substantial proportions working very long hours and short hours. The self-employed who work short hours in developing countries are more likely to be women (Lee et al. 2007: 140).

The ILO applies a threshold of 35 hours for short hours. In some cases, the proportion of short hours is high, for example, Albania and Georgia, at 40 percent. Short hours are common in high-income countries, where they are often used to reconcile employment and family life; but the high incidence of short hours in developing countries is believed to be the result of a slack labor market and poor economic performance, although work–family reconciliation is a factor too. In developing countries with a high proportion of short-hours workers, short hours tend to be concentrated among self-employed women, often in informal jobs, for which self-employment is a proxy. Involuntary short-hours work, that is, due to slack work, ranges from 0.4 percent in Hungary to 20 percent in Peru in 2001 (2002 data in the case of Peru) among 39 countries compared by the ILO. The highest percentages are in Peru, Colombia (2002), Armenia, Guatemala (2002), Nicaragua, and Costa Rica, ranging from 20.1 to 10 percent (Lee et al. 2007: 55, 59). Rates of short-hours work among female employees in industrialized countries ranged from 10.6 percent in Cyprus to 73.3 percent in the Netherlands in 2004; in the transition countries, from 2.5 percent in Romania to 46 percent in Georgia; and, in the developing countries, from 6.2 percent in Thailand to 38.3 percent in Uruguay. Among women who were self-employed in industrialized countries, rates of short-hours work ranged from 0 in Malta to 70.3 percent in the Netherlands; 9.8 percent in Slovakia to 58.9 percent in Albania in the transition countries; and 13.5 percent in Thailand to 64.2 percent in Panama in the developing countries (Lee et al. 2007: 72–3). Short-hours work among women in developing and transition countries is believed to be the product of the same forces that promote short-hours work among women in industrialized countries: reconciliation of employment and family care.

Work Hours Preferences

Researchers (Reynolds 2004; Stier and Lewin-Epstein 2003) have used the ISSP dataset cited above to investigate the work hours preferences of workers in the industrialized and transition countries. Stier and Lewin-Epstein (2003) did the most comprehensive analysis, studying 1997 data for 23 countries.[9] They found a preference for more work time in the former socialist countries, particularly Russia and Bulgaria, and Mediterranean countries such as Spain and Israel. The proportion desiring more work hours was lowest in developed countries such as Sweden, Japan, the UK, and France. Generally, in the majority of countries, the percentage of those who wanted to decrease work time was higher than those who wanted to increase it. Women were more likely than men to be dissatisfied with their number of hours devoted to paid employment, but because the ISSP question was answered by the unemployed as well as the employed, it is difficult to know whether it is employed women who want to increase their work hours or unemployed women who want to increase their work hours, or some combination of the two. Among both men and women, there are two clearly defined groups of countries: those in which workers want to increase their work hours to earn more and those in which workers prefer to decrease work hours even at the expense of lower earnings. In the former group, the most notable are the post-communist countries in which almost all men and women prefer more work hours and higher income. This is true of the Mediterranean countries as well. Even in the English-speaking countries, which generally have the highest standard of living, a substantial proportion of workers preferred to increase work hours. On the other hand, in several countries workers preferred a reduction in work hours and were willing to lose earnings, particularly the Scandinavian countries, where the preference for reduced hours was more pronounced among men than women, and, for men particularly, also in Switzerland (Stier and Lewin-Epstein 2003: 315).

Reynolds (2004) found that workers in the US, Japan, former West Germany, and Sweden were more likely to desire to reduce than increase their work hours. Americans, however, were least likely to desire a reduction in work hours and more likely to desire more hours when compared to workers in the other three countries. A large number of Americans wanted more hours even if they were already working full time. Gender was an important determinant of hours mismatches. In the US, men and women were about equally likely to have a mismatch. In Sweden and Germany, by contrast, men were more satisfied with their current situation than women, while in Japan men were less satisfied with their current situation. In the US and Germany, where combining work and family is particularly difficult, women were more likely to desire reduced hours than men. Yet lone mothers, lone fathers, and male breadwinners tended to desire more hours; thus, it seems that family responsibilities seem to increase the appetite for work. The gender difference was much less pronounced in family-friendly Sweden, and it was reversed in Japan, where there is a weak welfare system, traditional family structures prevail, and female labor-force participation is low.

Conclusion

Our tour of work time around the world uncovered a variety of patterns and trends. As discussed above, work time is generally lower where productivity and income are high, such as the industrialized countries, but there are important differences within that group. Those differences are products of other factors, as we saw when we compared European countries, Canada, Japan, and the US. These factors influence work hours in transition and developing countries too, but level of economic development is the overriding condition because it determines the extent and nature of economic activity and employment beyond basic agriculture. In developing countries, informal self-employment, especially as it intersects the gender division of labor, is more important than in developed countries.

We will return to the US in chapter 6 to reconsider what we have learned about work time and to think about new features of a political economy of work time emerging in the twenty-first century. Work aided by electronic technologies is important, as are new ways of organizing and customizing work time, some for the benefit of workers and others in the interest of employers. The struggle over work time continues, taking on new dimensions as the economy, the nature of work, and the gender division of labor change.

6
A New Political Economy of Work Time

This book began by drawing a distinction between work time as private trouble and public issue and posed the question, what are the cultural norms, public policies, and business practices from which our current work-time conventions derive? Chapter 1 offered a broad overview of work time beginning with the "deep history" of early pre-industrial societies, challenging the notion that lack of material affluence meant long work hours and encouraging critical thinking about the nature of affluence itself. Long work hours, in fact, date to the Industrial Revolution, when the natural rhythms that had marked time in pre-industrial agricultural societies gave way to the fixed mechanical calibrations of the clock, and in the context of unequal class relations and the profit motive of industrial capitalism control of work time shifted from the relative autonomy of the pre-industrial peasant and crafter to the factory owner and boss. As wage-labor developed and employers assumed control of work time, time itself was commodified in the capital–labor exchange. Parallel to the factory system, unpaid work in the home, the specialty of women as men left the household to "go to work," was devalued because it was outside the wage-labor system. Although the industrial structure, occupational structure, and labor market have changed over the two and a half centuries since the English Industrial Revolution, and a layered-task time discipline applies in some occupations while an industrial time discipline applies in others, these fundamental principles of work time and gender persist.

In the United States, legislated reductions of work hours to 10 daily, then eight, and "finally" the 40-hour week were the result largely of dogged labor activism throughout the nineteenth and early twentieth centuries, rooted in the work-time regimes of craft shops and factories. Worker victories were local and incremental, and, in the case of the eight-hour day at Ford, granted by capital in an effort to disarm unions. The challenges in the last few decades to the now standard 40-hour week have come in the labor market, especially in the way employers hire and organize labor in the service economy to maximize flexibility without strong union opposition, but also from workers seeking better integration of paid work and the rest of life.

The labor market is increasingly composed of non-standard jobs, which have grown during the last several decades more rapidly than standard, full-time jobs, while the proportion of standard jobs declines. The forces driving the growth of non-standard jobs are complex, including employers' desire for a more flexible labor force and workers' desire for shorter and flexible hours. The latter is especially true of women, who have few options, especially in countries like the US, when seeking to integrate employment and family care. Employers reduce wages and avoid paying expensive benefits to non-standard workers, who labor outside the reach of many labor laws. In an economy of 24/7 retailing and services, employers cover more business hours and adjust to customer traffic flow by utilizing workers on flexible, often short-hours schedules. Increasingly, workers who are not qualified for or who cannot obtain regular, full-time jobs for other reasons land non-standard jobs, even if they prefer standard, full-time employment.

This growing proportion of short-hours workers is at one end of an increasingly bifurcated work-time distribution. At the other are a growing proportion of standard, full-time workers, typically salaried, who work in excess of 50 hours per week and are exempt from overtime protections of the FLSA. Expensive employee benefits, such as health care, are disincentives to hiring additional workers, and employers often expect those they have already hired to take on more work when the workload increases. These developments at the extremes of the work-time distribution are obscured by the statistical average, making it appear that the work-time regime established by the FLSA in 1938 remains current despite significant changes in the industrial structure, occupational structure, and labor market. The preponderance of evidence is that, in the aggregate, Americans work on average more hours annually today than several decades ago, explained largely by the increased contribution of women in the paid labor force. Mismatches in workers' actual and preferred hours lead many of the overworked to prefer shorter hours and many of the underemployed to prefer more hours, or at least better pay and benefits.

Mismatch is most profound, perhaps, among those who seek better integration of employment and family care. This type of mismatch became more evident as growing numbers of women with children entered the workforce. As family structures have changed, increasingly assuming the dual-earner and single-parent forms, workers often feel squeezed for time. This is especially true of women, who continue to perform more unpaid work in the home compared to men, although men's contributions have increased over the last few decades. In the US, the most common adaptations are private because public supports, with the exception of the Family and Medical Leave Act, are rare and uneven. Organizations vary in the nature and scope of the family-friendly benefits they offer, and those that are generous in this regard often do it to enhance recruitment and retention. Thus, these organizational efforts are aimed at a segment of the labor force in which there is labor market competition on the buyers' side, enhancing the power of workers with valuable skills. A few states have sought to go beyond the terms of the FMLA, and President Obama is on record supporting expansion of the law, but the US has a long way to go to approximate the family policies common in Europe. Program specifics and origins vary by country and in gender equity, and European family policies are framed by more extensive work-time regulation by comparison to the US, the product of stronger labor influences in these societies through the mechanisms of unions and political parties. In the US, lack of a labor party, despite Democrats' ties to organized labor, and the declining power of unions do not bode well for work-time regulation in workers' interests. Even in the midst of the Great Recession and persistent weak economy since, work-time reform is not being considered. Lessons from the Great Depression were Federal Reserve Chairman Ben Bernanke's guide in addressing the 2008 banking crisis in hopes of avoiding the mistakes that lengthened the 1930s crisis. Both the duration of the crisis and extent of unemployment (reaching 25 percent in the Great Depression) spawned the work-time reforms of the 1930s, but even with lingering high unemployment after the Great Recession we are far from those conditions today.

Work-time mismatches and the common US practice of private adaptation beg the question, why don't workers who don't like their hours just change jobs? The way I posed the question provides a clue to the answer. In the US, a job's hours are packaged with the job itself, and there are few government regulations, unlike the situation in Europe, of work time. US workers in some jobs can negotiate for flexibility at the margins or perhaps even reduced hours, and workers in highly autonomous jobs can manage their own time, but for the most part workers must change jobs to gain reduced hours and/or greater flexibility. These gains may be achieved at the expense of wages and benefits – tradeoffs few can afford. Thus, the lack of universal health care, the lack of widely available child care, and the high degree of wage inequality in the US inhibit the free mobility of labor and contribute to suboptimal allocation of the labor supply, in addition to ratifying gender and ethnic inequalities in the allocation of standard and non-standard jobs.

Work hours in transition and developing countries are further evidence of a truth long known by scholars of industrialization and work time. Early in the industrialization process work hours are long, but, as societies develop, increased productivity and social wealth tend to yield shorter work hours. Comparisons of work hours today in the developed and developing countries bear this out. But legislated reduction in hours stalled in the US as Americans preferred consumption after World War II. While many European countries made more progress in reducing weekly hours below 40, they too are experiencing the competitive pressures of service economies in an integrated global economy. Many

employers today prefer a flexible labor force and destandardization of legislated norms. And if globalization is a race to
the bottom, more workers in developed countries may return
to the days of low wages and long hours.

As public policy goes, systemic work-time reform would
be as difficult to achieve in the US as, say, health care or Social
Security reform. Workers do not have the same work-time
objectives, and there are plenty of obstacles in the form of
income and benefit needs, employer attitudes and interests,
workplace cultures, and the organization of work. Although
recent Social Security reform efforts failed and health-care
reform was enacted, the debates ebb and flow and the issues
are in the public's and policymakers' consciousness. The same
cannot be said for work-time reform.

Work time is not currently a major public issue, but it is
a private trouble shared by many. In addition to the work-
time conflicts that have been addressed throughout this book,
new forms of work, especially those aided by electronic technologies, have familiar and new work-time conflict and
control dilemmas.

The Electronic Cottage

Flexibility for whom? This question must be asked about all
forms of flexible work arrangements in an economy structured upon institutionalized inequalities (Pollert 1988, 1991).
Today electronic technologies abet flexible work-time regimes.
Developments in information and communication technologies have changed how and where we work. This electronic
workplace is a paradox, the source of both greater flexibility
and overwork, especially as it has facilitated the extension of
the office to the home, cafe, and beyond. Homework itself is
not new, however, in that traditional forms extend the factory
to the home, as in garment manufacturing and electronic
assembly.

About half of all American workers use a computer at
work, and about 80 percent of those who usually do job-
related work at home – about 14 million – use a computer
at home. Homeworkers in general work on average seven hours

per week at home if the arrangement is informal (i.e., just taking work home; these are the majority of homeworkers), or 19 hours with a formal arrangement (who are most likely to use a computer). Among occupational groups, managerial and professional workers are most likely to work at home, especially teachers, although many who work at home are self-employed in a home-based business. A small minority, 9 percent, arranged to work at home to coordinate work with personal or family needs (US Department of Labor 2005c).

Homework aided by a computer is only a subset of all telework. Other teleworkers work at telecenters, client offices, or other sites at a distance from the main office (Ellison 2004: 18; Gurstein 2001: 3). Information and communication technologies facilitate a mobile, flexible workforce, who commonly experience social isolation (Ellison 2004: 27, 103; Gurstein 2001: 71–4, 95). While their control of time was enhanced, some found it difficult to adjust to the freedom of working at home, manage the permeable boundaries of work and home, and negotiate demands and constraints of space and new rules and boundaries within the family (Ellison 2004: 31–3, 108–12, 117–23; Gurstein 2001: 57, 65, 95). Most home-based workers worked long hours; close to two thirds worked more than 40 hours a week on average and more than five days a week, in Gurstein's (2001: 62–3, 65, 90) study in San Francisco and Canada, often stretching out the workday with long breaks. Some researchers (Ellison 2004: 32–5) found more role conflict among women who worked at home compared to their male counterparts. Women, in fact, reported *increased* (emphasis mine) stress associated with teleworking, suggesting electronic flexibility is not a solution to work–life problems.

As employers become more comfortable with workers working off site, face time is becoming less important in evaluating workers' performance and productivity. Instead, organizations become results oriented, shifting from the prevailing clock-time orientation of the industrial era (Thompson 1967) as it has been applied, particularly in offices, to a renewed task orientation applied to the post-industrial workplace (Rubin 2007b). Workers on site and off are encouraged to "work smart" instead of long, that is, work efficiently to complete tasks in less time.

Customized Time: Two Forms

Destandardization of work hours and employment relations (Golden 2001; Negrey 1993) has two faces. On one side it offers flexibility and worker control of time, as in the case of part-time technical professionals studied by Meiksins and Whalley (2002) and job sharers I interviewed in the 1980s (Negrey 1993). On the other side, flexibility maximizes employers' use of the labor force at the expense of workers' control of time.

The engineers, computer professionals, and technical writers interviewed by Meiksins and Whalley (2002) had reduced their work time and customized their work arrangements, either through corporate part-time employment or independent contracting. They were satisfied part-time professionals who enjoyed their work and derived satisfaction from parenting or other non-work activities (Meiksins and Whalley 2002: 3–4). As skilled technical workers, they leveraged their power in the labor market to customize their work schedules. The respondents, approximately 80 percent of whom were women, 60 percent of whom had children, and 50 percent of whom had children under age five, resisted a view of work that was all-encompassing and all-consuming and also resisted cultural norms of intensive mothering (Meiksins and Whalley 2002: 35–6). Their motives varied, to some degree by gender, and they used different strategies of negotiation to customize their work schedules. Women were more likely to be motivated by family care; men generally had other reasons, some to ease into retirement. Individual managers exercised considerable discretion in permitting such customization, and managerial and organizational pressures to return to full time were formidable in some cases. In sum, however, the long-term and short-term part-timers were uncomfortable with the prevailing time structures of the contemporary workplace; they wanted flexible work schedules that were more than short-term solutions to specific problems. The ability to control one's time was a high priority among all respondents (Meiksins and Whalley 2002: 145). Thus, work-time customization can go beyond one-size-fits-all family-friendly policies to permit true control over one's work time by facilitating individual choice among a range of options (Meiksins and Whalley 2002: 151).

This personal form of customization is contrasted with a corporate form as exemplified by Walmart, the largest private employer in the US, which has begun using a new computerized scheduling system that moves many of its 1.3 million workers from predictable shifts to a system based on the number of customers in stores at any given time, to enhance productivity and customer satisfaction. The system was implemented initially in 2006 for some workers, including cashiers and accounting-office personnel. Software designed by Kronos tracks individual store sales, transactions, units sold, and customer traffic in 15-minute increments over seven weeks, and compares data to that of the prior year before scheduling workers. Such scheduling-optimization systems can integrate data ranging from the number of in-store customers at certain hours to the average time it takes to sell a television or unload a truck, and help predict how many workers will be needed at any given hour. In addition to Walmart, Payless ShoeSource, Radio Shack, and Mervyn's are among other companies using advanced scheduling systems. While these systems benefit retailers and customers, they create unpredictable work schedules and paychecks for workers. Workers may be asked to be on call to meet customer surges or sent home because of a lull. The new systems also alert managers when a worker is approaching full-time status or overtime, which would require higher wages and benefits, so they can reduce hours to keep the worker below those thresholds. In concert with the new system, Walmart asks hourly employees to complete a "personal availability" form indicating when they can work, noting that all full-time cashiers and customer-service workers are encouraged to consider a weekend shift every week. "Limiting your personal availability may restrict the number of hours you are scheduled," the form warns (Maher 2007).[1]

These tales reveal the promise and pitfalls of flexible work arrangements, especially as those arrangements intersect the differential power of workers in their respective occupations.

Recommendations for Change

Starting from a perspective of better integration of work time and family care, numerous scholars have proposed recommendations for work-time reform in the US. The unequal distribution of paid employment and unpaid household work across men and women, and unequal patterns of alternative work arrangements and reduced work, show that work time is gendered. So far, efforts to reorganize and/or reduce work time in the US and Europe have not degendered work time. Instead, alternative arrangements have ratified the conventional gender division of labor to the extent that women are more likely than men to avail themselves of reduced and flexible work-time options to integrate employment and family responsibilities (Appelbaum et al. 2002; Figart and Mutari 1998, 2000; Negrey 1993; Sirianni and Negrey 2000). Increasingly, gender is differentiated not by whether individuals have a job but the amount of time spent in paid employment. The expansion of overtime for men and part-time jobs for women reinforces the skewed division of domestic labor and occupational segregation (Figart and Mutari 1998, 2000). This skewed distribution of paid work time, domestic labor, and occupational segregation is at once a product of and reinforced by gender inequity in pay. The rational dual-earner household has less to lose financially – but much to lose in terms of gender equity – when it is the wife who reduces her paid work hours.

A number of recommendations for change have been proposed, from very specific calls for more vacation time, to shorter workdays and workweeks, to more comprehensive proposals that include reduced work time as one key component. For example, *Escape*, a travel magazine, formed a committee called Work to Live, whose goal is to increase vacation time in the US to three weeks by law after the first year on the job and four weeks after three years (Robinson 2000). Opponents to longer vacation time claim it would harm productivity, but such opposition is countered by productivity data from, for example, Germany, France, and Sweden, where productivity has been high despite long mandated vacations. Proponents of longer vacation time argue that mandated paid vacations level the playing field for companies and eliminate the current penalties against people who change jobs and lose vacation time as a result (Robinson 2000).

More vacation time is appealing on its face, and it is certainly in the interests of the travel industry, but it does not address the sense of daily time famine and the mismatches between actual and ideal work hours. These pressures require relief more immediately and regularly than vacations give – thus, calls for reductions in the workweek.

A recent argument for four eight-hour days (LaJeunesse 1999)[2] claimed that a shorter workweek would lead to higher productivity through more efficient use of work time (less fatigue and shirking) and less monitoring of shirking. A four-day workweek would require fewer days of child care per week and, if the length of the school day were increased to coincide with work hours, less need for before- and after-school care. A four-day week could also reduce commuting, no small matter in many large US metropolitan areas. Historically, major reductions of hours in Britain preceded, rather than followed, peaks of productivity growth, and in France in 1983, when legislation to reduce the workweek to 39 hours from 40 took effect, hourly productivity rose 6 percent compared to a 2 percent increase the year before (and less than 4 percent afterward) (LaJeunesse 1999: 100–1). Part-time work and job sharing have also been found to increase productivity (Bailyn 1993: 84).

Beechey and Perkins (1987: 107) argued that appeals for work-time reduction that focus on the length of the workweek instead of the workday are often masculine in their orienting assumptions. A feminist approach would emphasize reduction in the length of the workday (such as five six-hour days, especially to mesh with children's school days; although some advocate year-round school, for example, Heymann 2000); work-time flexibility; and limits on overtime, evening, night, and weekend work. Most of the examples of recommendations for change in box 6.1 recognize these principles by embedding calls for shorter work time within more comprehensive systemic changes that would include subsidized child and dependent care and universal health care. Tilly's (1996) recommendations focus on enhancing the quality of part-time jobs. Appelbaum et al. (2002), Gornick and Meyers (2003, 2009), Hartmann et al. (2007), Hartmann and Lovell (2009), and Jacobs and Gerson (2004) envision variants of a dual-earner/dual-caregiver society in the US as with European models. Sirianni's (1991) "Post-industrial New Deal" has self-management of time at its core.

Box 6.1:   Examples of recommendations for change

Sirianni 1991

- "Post-industrial New Deal" would have self-management of time at its core.
- Facilitate wide range of voluntary time–income tradeoffs through policies that support and legitimate options for temporary and partial withdrawal from the labor market by the employed.
- Full employment, even if only part-time jobs can be guaranteed and basic income supports are necessary.
- Free time for political participation.
- Financial and administrative support for activity outside the formal labor market (independent and community self-help and services; ecologically sound cooperative and craft production; aesthetic and leisure pursuits).

Tilly 1996

- Limit creation of "lousy" part-time jobs.
- Enhance quality of part-time jobs.
- Narrow compensation differentials of full- and part-time jobs.
- Support unionization, via multi-employer bargaining structures as necessary.
- Reduce work-time for all.
- Universal benefits, e.g., health care.
- Portability of worker pensions.
- Standardize eligibility for unemployment insurance and workers' compensation to include part-time and contingent workers.
- Universal system of child and dependent care.

Appelbaum et al. 2002

- Six cornerstones of a "shared work/valued care" model:
- Hours of work legislation to allow for a shorter standard workweek for all, flexibility for workers, longer part-time hours, and limits on mandatory overtime.
- Adjustment of hours legislation to allow workers to request up to a 20 percent reduction in hours and pro-rated reductions in pay and benefits that employers would have to honor unless there was a good business reason not to do so.

- Equal opportunity and non-discrimination provisions to protect workers on part-time schedules from discrimination in pay or benefits, to encourage private sector employers to make good part-time jobs widely available, and to reduce the gender gap in pay.
- Share the cost of care by investing in day care and elder care infrastructure and by providing subsidies for child care and elder care, short-term caregivers' leave, subsidized wages or tax credits for caregivers, universal pre-school, and after- and before-school programs for children.
- Untie benefits from individual employers by making access to health insurance available to everyone without regard to employment status and by establishing funds similar to unemployment insurance for maternity leave, parental leave, and long-term family medical leave; provide a floor under wages by indexing the minimum wage to the median wage.
- Update income security protections such as unemployment insurance and old age pensions so they are no longer geared toward an outdated model of work and care that assumes a full-time breadwinner and full-time homemaker.

Gornick and Meyers 2003, 2009

Dual-earner/dual caregiver society in US with policies borrowed from European models, particularly in areas of:

(1) paid family leave;
(2) work-time regulation (limit weekly hours, paid annual leave, part-time parity, right to shift from full-time to reduced or flexible hours); and
(3) early childhood education and care, to effect dissolution of gender specialization in paid work and unpaid care work.

Jacobs and Gerson 2004

1 Work-facilitating and family-support reforms:
  child care
    shorter workday
    paid parental leave
    high-quality child care
      smaller classes
      more adults per child
      less caretaker turnover through better training and pay
    night and weekend child care

(Continued)

after-school programs
income support
   living wage through combination of tax credits and
     increased minimum wage.
2 Equal opportunity reforms:
work flexibility
better enforcement of equal opportunity laws
comparable worth
job security for part-time workers.
3 Work-regulating reforms:
extend FLSA to professional, managerial and other salaried
   workers
pro-rate benefits for all workers
35-hour standard workweek
limit mandatory overtime
graduated bonuses for night and weekend work.

Hartmann et al. 2007

- Greater job flexibility à la European models.
- Paid caregiver leave.
- Subsidized child care, universal pre-k, and before- and after-school care.
- Extend FMLA to smaller firms, preferably all firms; and to care for elder in-laws, step-parents, and same-sex partners; create very short term leave for "small necessities" such as meetings at school.
- Require all employers to provide 10 paid sick days per year.
- Reduce standard workweek to 37.5 or 35 hours.
- Increase time off through mandated paid vacation and paid holidays.
- End discrimination in wages and benefits for workers on reduced hours.
- End mandatory overtime.
- Modernize tax policy to facilitate combination of paid work and caregiving among all workers.

Hartmann and Lovell 2009

- Paid sick leave as new minimum standard.
- Family care days.
- Advocate Healthy Families legislation.
- Advocate Family Leave Insurance legislation.

How realistic are these proposals, especially in the wake of the Great Recession? While President Obama supports expanding FMLA, and doing so would be a step in the right direction, expansion of FMLA is a small piece of the reforms recommended in box 6.1. Subsidized child care is a long way off given current public budget woes. Work-time reforms outside the scope of expanding FMLA, such as revising FLSA to reduce work hours, are not on the agenda. The recommendations illustrated in box 6.1 generally do not make work-sharing arguments for reducing work time. Sirianni (1991) is a noteworthy exception, advocating full employment even if only short-hours jobs can be guaranteed. Arguments for work sharing may (re)emerge among scholars and policy advocates and within the larger public if relatively high unemployment persists.[3] With so many workers on short hours even during periods of low unemployment, however, it is difficult to imagine a groundswell for work-time reduction. And the high cost of employer-provided health insurance is itself a barrier to additional hiring.

Economic growth is the mantra we hear, especially in periods of high unemployment, to create jobs and stimulate consumption, but can our planet support a lifestyle of unfettered consumption? Environmentalists say no. And what if a cultural backlash occurs against this, or if structural conditions can no longer support mass consumption for consumption's sake? With less consumption and shrinking demand, would there be enough jobs for everyone who wants one? Is work-time reform an important, but overlooked, dimension of going green?

Work Time and Environmental Sustainability

I don't understand how you can – if you're an American – embrace the green movement and not admit to yourself that it means you must consume less in your own life.
Jeff Yeager, author of *The Ultimate Cheapskate's Road Map to True Riches: A Practical (and Fun) Guide to Enjoying Life More by Spending Less* (Zak 2008)

Environmental concerns have been scientific matters for decades, and activists have raised awareness about the issues since the first Earth Day in 1970. Subsequent developments – not limited to community and corporate recycling programs, the devastation wrought by Hurricane Katrina, media devoted to environmental issues, widespread availability of compact fluorescent light bulbs and energy-efficient appliances, green construction, rooftop gardens, organic foods and farmers' markets, community and store bans on plastic bags – have created mass environmental awareness in recent years. None of these efforts, at least in the US, however, have promoted work-time reform as a central aspect of environmental stewardship.

Sirianni's (1991) call for self-management of time in a post-industrial New Deal asserted "ecologically sound cooperative and craft production," but left the argument tying work-time reform and environmentalism undeveloped. Others (Daly 1991; Hayden 1999; Schor 2001) address production and consumption directly, offering a critique of growth that implies a necessity for work-time reform. Hayden (1999: 2) notes that the debate regarding sustainable development focuses disproportionately on poorer nations of the global South and fears of overpopulation, but argues that the environmental crisis "is in fact deeply rooted in the overconsumption of resources in the wealthy nations of the North" and that Northern levels of consumption, also as the model of development in the global South, are unsustainable.

Technological fixes, by using more efficient alternative technologies and renewable resources, are the common approach to addressing resource depletion. Schor (2001: 8) argued that green technologies are an important and necessary component of sustainability, but ecological pressures stemming from growth repeatedly cancel out the benefits of better technology. Technological fixes are an incomplete solution to continuing environmental degradation and global inequality that must be accompanied by a new paradigm challenging the entire notion of economic growth.

Proponents of growth advocate unfettered growth, with little if any reflection on the nature, purpose, and costs of growth (Daly 1991; Douthwaite 1992). Proponents of sustainability advocate sufficiency and maintenance (Daly 1991;

Hayden 1999). If we adhere to the ecological dictum of "reduce, reuse, recycle," demand declines for certain goods, thereby reducing resource use. Reduction in consumption means reduction in production. In an economy in which consumer spending accounts for two thirds of total economic activity (Anonymous 2008a), long-term slack demand is recessionary from the perspective of unfettered growth. From the perspective of sustainability, such action represents a realignment of values, with an emphasis on quality of life instead of quantity of goods (Daly 1991; Douthwaite 1992; Hayden 1999; Schor 2001), and requires a new definition of affluence.

To date, ecologistic push-back against the forces of growth has been largely a matter of education and consciousness-raising. But the market itself may be nudging us in the direction of sustainability today. When I finished the first draft of this book in April 2008, oil was more than $100 per barrel. Due to political conflict in the Middle East and earthquake-related disaster in Japan, oil was more than $100 per barrel again in March 2011, although the price has fallen below $100 (September 2011) with the sluggish economy and European debt crisis. From 1987 to as recently as 2003, oil ranged from $10 to $40 per barrel, averaging $20 per barrel, one fifth of the April 2008 price. Energy analyst Charles T. Maxwell projected an average of $40 between 2005 and 2010, and $70 between 2011 and 2020, with a range of $50 to $100 during the latter period (Prestowitz 2005: 156). At the moment, we seem to be a decade ahead of this forecast. The high price of oil increased the price of gasoline and consumer goods, creating shrinking demand for some goods, limited production of alternative fuels, and mainstream political rhetoric in support of alternative fuels and "green" jobs. The economy has adapted to rising oil prices in the past, but today there is increasing competition for the resource from "three billion new capitalists" (Prestowitz 2005) in China and India, where growing middle classes want to consume like Americans.

When oil escalated to $147 per barrel in July 2008, American drivers shed their SUVs, mass transit ridership increased, and some employers offered workers the option of four-day workweeks (10-hour days) to reduce commutes. Grant

County in the state of Indiana proposed closing county offices on Fridays to save on utility costs. Most county employees worked a 35-hour week, from 8 a.m. to 4 p.m. Monday through Friday, with a one-hour lunch break. Under the proposal, they could work 8 a.m. to 5 p.m. Monday through Thursday – 32 hours a week – at the same pay (Anonymous, 2008b).

The credit crisis in fall 2008 caused the price of oil to nosedive as production was curtailed, workers were laid off, and consumer demand shrunk. During the Great Recession, workers faced reduced work hours because of recessionary conditions. Some companies cut full-time workers' hours to part time to avoid layoffs, and many state and local governments furloughed workers to reduce costs.

In the current crisis, there is opportunity to think critically about production and consumption, and shift to sustainability. Environmentalists would tell us we have no choice. Stagnant wages and price inflation were the practical and immediate impetus for consumer frugality in the summer of 2008. Job loss and declining wages with reduced work hours and tight credit are the impetus for such frugality now. But wage deflation is of long duration in the US, dating from the early 1970s. Real wages per worker in the 1990s returned to levels comparable to the late 1950s (*Economic Report of the President* 1994: 320), and an upturn in wages after the mid-1990s did not return them to their early 1970s peak (US Department of Labor, table B-47, Hours and Earnings in Private Nonagricultural Industries, 1960–2008). The median earnings of men ages 25 to 64 declined 28 percent from 1969 to 2009, 47 percent among men who completed high school but didn't go to college (Meyerson 2011). The purchasing power of one wage earner in the early 1970s requires two wage earners today – or lots of credit. That credit is no longer so freely available. Nor should it be, according to some economists (e.g., Stiglitz 2007) who argue our economy rested on too much debt before the 2008 financial crisis.

We have become accustomed to believing we can grow ourselves out of joblessness and poverty (Daly 1991; Douthwaite 1992; Hayden 1999; Schor 2001). But, in mature economies, poverty and joblessness are not due to shortage; they are distributional effects of the economy's normal operation.

Redistribution of jobs and income can address problems of joblessness and poverty while shifting to economic sustainability.[4] Advocates of work-time reduction believe it is a mechanism of job redistribution and consistent with a vision of sustainability (see for example, most recently, Schor 2010).

Conclusion

The discussion above of the shorter workweek vs workday points to the trenchant problem facing parents today: conflict between paid work routines and children's routines or what Williams (2000) has called the ideal worker norm and the family care norm. One option is to maintain the status quo in work hours and expand children's school days and years. While this option might relieve conflict between parent work routines and child care by extending the time children are in the custody of schools, it does not necessarily reduce the sense of time famine that many adults experience because they feel they spend too much time on the job and too little time with family, in leisure, in education and/or training, and in community with others. Nor does it address the difficulties of meshing employment and child care for preschoolers, although universal pre-kindergarten has been advocated in the US. The solution we choose – longer school days and years to better mesh with parents' long work hours, or a new, shorter, full-time work norm to better mesh with children's school hours – is ultimately a statement on our values as a society, for life, including its vast array of activities and possibilities, is a moral economy of time (Sirianni 1991). Long work hours and school routines mean we value market activity over almost everything else in life. A new, shorter, full-time work norm permits us to claim a larger sphere of non-market activity.

Hewlett and West (1998: 32) noted an important irony: that conservatives – the staunchest defenders of markets – who lament the decline of "family values" often fail to recognize the ways in which market values destroy family values. But liberals, who are generally less critical of recent changes in family demographics and less sanguine in their support of markets, often don't see the contradictions between the market and families either. As we pursue an economic agenda of unfettered market growth, we stretch family relationships – temporally, emotionally, and geographically – to a breaking point. And as the bonds of family break, we turn to market institutions and relationships, as inadequate as they may be, to fill the void. In the process, we undermine ties of community, and we literally trash our environment with the surplus stuff we feel compelled to make and sell. If it is time to check our market impulses, we must do so in ways that do not erode the advances made in recent decades toward gender equality and that improve the market standing of the un- and underemployed and working poor. Because the underemployed – as measured by work hours according to the current full-time norm – and the working poor are disproportionately women, both objectives can be pursued by improving the wages, benefits, and working conditions of workers in marginal jobs.

In redistributing our values from market to non-market activities, it is necessary to redistribute work time – good paid work from men to women, unpaid work from women to men, and overwork to the underemployed. The Universal Caregiver model espoused by Fraser (1996) encourages us to think in terms of *everyone* doing primary care work in addition to paid work, not just women predominantly. Our market work might be organized very differently if we begin from an assumption that all workers also (will) have caregiving responsibilities, instead of assuming that particular, mostly marginalized women, workers have such responsibilities. Such restructuring of market work necessitates deconstructing the ideal worker norm (Williams 2000).[5]

Figart and Mutari's (2000) account of work-time regimes in Europe (and implicitly the US) indicates that we have yet to step on the high road to flexibilization. This high road would provide the institutional basis for restructuring gender relations by utilizing a variety of approaches to work hours and the workweek to balance paid and unpaid labor. Such flexibilization would be built upon a foundation of work-hours reductions from the current full-time standard, not just more flexibility around it. Their analysis of work-time regimes in European countries found that countries with shorter workweeks have a lower gap between men's and women's labor market behavior. "High road flexibilization" lies in combining shorter hours for both men and women with diverse work-time schedules, thereby degendering part-time work and providing more opportunities for employees to control their work routines.

More than 70 years after the FLSA, it is worth reflecting on the New Deal reforms that created a regulated form of capitalism in the US that stabilized economic conditions after the Great Depression to the benefit of the many (Kuttner 2007), admittedly with limited global competition. Those reforms included banking and financial regulations, a social safety net, and basic labor standards as defined in the FLSA. Americans have come to take these reforms for granted; have resisted their undoing (e.g., privatization of Social Security); and are shocked by stories of financial speculation, stock manipulation, self-dealing, and creative accounting by the avaricious privileged few who operate at the margins of regulation, who can bring down the many with the few when their risky ventures fail. I first wrote those words almost six months before the credit crisis and stock-market crash in the fall of 2008. Shock gave way to outrage, and their meaning is even more profound today as our economy reckons with the consequences of subprime lending, home foreclosures, and speculative mortgage-backed securities.

Deregulation eroded the regulatory structure governing the financial sector (Kuttner 2007). Demographics, federal taxation and spending priorities, and global free trade with countries whose living and labor standards are considerably less than our own threaten to undermine the social safety net and labor standards established by the New Deal. Some adherents to the Federalist Society agenda (Greider 2001) would repeal those standards to further corporate goals of flexibility and competitiveness. Alternatively, preservation of some measure of security in the new global economy requires adapting the labor standards, taking into consideration changes in recent decades in the gender division of labor, family structure, and the complexities of social life.

The New Deal reforms originated in an era when manufacturing was the dominant sector in the US economy. The industrial clock-time regime generalized from the shop floor to most jobs as the industrial and occupational structures changed to include more offices, schools, health-care facilities, stores, and restaurants. However, the industrial clock-time regime does not mesh well with more task-oriented creative and knowledge work in the arts, technology, and professions in which the requisite creative inspiration cannot be forced by, and may in fact be squelched by, the clock. Unpaid care work has never meshed well with the rigidity of industrial clock time. Many jobs, however, will remain packaged by fractions of the clock and remain subject to Taylorist notions of productivity even outside the factory setting. The marriage of Taylorism and electronic technologies likely will subject increasing numbers of workers to the Walmart model of scheduling. As discussed above, this model has its pitfalls, and without strong union opposition and regulation corporations can adopt the Walmart model with impunity. The absence of resistance does not mean workers will be complicit, however, only weak in their silence. As in times past, such workers will wait and hope for the state to intervene.

Work time is a basic organizing structure of society, and time is a resource we all share. However, our position in society largely determines what we do with our time and the degree to which we feel we have enough of it and can control it. Capitalism creates inequalities in class and across and within nations, and reinforces inequalities of gender and race and ethnicity. These inequalities are expressed in part in the distribution and control of work time. Work time has been the basis of social conflict in the past and continues to be so, although today the conflict has not spilled into the streets so much as it has remained isolated in workplaces and homes. Collective action and state intervention brought forth work-time remedies in the past, but those remedies are at their social limits in the twenty-first-century global economy. Today's conflicts about work time constitute an emergent new political economy of work time. What role will you play in shaping it?

Notes

Chapter 1 From Field to Factory and Beyond

1 For a history of the week, see Zerubavel (1985).
2 A particularly good application of Marxian concepts to work in contemporary American society appears in Walsh and Zacharias-Walsh (1998).
3 Saint Monday and Saint Tuesday were informal workers' holidays and exemplify the irregular work rhythms that were common in some settings and trades. According to Thompson (1967: 72–6), Monday was often treated as an extension of Sunday (hence the prefix "Saint") and used by workers as a day of rest. In some cases when workers did go to work on Monday and Tuesday, the pace of work was slow, the workday shorter, and a holiday feeling prevailed.

Chapter 2 Work-time Reduction in the US

1 See Roediger and Foner (1989) for a thorough historical treatment of the 10-hour movement, the eight-hour movement, and the varied and numerous strikes and labor actions, as well as the numerous legislative successes and failures. The book is essential reading in American labor history.
2 The full-time workweek at my university is 37.5 hours, with benefits.
3 For a detailed account of the Haymarket incident and the history of the eight-hour campaign in Chicago, see Green (2006).

4   See Vittoz (1987) for in-depth analysis of labor, business, and legislative politics surrounding the National Industrial Recovery Act.

5   For more information on the politics surrounding the formulation and passage of the Fair Labor Standards Act of 1938, see Phelps (1939), Grossman (1978), and Steinberg (1982).

6   For further discussion of the pros and cons of work-time reduction, see Cuvillier (1984), and Ehrenberg and Schumann (1982).

7   Goodyear, Sears Roebuck, General Motors at Tarrytown, Standard Oil of New Jersey, Hudson Motors, and several cotton manufacturers in New England also instituted six-hour systems. By 1937, the longshoremen on the Pacific Coast had won the 30-hour week, and about 5 percent of organized building construction workers had 30-hour agreements (Hunnicutt 1996: 207 n.42).

8   Chapter 7 in Hunnicutt's (1996) book is a fascinating account of workers' sentiments, both positive and negative, regarding the six-hour system, and by using workers' own words illustrates the emergence of new work rhetoric in the post-World War II period to justify longer hours for men, while feminizing short hours.

9   This summary of Metro Plastics' 30/40 experiment is drawn from Negrey (1998).

Chapter 3   Current Trends

1   Workers in non-agricultural industries.

2   In studies based upon self-reported estimates, researchers calculate annual hours by multiplying the number of reported hours worked during the reference week by the number of reported weeks worked during the reference year. The Current Population Survey, for example, asks respondents how many hours they worked "last week." If they didn't work the previous week, they are asked how many hours they usually work. By contrast, Robinson and Godbey (1997) used data from time diaries, in which respondents recorded their activities throughout a single day and from which researchers constructed "synthetic weeks" by adding days together. Such time budgets are the oldest and most established studies of time in sociology (Adam 1990: 94; Perlow 1999). Proponents of time diaries (Robinson and Bostrom 1994; Robinson and Godbey 1997) argue that self-report estimates may be inaccurate because respondents may not recall correctly their work hours, be reluctant to respond truthfully, and have difficulty knowing how to include or exclude

particular activities (such as work breaks, machine down time, work brought home, etc.). Additionally, the previous week may not be a typical week, leading some to respond based on what they perceive to be their normal or typical week. Time diaries, by contrast, ask respondents to report activities as they occur throughout a 24-hour period; and proponents believe they are more accurate than retrospective or prospective estimates.

Comparing 1985 CPS data to 1985 time diaries showed a similar percentage distribution of weekly work hours (Robinson and Bostrom 1994: 16). Yet comparison of individuals' diary-recorded work time to their own estimates of work hours gathered in the time-diary project showed a systematic tendency for respondents to exaggerate the length of their workweek, a tendency that increased as the length of the workweek increased. Women were more likely to overestimate their paid work hours than men, despite working shorter weeks (Robinson and Bostrom 1994; Robinson and Godbey 1997: 89–93). Diaries and estimates were most accurate when work hours were in the "normal" range of 35 to 45 hours (Robinson and Godbey 1997: 93).

Beeper studies and observational studies are other, less common methods of data collection on time use, generally applied to small samples. In beeper studies, participants record their activities and their state of mind when the beeper they are wearing goes off randomly. Such studies permit getting information close to the event, and repeated measures give a broad overview of time use and experience of time. In observational studies, an unbiased observer reports what he or she sees. All self-reports, including surveys and time diaries as well as beeper studies, are subject to distortion as a result of underestimation or exaggeration of particular activities, depending on their perceived level of social acceptability, or failed memory in the case of surveys (Jacobs and Gerson 2004: 15).

3   Some business groups have advocated greater availability of compensatory time instead of overtime pay for overtime work, but labor leaders and other critics are skeptical that such proposals are just a ploy to permit companies to avoid paying overtime wages while lengthening working time. Critics also fear that workers would be pressured to take compensatory time rather than overtime pay, or might not be able to actually take the compensatory time they have accumulated, or that employers would restrict when compensatory time could be taken or cut back on sick leave and vacation time (Eisenbrey 2003; Golden 2003; Strope 2003).

4   I thank Vernon Smith, Urban Studies Institute, University of Louisville, for obtaining these unpublished data from BLS.

5 This section was adapted from a literature review co-authored in 2001 with Sunhwa Lee, Study Director, Institute for Women's Policy Research, Washington, DC.

6 The National Association of Temporary and Staffing Services (NATSS) reported that temporary workers increasingly participate in fringe benefits plans offered by temporary agencies. The percentages of workers subscribing to these plans, however, still seem to be low (NATSS 1998 at <http://www.natss.org/staff-stats/releases4-3-98.htm>).

7 See Presser (2003) for more detailed analysis of non-standard schedules by occupation, industry, age, gender, race and ethnicity, educational attainment, marital status, and parental status.

8 For more detail on the relationship between occupation, industry, education, age, marital status, parental status, and work time preferences, see Jacobs and Gerson 2004: 67–73, and Golden and Gebreselassie 2007.

Chapter 4 Work–Family, Work–Life

1 Perry-Jenkins et al. (2000) is a good retrospective of scholarship on work and family. MacDermid (2005) assesses the theoretical utility of the conflict construct.

2 For a more complete account of US exceptionalism in family policy and publicly subsidized child care, see O'Connor, Orloff, and Shaver (1999). Fried (1998: 140–9) provides a discussion of the history of maternity and parental leave in Europe and the US, including debate over FMLA leading up to its enactment. A summary of cost–benefit arguments for parental leave can be found in Fried (1998: 26–8).

Chapter 5 Work Time outside the US

1 The full text of EU directives is available at Europa, the official EU website (<www.europa.eu.int>).

2 This estimate predates the 2004 changes in overtime regulations.

3 See Anonymous (2006).

4 For more on part-time employment in Europe and Japan, see Gleason (2006), and Houseman and Osawa (2003).

5 Denmark, Finland, Norway, Sweden.

6 Belgium, France, Germany, Luxembourg, the Netherlands.

7 Australia, Austria, Canada, Denmark, Finland, Germany, Iceland, Japan, the Netherlands, Norway, Singapore, Sweden,

Switzerland, the UK, and the US, based on World Economic Forum rankings 1999–2008 (Heymann and Earle 2010: 56).

8 Austria, Denmark, Iceland, Ireland, Japan, Republic of Korea, Luxembourg, Mexico, the Netherlands, Norway, Switzerland, the UK, and the US, based on OECD unemployment rates 1998–2007 (Heymann and Earle 2010: 28).

9 Canada, the US, the UK, Germany (East and West), France, Switzerland, the Netherlands, Sweden, Norway, Denmark, Italy, Spain, Portugal, Israel, New Zealand, Japan, Russia, the Czech Republic, Poland, Bulgaria, Hungary, and Slovenia.

Chapter 6   A New Political Economy of Work Time

1 My mother worked for many years as a head cashier for a supermarket chain before she retired in the 1980s. She did a low-tech version of this each week, with papers spread out on our kitchen table, when she created the next week's work schedule for cashiers in her store. She used sales and scheduling data from the same week the previous year to inform her plans for the coming week, along with any special scheduling requests from individual part-time and full-time cashiers. The unpredictability anticipated for Walmart workers subject to the electronic scheduling-optimization system is not unlike the unpredictability experienced by temporary workers I interviewed in the 1980s (Negrey 1993). Temps with intermittent jobs told me of staying home to be near the phone in case the THS service called with an assignment. Equipped with cell phones today, of course, workers need not stay home, but they need to stay geographically close to their employer. Unpredictable work schedules also make it difficult to coordinate dependent care.

2 Over the years, numerous writers have argued for shorter workweeks, most often during times of high unemployment as a strategy to create jobs. Among my favorites is a small book dating from the turn of the twentieth century by Lafargue (1907). The historical evidence, however, is that work-time reductions have been instituted during times of labor shortage, when worker power is maximized. On this point, see Cross (1988b).

3 In 2011, unemployment is stuck near 9 percent in the US, two years after the Great Recession's end.

4 Daly (1991) offered detailed policy principles. Lest one think he is just another crackpot tree-hugger, Daly is an economist who was employed at the World Bank at the time he wrote the book.

His insider's critique of growth, and the economics profession, is compelling reading. Douthwaite and Schor are also professional economists. Hayden is a community activist in Canada.

5 For an account of organizational experiments along this line, see Rapoport et al. (2002).

References

Abraham, Katharine G. and Susan N. Houseman. 2009. "Short-Time Compensation is a Missing Safety Net for U.S. Economy in Recessions." *Upjohn Institute Employment Research* (July). Kalamazoo, MI: W. E. Upjohn Institute for Employment Research.

Acker, Joan. 1990. "Hierarchies, Jobs, and Bodies: A Theory of Gendered Organizations." *Gender & Society* 4(2): 139–58.

Acker, Joan. 1992. "Gendered Institutions: From Sex Roles to Gendered Institutions." *Contemporary Sociology* 21: 139–58.

Adam, Barbara. 1990. *Time and Social Theory*. Philadelphia, PA: Temple University Press.

Adam, Barbara. 1998. *Timescapes of Modernity: The Environment and Invisible Hazards*. London: Routledge.

Alesina, Alberto, Edward Glaeser, and Bruce Sacerdote. 2005. "Work and Leisure in the U.S. and Europe: Why So Different?" Working Paper 11278 (April). Cambridge, MA: National Bureau of Economic Research.

Altman, Morris and Lonnie Golden. 2007. "The Economics of Flexible Work Scheduling: Theoretical Advances and Contemporary Paradoxes." In Beth A. Rubin, ed., *Workplace Temporalities: Research in the Sociology of Work, Vol. 17*. Oxford: Elsevier JAI, pp. 313–41.

Anonymous. 2006. "Berlin Adding to Store Hours." *The Courier-Journal* (November 12): D4.

Anonymous. 2008a. "Consumers Cut Back Spending." *The Courier-Journal* (March 29): D1.

Anonymous. 2008b. "Grant May Extend Hours But Reduce Days for County Offices." *The Courier-Journal* (June 26): B2.

Appelbaum, Eileen, Thomas Bailey, Peter Berg, and Arne Kalleberg. 2002. "Shared Work/Valued Care: New Norms for Organizing Market Work and Unpaid Care Work." In Gunther Schmid, Jacqueline O'Reilly, Klaus Schomann, and Hugh Mosley, eds, *Labour Markets, Gender, and Institutional Change: Essays in Honour of Gunther Schmid*. Cheltenham: Edward Elgar.

Apter, Jeff. 1997. "France Plans 35-Hour Week by 2000 – Without Pay Loss." *UE News*, December (retrieved from <http://ranknfile-ue.org/uen 1297 france.html>).

Arens, Marianne and Francoise Thull. 1999. "The Fraud of the 35-Hour Workweek in France." *World Socialist Website*, November 9 (retrieved from <http://www.wsws.org/articles/1999/nov1999/fran-n09_prn.shtml>).

Autor, David H., Frank Levy, and Richard J. Murnane. 1999. "Skills Training in the Temporary Help Sector: Employer Motivations and Worker Impacts." A Report to the US Department of Labor, Employment and Training Administration.

Baca Zinn, Maxine and D. Stanley Eitzen. 1993. *Diversity in Families*, 3rd edn. New York: HarperCollins.

Bailyn, Lotte. 1993. *Breaking the Mold: Women, Men, and Time in the New Corporate World*. New York: The Free Press.

Barker, Kathleen and Kathleen Christensen. 1998. *Contingent Work: American Employment Relations in Transition*. Ithaca, NY: ILR Press/Cornell University Press.

Barnett, Rosalind Chait and Douglas T. Hall. 2001. "How to Use Reduced Hours to Win the War for Talent." *Organizational Dynamics* 29(3): 192–210.

Barnett, W. S., J. T. Hustedt, K. B. Robin, and K. L. Schulman. 2004. "The State of Preschool: 2004 State Preschool Yearbook." New Brunswick, NJ: National Institute for Early Education Research.

Becker, Gary. 1965. "A Theory of the Allocation of Time." *Economic Journal* 75: 493–517.

Becker, Gary. 1981. *A Treatise on the Family*. Cambridge, MA: Harvard University Press.

Beechey, Veronica and Tessa Perkins. 1987. *A Matter of Hours*. Minneapolis, MN: University of Minnesota Press.

Beers, Thomas M. 2000. "Flexible Schedules and Shift Work: Replacing the '9-to-5' Workday?" *Monthly Labor Review* 123 (June): 33–40.

Bell, Linda A. 1998. "Differences in Work Hours and Hours Preferences by Race in the U.S." *Review of Social Economy* LVI(4): 481–500.

Belous, Richard. 1989. "The Contingent Economy: The Growth of the Temporary, Part-Time, and Subcontracted Workforce." McLean, VA: National Planning Association.

Benner, Chris. 1996. "Shock Absorbers in the Flexible Economy: The Rise of Contingent Employment in Silicon Valley." San Jose, CA: Working Partnerships USA.

Benner, Chris, Bob Brownstein, Laura Dresser, and Laura Leete. 2001. "Staircases and Treadmills: The Role of Labor Market Intermediaries in Placing Workers and Fostering Upward Mobility." Paper presented at the annual meeting of the Industrial Relations Research Association, New Orleans, LA, January.

Bennhold, Katrin. 2008. "French Unions Losing Influence in Downturn." *The New York Times* (December 25). At: <http:www.nytimes.com/2008/12/26/business/worldbusiness/26union.html?pagewanted=all>.

Berg, Peter, Eileen Appelbaum, Tom Bailey, and Arne L. Kalleberg. 2004. "Contesting Time: International Comparisons of Employee Control of Working Time." *Industrial and Labor Relations Review* 57(3): 331–49.

Berger, Peter L. 1963. *An Invitation to Sociology.* New York: Anchor Books.

Berk, Sarah Fenstermaker. 1985. *The Gender Factory: The Apportionment of Work in American Households.* New York: Plenum.

Bernstein, Jared. 2004. "The Low-Wage Labor Market: Trends and Policy Implications." In Ann C. Crouter and Alan Booth, eds, *Work–Family Challenges for Low-Income Parents and Their Children.* Mahwah, NJ: Lawrence Erlbaum Associates, pp. 3–34.

Bianchi, Suzanne M., John P. Robinson, and Melissa A. Milkie. 2006. *Changing Rhythms of American Family Life.* New York: Russell Sage Foundation.

Blair-Loy, Mary. 2003. *Competing Devotions: Career and Family among Women Executives.* Cambridge, MA: Harvard University Press.

Blank, Rebecca M. 1998. "Contingent Work in a Changing Labor Market." In Richard B. Freeman and Peter Gottschalk, eds, *Generating Jobs: How to Increase Demand for Less-Skilled Workers.* New York: Russell Sage Foundation, pp. 258–94.

Blau, Francine D. and Ronald G. Ehrenberg. 1997. *Gender and Family Issues in the Workplace.* New York: Russell Sage Foundation.

Blau, Francine D., Marianne A. Ferber, and Anne E. Winkler. 2002. *The Economics of Women, Men, and Work.* Upper Saddle River, NJ: Prentice-Hall.

Blossfeld, Hans-Peter and Catherine Hakim, eds. 1997. *Between Equalization and Marginalization: Women Working Part-Time in Europe and the United States of America*. New York: Oxford University Press.

Bluedorn, Allen C. 2002. *The Human Organization of Time: Temporal Realities and Experience*. Stanford, CA: Stanford Business Books.

Bluestone, Barry and Bennett Harrison. 1982. *The Deindustrialization of America*. New York: Basic Books.

Bluestone, Barry and Stephen Rose. 1998. "The Macroeconomics of Work Time." *Review of Social Economy* LVI(4): 425–41.

Blum, Alexander B., Farbod Raiszakeh, Sandra Shea, David Mermin, Peter Lurie, Christopher P. Landrigan, and Charles A. Czeisler. 2010. "US Public Opinion Regarding Proposed Limits on Resident Physician Work Hours." *BMC Medicine*, June 1 (retrieved March 28, 2011 from <http://www.biomedcentral.com/1741-7015/8/33>).

Bond, James T., Ellen Galinsky, and Jennifer E. Swanberg. 1998. *The 1997 National Study of the Changing Workforce*. New York: Families and Work Institute.

Bond, James T. with Cynthia Thompson, Ellen Galinsky, and David Prottas. 2003. *Highlights of the National Study of the Changing Workforce 2002*. New York: Families and Work Institute.

Boris, Eileen and Carolyn Herbst Lewis. 2006. "Caregiving and Wage-Earning: A Historical Perspective on Work and Family." In Marcie Pitt-Catsouphes, Ellen Ernst Kossek, and Stephen Sweet, eds, *The Work and Family Handbook*. Mahwah, NJ: Lawrence Erlbaum Associates Inc., pp. 73–97.

Bowles, Samuel and Yongjin Park. 2005. "Emulation, Inequality, and Work Hours: Was Thorstein Veblen Right?" *The Economic Journal* 115 (November): F397–F412.

Brannen, Julia. 2005. "Time and the Negotiation of Work–Family Boundaries: Autonomy or Illusion?" *Time & Society* 14(1): 113–31.

Brayfield, April. 1995. "Juggling Jobs and Kids: The Impact of Employment Schedules on Fathers' Caring for Children." *Journal of Marriage and the Family* 57 (May): 321–32.

Budig, Michelle J. and Paula England. 2001. "The Wage Penalty for Motherhood." *American Sociological Review* 66(2): 204–25.

Callaghan, Polly and Heidi Hartmann. 1991. *Contingent Work: A Chart Book on Part-Time and Temporary Employment*. Washington, DC: Economic Policy Institute.

Cantor, D., J. Waldfogel, J. Kerwin, M. McKinley Wright, K. Levin, and J. Rauch. 2001. *Balancing the Needs of Families and Employ-*

ers: The Family and Medical Leave Surveys 2000 Update. Washington, DC: US Department of Labor, Office of the Assistant Secretary for Policy.

Capizzano, Jeffrey, Gina Adams, and Freya Sonenstein. 2000. *Child Care Arrangements for Children under Five: Variation across States*. Washington, DC: Urban Institute.

Caputo, Richard K. and Mary Cianni. 2001. "Correlates of Voluntary vs. Involuntary Part-time Employment among U.S. Women." *Gender, Work and Organization* 8(3): 311–25.

Carey, Max L. and Kim L. Hazelbaker. 1986. "Employment Growth in the Temporary Help Industry." *Monthly Labor Review* 109 (April): 37–44.

Carnevale, Anthony P., Lynn A. Jennings, and James M. Eisenmann. 1998. "Contingent Workers and Employment Law." In Kathleen Barker and Kathleen Christensen, eds, *Contingent Work: American Employment Relations in Transition*. Ithaca, NY: ILR Press/Cornell University Press, pp. 281–305.

Carre, Francoise, Marianne A. Ferber, Lonnie Golden, and Stephen A. Herzenberg, eds. 2000. *Nonstandard Work: The Nature and Challenges of Changing Employment Arrangements*. Champaign, IL: Industrial Relations Research Association.

Cassirer, Naomi. 1995. "The Restructuring of Work in the United States: Occupational and Industrial Determinants of Contingent Employment." Paper presented at the annual meeting of the American Sociological Association, Washington, DC.

Charles, Maria and David B. Grusky. 2004. *Occupational Ghettos: The Worldwide Segregation of Women and Men*. Stanford, CA: Stanford University Press.

Charpentier, Pascal, Michel Lallement, Florence Lefresne, and Jocelyne Loos-Baroin. 2006. "The French 35-hour Week: A Decent Working Time Pattern? Lessons from Case Studies." In Jean-Yves Boulin, Michel Lallement, Jon C. Messenger, and Francois Michon, eds, *Decent Working Time*. Geneva: International Labour Office, pp. 181–208.

Christopher, Karen. 2004. "Welfare As We [Don't] Know It: A Review and Feminist Critique of Welfare Reform Research in the United States." *Feminist Economics* 10(2): 143–71.

Clarkberg, Marin. 2000. "The Time Squeeze in American Families: From Causes to Solutions." In Eileen Appelbaum, ed., *Balancing Acts: Easing the Burdens and Improving the Options for Working Families*. Washington, DC: Economic Policy Institute.

Clawson, Dan. 1980. *Bureaucracy and the Labor Process*. New York: Monthly Review Press.

Cleaver, Harry. 1979. *Reading Capital Politically*. Austin, TX: University of Texas Press.

CNNMoney.com. 2004. "Battle Engaged Over New OT Rules" (August 23).

Cobble, Dorothy Sue. 2007. "Introduction." In Dorothy Sue Cobble, ed., *The Sex of Class: Women Transforming American Labor*. Ithaca, NY: ILR Press/Cornell University Press, pp. 1–12.

Cohany, Sharon R. 1998. "Workers in Alternative Employment Arrangements: A Second Look." *Monthly Labor Review* 121 (November): 3–21.

Cohany, Sharon R., Steven F. Hipple, Thomas J. Nardone, Anne E. Polivka, and Jay C. Stewart. 1998. "Counting the Workers: Results of a First Survey." In Kathleen Barker and Kathleen Christensen, eds, *Contingent Work: American Employment Relations in Transition*. Ithaca, NY: ILR Press/Cornell University Press, pp. 41–68.

Cohen, Philip N. and Suzanne M. Bianchi. 1999. "Marriage, Children, and Women's Employment: What Do We Know?" *Monthly Labor Review* 122 (December): 22–31.

Coleman, Mary T. and John Pencavel. 1993. "Changes in Work Hours of Male Employees, 1940–1988." *Industrial and Labor Relations Review* 46(2): 262–83.

Collinson, David A. 1992. *Managing the Shopfloor*. New York: Walter de Gruyter.

Coltrane, Scott. 2000. "Research on Household Labor: Modeling and Measuring the Social Embeddedness of Routine Family Work." *Journal of Marriage and the Family* 62 (November): 1208–33.

Coltrane, Scott. 2009. "Fatherhood, Gender, and Work–Family Policies." In Janet C. Gornick and Marcia K. Meyers, *Gender Equality: Transforming Family Divisions of Labor*. London and New York: Verso, pp. 385–409.

Commission on Family and Medical Leave. 1996. *A Workable Balance: Report to Congress on Family and Medical Leave Policies*. Washington, DC: US Department of Labor, Women's Bureau.

Connolly, Catherine. 2000. "Part-Time Work and Federal Employment Policy." In Randy Hodson, ed., *Marginal Employment*. Stamford, CT: JAI Press, pp. 147–63.

Cooper, Marianne. 2000. "Being the 'Go-To Guy': Fatherhood, Masculinity, and the Organization of Work in Silicon Valley." *Qualitative Sociology* 23(4): 379–405.

Corral, A. and I. Isusi. 2004. *Part-time Work in Europe*. Dublin: European Foundation for the Improvement of Living and Working Conditions.

Correll, Shelley J., Stephen Benard, and In Paik. 2007. "Getting a Job: Is There a Motherhood Penalty?" *American Journal of Sociology* 112(5): 1297–1338.

Cousins, Christine R. and Ning Tang. 2004. "Working Time and Work and Family Conflict in the Netherlands, Sweden, and the UK." *Work, Employment and Society* 18(3): 531–49.

Cowan, Ruth Schwartz. 1983. *More Work for Mother*. New York: Basic Books.

Crompton, Rosemary. 2006. *Employment and the Family: The Reconfiguration of Work and Family Life in Contemporary Societies*. Cambridge: Cambridge University Press.

Cross, Gary. 1988a. "Worktime and Industrialization: An Introduction." In Gary Cross, ed., *Worktime and Industrialization: An International History*. Philadelphia, PA: Temple University Press, pp. 3–19.

Cross, Gary. 1988b. "Worktime in International Discontinuity." In Gary Cross, ed., *Worktime and Industrialization: An International History*. Philadelphia, PA: Temple University Press, pp. 155–81.

Cutler, Jonathan. 2004. *Labor's Time: Shorter Hours, the UAW, and the Struggle for American Unionism*. Philadelphia, PA: Temple University Press.

Cuvillier, Rolande. 1984. *The Reduction of Working Time*. Geneva: International Labour Office.

Daly, Herman E. 1991. *Steady-State Economics*, 2nd edn. Washington, DC: Island Press.

Davies, Scott. 1990. "Inserting Gender into Burawoy's Theory of the Labor Process." *Work, Employment and Society* 4: 391–406.

Degler, Carl. 1980. *At Odds: Women and the Family in America from the Revolution to the Present*. New York: Oxford University Press.

Deutermann, William V., Jr. and Scott Campbell Brown. 1978. "Voluntary Part-Time Workers: A Growing Part of the Labor Force." *Monthly Labor Review* 101 (June): 3–10.

Dobuzinskis, Caroline. 2011. "IWPR Helps Inform Historic Vote to Legislate Paid Sick Days in Connecticut." *IWPR Quarterly Newsletter* (spring/summer). Washington, DC: Institute for Women's Policy Research, p. 1.

Dohse, Knuth, Ulrich Jurgens, and Thomas Malsch. 1985. "From 'Fordism' to 'Toyotism'? The Social Organization of the Labor Process in the Japanese Automobile Industry." *Politics & Society* 14(2): 115–46.

Douthwaite, Richard. 1992. *The Growth Illusion*. Tulsa, OK: Council Oaks Books.

Drew, Eileen and Ruth Emerek. 1998. "Employment, Flexibility, and Gender." In Eileen Drew, Ruth Emerek, and Evelyn Mahon, eds, *Women, Work and the Family in Europe*. London and New York: Routledge, pp. 89–99.

Dupuy, Max and Mark E. Schweitzer. 1995. "Another Look at Part-Time Employment." *Economic Commentary* (Federal Reserve Bank of Cleveland), February 1.

duRivage, Virginia L., Francoise J. Carre, and Chris Tilly. 1998. "Making Labor Law Work for Part-Time and Contingent Workers." In Kathleen Barker and Kathleen Christensen, eds, *Contingent Work: American Employment Relations in Transition*. Ithaca, NY: ILR Press/Cornell University Press, pp. 263–80.

Economic Report of the President. 1994. Washington, DC: Council of Economic Advisers.

Edwards, Richard. 1979. *Contested Terrain: The Transformation of the Workplace in the Twentieth Century*. New York: Basic Books.

Ehrenberg, Ronald G. and Paul L. Schumann. 1982. *Longer Hours or More Jobs? An Investigation of Amending Hours Legislation to Create Employment*. Ithaca, NY: New York State School of Industrial and Labor Relations, Cornell University.

Ehrle, Jennifer, Gina Adams, and Kathryn Tout. 2001. *Who's Caring for Our Youngest Children? Child Care Patterns of Infants and Toddlers*. Washington, DC: Urban Institute.

Eisenbrey, Ross. 2003. "The Naked Truth about Comp Time." *EPI Issue Brief*. Washington, DC: Economic Policy Institute.

Eisenbrey, Ross. 2004. *Longer Hours, Less Pay: Labor Department's New Rules Could Strip Overtime Protection from Millions of Workers*. Briefing Paper. Washington, DC: Economic Policy Institute.

Elder, Peyton K. and Heidi D. Miller. 1979. "The Fair Labor Standards Act: Changes of Four Decades." *Monthly Labor Review* 102 (July): 10–16.

Ellison, Nicole B. 2004. *Telework and Social Change: How Technology is Reshaping the Boundaries between Home and Work*. Westport, CT: Praeger.

Estes, Sarah Beth. 2003. "Growing Pains and Progress in the Study of Working Families." *Work and Occupations* 30(4): 479–93.

Estevão, Marcello and Saul Lach. 2000. "The Evolution of the Demand for Temporary Help Supply Employment in the United States." In Francoise Carre, Marianne A. Ferber, Lonnie Golden, and Stephen A. Herzenberg, eds, *Nonstandard Work: The Nature and Challenges of Changing Employment Arrangements*. Champaign, IL: Industrial Relations Research Association, pp. 123–43.

Estey, Marten S. 1968. "The Grocery Clerks: Center of Retail Unionism." *Industrial Relations* 7: 249–61.

Evans, John M., Douglas C. Lippoldt, and Pascal Marianna. 2001. "Trends in Working Hours in OECD Countries." *Labour Market and Social Policy Occasional Papers No. 45* (March 30). Paris: OECD.

Everingham, Christine. 2002. "Engendering Time: Gender Equity and Discourses of Workplace Flexibility." *Time & Society* 11(2/3): 335–51.

Fagan, Colette. 2001. "The Temporal Organization of Employment and the Household Rhythm of Work Schedules." *American Behavioral Scientist* 44(7): 1199–1212.

Fallick, Bruce C. 1999. "Part-Time Work and Industry Growth." *Monthly Labor Review* 122 (March): 22–9.

Ferber, Marianne A. and Jane Waldfogel. 1998. "The Long-Term Consequences of Nontraditional Employment." *Monthly Labor Review* 121 (May): 3–12.

Figart, Deborah M. and Lonnie Golden. 1998. "The Social Economics of Work Time." *Review of Social Economy* LVI(4): 411–24.

Figart, Deborah M. and Ellen Mutari. 1998. "Degendering Work Time in Comparative Perspective: Alternative Policy Frameworks." *Review of Social Economy* LVI(4): 460–80.

Figart, Deborah M. and Ellen Mutari. 2000. "Work Time Regimes in Europe: Can Flexibility and Gender Equity Coexist?" *Journal of Economic Issues* XXXIV(4): 847–71.

Firestein, Netsy and Nicola Dones. 2007. "Unions Fight for Work and Family Policies – Not for Women Only." In Dorothy Sue Cobble, ed., *The Sex of Class: Women Transforming American Labor*. Ithaca, NY: ILR Press/Cornell University Press, pp. 140–54.

Florida, Richard and Martin Kenney. 1991. "Transplanted Organizations: The Transfer of Japanese Industrial Organization to the U.S." *American Sociological Review* 56 (June): 381–98.

Ford, Peter. 1998. "France Cuts Hours to Make Jobs." *The Christian Science Monitor*, February 11 (retrieved from <http://csmweb2.emcweb.com/durable/1998/02/11/intl/intl.1>).

Fouarge, Didier and Christine Baaijens. 2006. "Labour Supply Preferences and Job Mobility of Dutch Employees." In Jean-Yves Boulin, Michel Lallement, Jon C. Messenger, and Francois Michon, eds, *Decent Working Time*. Geneva: International Labour Office, pp. 155–79.

Fraser, Nancy. 1996. *Justice Interruptus: Critical Reflections on the "Postsocialist" Condition*. London and New York: Routledge.

210   *References*

Freedman, Audrey. 1985. "The New Look in Wage Policy and Employee Relations." Conference Board Report No. 865. New York: The Conference Board.

Fried, Mindy. 1998. *Taking Time: Parental Leave Policy and Corporate Culture*. Philadelphia, PA: Temple University Press.

Frost, Laurence. 2005. "France Waters Down 35-Hour Workweek." *The Courier-Journal* (March 23): D2.

Gadrey, Nicole, Florence Jany-Catrice, and Martine Pernod-Lemattre. 2006. "The Working Conditions of Blue-Collar and White-Collar Workers in France Compared: A Question of Time." In Jean-Yves Boulin, Michel Lallement, Jon C. Messenger, and Francois Michon, eds, *Decent Working Time*. Geneva: International Labour Organization, pp. 265–87.

Galinsky, Ellen, James T. Bond, Stacy S. Kim, Lois Backon, Erin Brownfield, and Kelly Sakai. 2004. *Overwork in America: When the Way We Work Becomes Too Much*. New York: Families and Work Institute.

Galinsky, Ellen, James T. Bond, and E. Jeffrey Hill. 2005. *When Work Works: A Project on Workplace Effectiveness and Workplace Flexibility*. New York: Families and Work Institute.

Gardner, Jennifer. 1996. "Hidden Part-Timers: Full-Time Work Schedules, but Part-Time Jobs." *Monthly Labor Review* 119 (September): 43–4.

Gault, Barbara and Vicky Lovell. 2006. "The Costs and Benefits of Policies to Advance Work/Life Integration." *American Behavioral Scientist* 49(9): 1152–64.

Gergen, Kenneth J. 1991. *The Saturated Self: Dilemmas of Identity in Contemporary Life*. New York: Basic Books.

Gershuny, Jonathan. 2000. *Changing Times: Work and Leisure in Postindustrial Society*. Oxford: Oxford University Press.

Gershuny, Jonathan, Michael Godwin, and Sally Jones. 1994. "The Domestic Labour Revolution: A Process of Lagged Adaptation." In Michael Anderson, Frank Bechhofer, and Jonathan Gershuny, eds, *The Social and Political Economy of the Household*. Oxford: Oxford University Press, pp. 151–97.

Gerson, Kathleen. 2010. *The Unfinished Revolution: How a New Generation is Reshaping Family, Work, and Gender in America*. New York: Oxford University Press.

Gerstel, Naomi and Dan Clawson. 2002. "Unions' Responses to Family Concerns." In Naomi Gerstel, Dan Clawson, and Robert Zussman, eds, *Families at Work: Expanding the Boundaries*. Nashville, TN: Vanderbilt University Press, pp. 317–42.

Gerstel, Naomi, Dan Clawson, and Dana Huyser. 2007. "Explaining Job Hours of Physicians, Nurses, EMTs, and Nursing Assistants: Gender, Class, Jobs, and Families." In Beth A. Rubin, ed., *Workplace Temporalities: Research in the Sociology of Work, Vol. 17.* Oxford: Elsevier JAI, pp. 369–401.

Gewirtz, Mindy L. and Mindy Fried. 2007. "Organizational Strategies for Network Weaving Work–Life Integration into 24/7 Cultures." In Beth A. Rubin, ed., *Workplace Temporalities: Research in the Sociology of Work, Vol. 17.* Oxford: Elsevier JAI, pp. 497–525.

Gianarelli, L. and J. Barsimantov. 2000. *Child Care Expenses of America's Families.* Washington, DC: Urban Institute.

Glass, Jennifer and Sarah Beth Estes. 1997. "The Family Responsive Workplace." *Annual Review of Sociology* 23: 289–313.

Glass, Jennifer and Tetsushi Fujimoto. 1995. "Employer Characteristics and the Provision of Family Responsive Policies." *Work and Occupations* 22: 380–411.

Gleason, Sandra, ed. 2006. The Shadow Workforce: Perspectives on Contingent Work in the United States, Japan, and Europe. Kalamazoo, MI: W. E. Upjohn Institute for Employment Research.

Gleick, James. 1999. *Faster: The Acceleration of Just About Everything.* New York: Pantheon Books.

Golden, Lonnie. 2001. "Flexible Work Schedules: What Are We Trading Off to Get Them?" *Monthly Labor Review* 124 (March): 50–67.

Golden, Lonnie. 2003. *Comp Time Bills Off Target.* Briefing Paper. Washington, DC: Economic Policy Institute.

Golden, Lonnie and Deborah M. Figart, eds. 2000. *Working Time: International Trends, Theory, and Policy Perspectives.* New York: Routledge.

Golden, Lonnie and Tesfayi Gebreselassie. 2007. "Overemployment Mismatches: The Preference for Fewer Work Hours." *Monthly Labor Review* 130 (April): 18–37.

Goldfield, Michael. 1987. *The Decline of Organized Labor in the United States.* Chicago, IL: University of Chicago Press.

Goodstein, Jerry D. 1994. "Institutional Pressures and Strategic Responsiveness: Employer Involvement in Work–Family Issues." *Academy of Management Journal* 37: 350–82.

Gornick, Janet C. and Marcia K. Meyers. 2003. *Families That Work: Policies for Reconciling Parenthood and Employment.* New York: Russell Sage Foundation.

Gornick, Janet C. and Marcia K. Meyers. 2009. "Institutions that Support Gender Equality in Parenthood and Employment." In Janet C. Gornick and Marcia K. Meyers, eds, *Gender Equality: Transforming Family Divisions of Labor.* London and New York: Verso, pp. 3–64.

Gottfried, Heidi. 1991. "Mechanisms of Control in the Temporary Help Service Industry." *Sociological Forum* 6: 699–713.

Graham, Laurie. 1993. "Inside a Japanese Transplant: A Critical Perspective." *Work and Occupations* 20(2): 147–73.

Green, Francis. 2004. "Why Has Work Effort Become More Intense?" *Industrial Relations* 43(4): 709–41.

Green, James. 2006. *Death in the Haymarket: A Story of Chicago, the First Labor Movement and the Bombing That Divided Gilded Age America*. New York: Pantheon Books.

Greider, William. 2001. "The Right and US Trade Law: Invalidating the 20th Century." *The Nation* (November 17). At: <http: www.thenation.com/article/right-and-us-trade-law-invalidating-20th-century>.

Grimsley, Kirstin Downey. 2000. "Revenge of the Temps: Independent Contractors' Victory in Microsoft Case May Have Wide Impact." *The Washington Post* (January 16): H1.

Grossman, Jonathan. 1978. "Fair Labor Standards Act of 1938: Maximum Struggle for a Minimum Wage." *Monthly Labor Review* 101 (June): 22–30.

Gurstein, Penny. 2001. *Wired to the World, Chained to the Home*. Vancouver: UBC Press.

Hacker, Jacob S. 2006. *The Great Risk Shift: The Assault on American Jobs, Families, Health Care, and Retirement And How You Can Fight Back*. Oxford: Oxford University Press.

Hamermesh, Daniel S. 1999. "The Timing of Work over Time." *The Economic Journal* 109 (January): 37–66.

Hamermesh, Daniel. 2000. "12 Million Salaried Workers Are Missing." *Industrial and Labor Relations Review* 55: 649–75.

Haraven, Tamara K. 1990. "A Complex Relationship: Family Strategies and the Processes of Economic and Social Change. In R. Friedland and A. F. Robertson, eds, *Beyond the Marketplace: Rethinking Economy and Society*. New York: Degruyter, pp. 215–44.

Harrington, Mona. 1999. *Care and Equality: Inventing a New Family Politics*. New York: Alfred A. Knopf.

Hartmann, Heidi. 1976. "Capitalism, Patriarchy, and Job Segregation by Sex." *Signs* 1(3): 137–69.

Hartmann, Heidi. 1981. "The Family as the Locus of Gender, Class, and Political Struggle: The Example of Housework." *Signs* 6(3): 366–94.

Hartmann, Heidi. 2001. "Economic Security for Women and Children: What Will It Take?" In Robert L. Borosage and Roger Hickey, eds, *The Next Agenda*. Boulder, CO: Westview Press.

Hartmann, Heidi, Ariane Hegewisch, and Vicky Lovell. 2007. *An Economy that Puts Families First: Expanding the Social Contract to Include Family Care*. EPI Briefing Paper, May 24. Washington, DC: Economic Policy Institute.

Hartmann, Heidi and Vicky Lovell. 2009. "A US Model for Universal Sickness and Family Leave: Gender-Egalitarian and Cross-Class Caregiving Support for All." In Janet C. Gornick and Marcia K. Meyers, eds, *Gender Equality: Transforming Family Divisions of Labor*. London and New York: Verso, pp. 231–51.

Harvey, David. 1985. *Consciousness and the Urban Experience*. Baltimore, MD: Johns Hopkins University Press.

Haskins, Ron and Wendell Primus. 2002. "Welfare Reform and Poverty." In Andrea Kane, Isabel V. Sawhill, Kent R. Weaver, and Ron Haskins, eds, *Welfare Reform and Beyond: The Future of the Safety Net*. Washington, DC: Brookings Institution, pp. 59–70.

Haugen, Steven E. 1986. "The Employment Expansion in Retail Trade, 1973–85." *Monthly Labor Review* 109 (August): 9–16.

Hawkins, Daniel N. and Shawn D. Whiteman. 2004. "Balancing Work and Family: Problems and Solutions for Low-Income Families." In Ann C. Crouter and Alan Booth, eds, *Work–Family Challenges for Low-Income Parents and Their Children*. Mahwah, NJ: Lawrence Erlbaum Associates, pp. 273–86.

Hayden, Anders. 1999. *Sharing the Work, Sparing the Planet: Work Time, Consumption, & Ecology*. London and New York: Zed Books Ltd.

Hayghe, Howard V. 1988. "Employers and Child Care: What Roles Do They Play?" *Monthly Labor Review* 111 (September): 38–44.

Heldrich Center for Workforce Development. 1999. "Work Trends: America's Attitudes about Work, Employers and Government." New Jersey: Heldrich Center, Rutgers University.

Henson, Kevin. 1996. *Just a Temp*. Philadelphia, PA: Temple University Press.

Hetrick, Ron L. 2000. "Analyzing the Recent Upward Surge in Overtime Hours." *Monthly Labor Review* 123 (February): 30–3.

Hewitt Associates. 1991. *Work and Family Benefits Provided by Major U.S. Employers in 1991*. Lincolnshire, IL: Hewitt Associates.

Hewlett, Sylvia Ann and Cornel West. 1998. *The War against Parents*. New York: Houghton Mifflin.

Heymann, Jody. 2000. *The Widening Gap*. New York: Basic Books.

Heymann, Jody and Alison Earle. 2010. *Raising the Global Floor: Dismantling the Myth that We Can't Afford Good Working Conditions for Everyone*. Stanford, CA: Stanford Politics and Policy (Stanford University Press).

Hill, E. Jeffrey, Andre'a D. Jackson, and Giuseppe Martinengo. 2006. "Twenty Years of Work and Family at International Business Machines Corporation." *American Behavioral Scientist* 49(9): 1165–83.

Hill, Kim, Hillard Kaplan, Kristen Hawkes, and Ana Magdelena Hurtado. 1985. "Men's Time Allocation to Subsistence Work among the Ache of Eastern Paraguay." *Human Ecology* 13(1): 29–47.

Hill, Richard C. and Cynthia Negrey. 1989. "Deindustrialization and Racial Minorities in the Great Lakes Region, USA." In D. Stanley Eitzen and Maxine Baca Zinn, eds, *The Reshaping of America: Social Consequences of the Changing Economy*. Englewood Cliffs, NJ: Prentice-Hall, pp. 168–78.

Hinrichs, Karl, William Roche, and Carmen Sirianni. 1991. *Working Time in Transition: The Political Economy of Working Hours in Industrial Nations*. Philadelphia, PA: Temple University Press.

Hipple, Steven. 1998. "Contingent Work: Results from the Second Survey." *Monthly Labor Review* 121 (November): 22–35.

Hipple, Steven and Jay Stewart. 1996a. "Earnings and Benefits of Contingent and Noncontingent Workers." *Monthly Labor Review* 119 (October): 22–30.

Hipple, Steven and Jay Stewart. 1996b. "Earnings and Benefits of Workers in Alternative Work Arrangements." *Monthly Labor Review* 119 (October): 46–54.

Hochschild, Arlie Russell. 1997. *The Time Bind: When Work Becomes Home and Home Becomes Work*. New York: Metropolitan Books.

Hochschild, Arlie Russell. 2008. "On the Edge of the Time Bind: Time and Market Culture." In Chris Warhurst, Doris Ruth Eikhof, and Axel Haunschild, eds, *Work Less, Live More? Critical Analysis of the Work–Life Boundary*. Basingstoke: Palgrave Macmillan, pp. 80–91.

Hochschild, Arlie Russell with Anne Machung. 1989. *The Second Shift: Working Parents and the Revolution at Home*. New York: Viking.

Hodson, Randy, ed. 2000. *Marginal Employment*. Stanford, CA: JAI Press.

Hodson, Randy and Teresa A. Sullivan. 2008. *The Social Organization of Work*, 4th edn. Belmont, CA: Thomson Wadsworth.

Houseman, Susan and George Erickcek. 2002. "Temporary Services and Contracting Out: Effects on Low-Skilled Workers." *Upjohn Institute Employment Research*, July. Kalamazoo, MI: W. E. Upjohn Institute for Employment Research.

Houseman, Susan and Machiko Osawa. 1995. "Part-time and Temporary Employment in Japan." *Monthly Labor Review* 118 (October): 10–18.

Houseman, Susan and Machiko Osawa. 2003. *Nonstandard Work in Developed Economies*. Kalamazoo, MI: W. E. Upjohn Institute for Employment Research.

Houseman, Susan N. and Anne E. Polivka. 1999. "The Implications of Flexible Staffing Arrangements for Job Stability." *Upjohn Institute Staff Working Paper No. 99–056*. Kalamazoo, MI: W. E. Upjohn Institute for Employment Research.

Howington, Patrick. 2009. "Teamster Deal May Avert UPS Layoffs." *The Courier-Journal* (June 20): B8.

Hudson, Ken. 1999. *No Shortage of "Nonstandard" Jobs*. Washington, DC: Economic Policy Institute.

Hunnicutt, Benjamin Kline. 1988. *Work Without End: Abandoning Shorter Hours for the Right to Work*. Philadelphia, PA: Temple University Press.

Hunnicutt, Benjamin Kline. 1996. *Kellogg's Six-Hour Day*. Philadelphia, PA: Temple University Press.

Huston, Aletha C. 2004. "Childcare for Low-Income Families: Problems and Promises." In Ann C. Crouter and Alan Booth, eds, *Work–Family Challenges for Low-Income Parents and Their Children*. Mahwah, NJ: Lawrence Erlbaum Associates, pp. 139–64.

International Labour Organization (ILO). 2006. "Bridging the Decent Work Gap: The Netherlands." *World of Work* 57 (September): 31.

Ishii-Kuntz, Masako and Scott Coltrane. 1992. "Predicting the Sharing of Household Labor: Are Parenting and Housework Distinct?" *Sociological Perspectives* 35(4): 629–47.

Jacobs, Jerry A. 1998. "Measuring Time at Work: Are Self-Reports Accurate?" *Monthly Labor Review* 121 (December): 42–53.

Jacobs, Jerry A. and Kathleen Gerson. 1998. "Who are the Overworked Americans?" *Review of Social Economy* LVI(4): 442–59.

Jacobs, Jerry A. and Kathleen Gerson. 2004. *The Time Divide: Work, Family, and Gender Inequality*. Cambridge, MA: Harvard University Press.

Kalleberg, Arne L. 2000. "Nonstandard Employment Relations: Part-Time, Temporary, and Contract Work." *Annual Review of Sociology* 26: 341–65.

Kalleberg, Arne L. 2007. *The Mismatched Worker*. New York: W. W. Norton and Company.

Kalleberg, Arne L., Barbara Reskin, and Ken Hudson. 2000. "Bad Jobs in America: Standard and Nonstandard Employment Relations and Job Quality in the United States." *American Sociological Review* 65(2): 256–78.

Kanter, Rosabeth Moss. 1977. *Men and Women of the Corporation*. New York: Basic Books.

Kern, Stephen. 1983. *The Culture of Time and Space, 1880–1918*. Cambridge, MA: Harvard University Press.

Kessler-Harris, Alice. 1982. *Out to Work: A History of Wage-Earning Women in the United States*. New York: Oxford University Press.

Kossek, Ellen Ernst and Susan J. Lambert. 2005. "Work–Family Scholarship: Voice and Context." In Ellen Ernst Kossek and Susan J. Lambert, eds, *Work and Life Integration: Organizational, Cultural, and Individual Perspectives*. Mahwah, NJ: Lawrence Erlbaum Associates, pp. 3–11.

Kuttner, Robert. 2007. *The Squandering of America: How the Failure of Our Politics Undermines Our Prosperity*. New York: Alfred A. Knopf.

Lafargue, Paul. 1907. *The Right to be Lazy, and Other Studies*. Chicago, IL: C. H. Kerr and Company.

LaJeunesse, Robert. 1999. "Toward an Efficiency Week." *Challenge* 42 (January–February): 92–109.

Lambert, Susan J. 1993. "Workplace Policies as Social Policy." *Social Service Review* 67(2): 237–60.

Lambert, Susan J. 2008. "Passing the Buck: Labor Flexibility Practices that Transfer Risk onto Hourly Workers." *Human Relations* 61(9): 1203–27.

Lambert, Susan J. and Ellen Ernst Kossek. 2005. "Future Frontiers: Enduring Challenges and Established Assumptions in the Work–Life Field." In Ellen Ernst Kossek and Susan J. Lambert, eds, *Work and Life Integration: Organizational, Cultural, and Individual Perspectives*. Mahwah, NJ: Lawrence Erlbaum Associates, pp. 513–32.

Landes, David S. 1983. *Revolution in Time: Clocks and the Making of the Modern World*. Cambridge, MA: Harvard University Press.

Landler, Mark. 2004. "Europeans Rethink Workweek." *The Courier-Journal* (July 19): D5.

Lee, Ching Kwan. 1998. *Gender and the South China Miracle*. Berkeley, CA: University of California Press.

Lee, Sangheon, Deirdre McCann, and Jon C. Messenger. 2007. *Working Time Around the World: Trends in Working Hours, Laws and Policies in a Global Comparative Perspective*. London, New York, and Geneva: Routledge and International Labour Organization.

Leete, Laura and Juliet B. Schor. 1994. "Assessing the Time Squeeze Hypothesis: Hours Worked in the United States, 1969–89." *Industrial Relations* 33(1): 25–43.

Le Goff, Jacques. 1980. *Time, Work, and Culture in the Middle Ages*. Chicago, IL: University of Chicago Press.

Lemaitre, Georges, Pascal Marianna, and Alois van Bastelaer. 1997. "International Comparisons of Part-time Work." *OECD Economic Studies* 29: 139–52.

Lettau, Michael K. and Thomas C. Buchmueller. 1999. "Comparing Benefit Costs for Full- and Part-time Workers." *Monthly Labor Review* 122 (March): 30–5.

Lewis, Suzan. 2003. "The Integration of Paid Work and the Rest of Life: Is Post-Industrial Work the New Leisure?" *Leisure Studies* 22: 343–55.

Linder, Marc. 2004. *"Time and a Half's the American Way": A History of the Exclusion of White-Collar Workers from Overtime Regulation, 1868–2004*. Iowa City, IO: Fanpihua Press.

Linder, Steffan. 1970. *The Harried Leisure Class*. New York: Columbia University Press.

Lovell, Vicky. 2004. *No Time to be Sick: Why Everyone Suffers When Workers Don't Have Paid Sick Leave*. Washington, DC: Institute for Women's Policy Research.

Lovell, Vicky. 2008. *Some Small and Medium-Size Establishments Join Large Ones in Offering Paid Sick Days*. Washington, DC: Institute for Women's Policy Research.

McAllister, Jean. 1998. "Sisyphus at Work in the Warehouse: Temporary Employment in Greenville, SC." In Kathleen Barker and Kathleen Christensen, eds, *Contingent Work: American Employment Relations in Transition*. Ithaca, NY: ILR Press/Cornell University Press, pp. 221–42.

McCammon, Holly J. 1990. "Legal Limits on Labor Militancy: U.S. Labor Law and the Right to Strike since the New Deal." *Social Problems* 32(2): 206–29.

McCammon, Holly J. 1993. "From Repressive Intervention to Integrative Prevention: The U.S. State's Legal Management of Labor Militancy, 1881–1978." *Social Forces* 71(3): 569–601.

McCammon, Holly J. 1994. "Disorganizing and Reorganizing Conflict: Outcomes of the State's Legal Regulation of the Strike since the Wagner Act." *Social Forces* 72(4): 1011–49.

McCammon, Holly J. 1995. "The Politics of Protection: State Minimum Wage and Maximum Hours Laws for Women in the United States, 1870–1930." *Sociological Quarterly* 36(2): 217–49.

McCammon, Holly J. 1996. "Protection for Whom?" *Work and Occupations* 23(2): 132–64.

MacDermid, Shelley M. 2005. "(Re)Considering Conflict Between Work and Family." In Ellen Ernst Kossek and Susan J. Lambert, eds, *Work and Life Integration: Organizational, Cultural, and Individual Perspectives*. Mahwah, NJ: Lawrence Erlbaum Associates, pp. 19–40.

Macdonald, Cameron. 2009. "What's Culture Got to Do with It? Mothering Ideologies as Barriers to Gender Equity." In Janet C. Gornick and Marcia K. Meyers, eds, *Gender Equality: Transforming Family Divisions of Labor*. London and New York: Verso, pp. 3–64.

McGaughey, William, Jr. 1981. *A Shorter Workweek in the 1980s*. White Bear Lake, MN: Thistlerose Publications.

McGrattan, Ellen R. and Richard Rogerson. 1998. "Changes in Hours Worked Since 1950." *Federal Reserve Bank of Minneapolis Quarterly Review* 22(1): 2–19.

McMenamin, Terence M. 2007. "A Time to Work: Recent Trends in Shift Work and Flexible Schedules." *Monthly Labor Review* 130 (December): 3–15.

McRae, Susan. 1998. "Part-Time Employment in a European Perspective." In Eileen Drew, Ruth Emerek, and Evelyn Mahon, eds, *Women, Work and the Family in Europe*. London and New York: Routledge, pp. 100–11.

Maher, Kris. 2007. "Wal-Mart Plans to Schedule Workers Based on Shoppers." *The Courier-Journal* (January 4): D1.

Mansfield, Howard. 2011. "Does Anybody Really Know What Time It Is?" *Cleveland Plain Dealer* (March 13): G2.

Martin, James E. with Thomas D. Heetderks. 1990. *Two-Tier Compensation Structures*. Kalamazoo, MI: W. E. Upjohn Institute for Employment Research.

Marx, Karl. 1971. *The Grundrisse*. New York: Harper Torchbooks.

Marx, Karl. 1977. *Capital*. Volume 1. New York: Vintage Books.

Maume, David J. 2006. "Gender Differences in Restricting Work Efforts Because of Family Responsibilities." *Journal of Marriage and Family* 68 (November): 859–69.

Maume, David J. and David A. Purcell. 2007. "The 'Over-paced' American: Recent Trends in the Intensification of Work." In Beth A. Rubin, ed., *Workplace Temporalities: Research in the Sociology of Work, Vol. 17*. Oxford: Elsevier JAI, pp. 251–83.

Meiksins, Peter and Peter Whalley. 2002. *Putting Work in Its Place: A Quiet Revolution*. Ithaca and London: Cornell University Press.

Meyers, M. K., L. R. Peck, E. E. Davis, A. Collins, J. L. Kreader, A. Georges, R. Weber, D. T. Schexnayder, D. G. Schroeder, and

J. A. Olson. 2002. *The Dynamics of Childcare Subsidy Use: A Collaborative Study of Five States*. New York: National Center for Children in Poverty.

Meyerson, Harold. 2011. "America's Post-Industrial Economy has Failed." *The Courier-Journal* (September 7): A9.

Milkman, Ruth and Eileen Applebaum. 2004. *Paid Family Leave in California: New Research Findings: The State of California Labor 2004*. Berkeley, CA: University of California Press.

Mills, C. Wright. 1959. *The Sociological Imagination*. New York: Oxford University Press.

Minge-Klevana, Wanda. 1980. "Does Labor Time Decrease with Industrialization? A Survey of Time-Allocation Studies." *Current Anthropology* 21(3): 279–98.

Mishel, Lawrence, Jared Bernstein, and Heidi Shierholz. 2009. *The State of Working America 2008/2009*. An Economic Policy Institute book. Ithaca, NY: Cornell University Press.

Moen, Phyllis, ed. 2003. *It's About Time: Couples and Careers*. Ithaca, NY: Cornell University Press.

Moonesinghe, S. R., J. Lowery, N. Shahi, A. Millen, and J. D. Beard. 2011. "Impact of Reduction in Working Hours for Doctors in Training on Postgraduate Medical Education and Patients' Outcomes: Systematic Review." *BMJ 2011; 342:d1580* (retrieved March 30, 2011, from <www.bmj.com>).

Mountford, Charles P., ed. 1960. *Records of the Australian-American Expedition to Arnhem Land, Volume 2: Anthropology and Nutrition*. Melbourne: Melbourne University Press.

Murphy, Teresa. 1988. "Work, Leisure, and Moral Reform: The Ten-Hour Movement in New England, 1830–1850." In Gary Cross, ed., *Worktime and Industrialization: An International History*. Philadelphia, PA: Temple University Press, pp. 59–76.

National Association of Temporary and Staffing Services (NATSS) website. At: <http://www.natss.org/staffstats/staffingfacts/shtml>; accessed April 2001.

Negrey, Cynthia. 1993. *Gender, Time, and Reduced Work*. Albany, NY: State University of New York Press.

Negrey, Cynthia. 1994. "Labor Process and Working Time: Part-Time Employment in the U.S. Supermarket Industry." Paper presented at the annual meeting of the American Sociological Association, Los Angeles, CA.

Negrey, Cynthia. 1998. "The Political Economy of Work-Time Reduction: Labor Shortage and Employer Queues." Paper presented at the annual meeting of the American Sociological Association, San Francisco, CA, August.

Negrey, Cynthia, Ramona Stone, Sunhwa Lee, and Gerard Barber. 2007. "Mobility from Part-Time to Full-Time Employment among Kentucky Welfare Leavers." *Journal of Poverty* 11(2): 47–71.

Nippert-Eng, Christena E. 1996. *Home and Work: Negotiating Boundaries through Everyday Life*. Chicago, IL: University of Chicago Press.

Nussbaum, Karen. 2007. "Working Women's Insurgent Consciousness." In Dorothy Sue Cobble, ed., *The Sex of Class: Women Transforming American Labor*. Ithaca, NY: ILR Press/Cornell University Press, pp. 159–76.

O'Connor, Julia S., Ann Shola Orloff, and Sheila Shaver. 1999. *States, Markets, Families*. Cambridge: Cambridge University Press.

Organisation for Economic Co-operation and Development (OECD). 2004. "Clocking In and Clocking Out: Recent Trends in Working Hours." *OECD Policy Brief* (October). At: <http: www.oecd.org/dataoecd/42/49/33821328.pdf>.

Osterman, Paul. 1995. "Work/Family Programs and the Employment Relationship." *Administrative Science Quarterly* 40: 681–700.

Paden, Shelley L. and Cheryl Buehler. 1995. "Coping with the Dual-Income Lifestyle." *Journal of Marriage and the Family* 57 (February): 101–10.

Pahl, R. E. 1984. *Divisions of Labour*. Oxford: Blackwell.

Parker, Robert. 1994. *Flesh Peddlers and Warm Bodies: The Temporary Help Industry and Its Workers*. New Brunswick, NJ: Rutgers University Press.

Patterson, James. 1969. *The New Deal and the States*. Princeton, NJ: Princeton University Press.

Perlow, Leslie A. 1999. "The Time Famine: Toward a Sociology of Work Time." *Administrative Science Quarterly* 44: 57–81.

Perry-Jenkins, Maureen, Rena L. Repetti, and Ann C. Crouter. 2000. "Work and Family in the 1990s." *Journal of Marriage and the Family* 62 (November): 981–98.

Phelps, Orme Wheelock. 1939. *The Legislative Background of the Fair Labor Standards Act*. Chicago, IL: University of Chicago Press.

Phillips, Deborah A. and Anne Bridgman. 1995. *Childcare for Low-Income families: Summary of Two Workshops*. Washington, DC: National Academy Press.

Phillips, Jill. 2008. "To-Do List for 2008." *The Courier-Journal* (January 28): C-J Job Journal: 1.

Pitts, Melinda K. 1998. "Demand for Part-time Workers in the U.S. Economy: Why is the Distribution across Industries Uneven?" *Social Science Research* 27: 87–108.

Pitt-Catsouphes, Marcie, Ellen Ernst Kossek, and Stephen Sweet. 2006. "Charting New Territory: Advancing Multi-Disciplinary Perspectives, Methods, and Approaches in the Study of Work and Family." In Marcie Pitt-Catsouphes, Ellen Ernst Kossek, and Stephen Sweet, eds, *The Work and Family Handbook*. Mahwah, NJ: Lawrence Erlbaum Associates Inc, pp. 1–16.

Piven, Frances Fox and Richard Cloward. 1971. *Regulating the Poor: The Functions of Social Welfare*. New York: Pantheon Books.

Pleck, Joseph H., Graham L. Staines, and Linda Lang. 1980. "Conflicts between Work and Family Life." *Monthly Labor Review* 103 (March): 29–32.

Polivka, Anne E. 1996. "Into Contingent and Alternative Employment: By Choice?" *Monthly Labor Review* 119 (October): 55–74.

Polivka, Anne E. and Thomas Nardone. 1989. "On the Definition of Contingent Work." *Monthly Labor Review* 112 (December): 9–16.

Pollert, Anna. 1988. "Dismantling Flexibility." *Capital & Class* 34(1) 42–75.

Pollert, Anna. 1991. "The Orthodoxy of Flexibility." In Anna Pollert, ed., *Farewell to Flexibility?* Oxford: Blackwell, pp. 3–31.

Poster, Winifred Rebecca. 2007. "Saying 'Good Morning' in the Night: The Reversal of Work Time in Global ICT Service Work." In Beth A. Rubin, ed., *Workplace Temporalities: Research in the Sociology of Work, Vol. 17*. Oxford: Elsevier JAI, pp. 55–112.

Presser, Harriet B. 1994. "Employment Schedules among Dual-Earner Spouses and the Division of Household Labor by Gender." *American Sociological Review* 59: 348–64.

Presser, Harriet B. 1995. "Job, Family, and Gender: Determinants of Nonstandard Work Schedules among Employed Americans in 1991." *Demography* 32: 577–98.

Presser, Harriet B. 2003. *Working in a 24/7 Economy: Challenges for American Families*. New York: Russell Sage Foundation.

Presser, Harriet B. 2004. "Employment in a 24/7 Economy: Challenges for the Family." In Ann C. Crouter and Alan Booth, eds, *Work–Family Challenges for Low-Income Parents and Their Children*. Mahwah, NJ: Lawrence Erlbaum Associates, pp. 83–105.

Prestowitz, Clyde. 2005. *Three Billion New Capitalists: The Great Shift of Wealth and Power to the East*. New York: Basic Books.

Rangarajan, A. and T. Novak. 1999. *The Struggle to Sustain Employment: The Effectiveness of the Post-Employment Services Demonstration*. Princeton, NJ: Mathematica Policy Research, Inc.

Rangarajan, A., P. Schochet, and D. Chu. 1998. *Employment Experiences of Welfare Recipients Who Find Jobs: Is Targeting Possible?* Princeton, NJ: Mathematica Policy Research, Inc.

Rapoport, Rhona, Lotte Bailyn, Joyce K. Fletcher, and Bettye H. Pruitt. 2002. *Beyond Work–Family Balance: Advancing Gender Equity and Workplace Performance.* San Francisco, CA: Jossey-Bass.

Ratner, Ronnie Steinberg. 1980. "The Paradox of Protection: Maximum Hours Legislation in the United States." *International Labour Review* 119(2): 185–98.

Reskin, Barbara and Irene Padavic. 1994. *Women and Men at Work.* Thousand Oaks, CA: Pine Forge Press.

Reynolds, Jeremy. 2003. "You Can't Always Get the Hours You Want: Mismatches between Actual and Preferred Work Hours in the U.S." *Social Forces* 81(4): 1171–99.

Reynolds, Jeremy. 2004. "When Too Much is Not Enough: Actual and Preferred Work Hours in the United States and Abroad." *Sociological Forum* 19(1): 89–120.

Reynolds, Jeremy and Lydia Aletraris. 2007. "For Love or Money? Extrinsic Rewards, Intrinsic Rewards, Work–Life Issues, and Hour Mismatches." In Beth A. Rubin, ed., *Workplace Temporalities: Research in the Sociology of Work, Vol. 17.* Oxford: Elsevier JAI, pp. 285–311.

Robinson, Joe. 2000. "Four Weeks Vacation for Everyone." *Utne Reader* (September–October): 49–54.

Robinson, John P. and Ann Bostrom. 1994. "The Overestimated Workweek? What the Time Diary Measures Suggest." *Monthly Labor Review* 117 (August): 11–23.

Robinson, John and Geoffrey Godbey. 1997. *Time for Life.* University Park, PA: Pennsylvania State University Press.

Rock, Howard. 1988. "Independent Hours: Time and the Artisan in the New Republic." In Gary Cross, ed., *Worktime and Industrialization: An International History.* Philadelphia, PA: Temple University Press, pp. 21–39.

Roediger, David R. 1988. "The Limits of Corporate Reform: Fordism, Taylorism, and the Working Week in the United States, 1914–1929." In Gary Cross, ed., *Worktime and Industrialization: An International History.* Philadelphia, PA: Temple University Press, pp. 135–54.

Roediger, David R. and Philip S. Foner. 1989. *Our Own Time: A History of American Labor and the Working Day.* London and New York: Verso.

Rogers, Jackie Krasas. 1995. "Just a Temp: Experience and Structure of Alienation in Temporary Clerical Employment." *Work and Occupations* 22: 137–66.

Rogers, Jackie Krasas and Kevin Henson. 1997. "Hey, Why Don't You Wear a Shorter Skirt? Vulnerability and the Organization of Sexual Harassment in Temporary Clerical Employment." *Gender & Society* 11: 215–37.

Rones, Philip L., Randy E. Ilg, and Jennifer M. Gardner. 1997. "Trends in Hours of Work since the Mid-1970s." *Monthly Labor Review* 120 (April): 3–14.

Rosenzweig, Roy. 1983. *Eight Hours for What We Will: Workers and Leisure in an Industrial City, 1870–1920.* Cambridge: Cambridge University Press.

Ross, Robert J. S. 2004. *Slaves to Fashion: Poverty and Abuse in the New Sweatshops.* Ann Arbor, MI: University of Michigan Press.

Rothstein, Donna S. 1996. "Entry Into and Consequences of Nonstandard Work Arrangements." *Monthly Labor Review* 119 (October): 75–82.

Rubery, Jill, Mark Smith, and Colette Fagan. 1998. "National Working-Time Regimes and Equal Opportunities." *Feminist Economics* 4(1): 71–101.

Rubin, Beth A. 1996. *Shifts in the Social Contract.* Thousand Oaks, CA: Pine Forge Press.

Rubin, Beth A. 2007a. "New Times Redux: Layering Time in the New Economy." In Beth A. Rubin, ed., *Workplace Temporalities: Research in the Sociology of Work, Vol. 17.* Oxford: Elsevier JAI, pp. 527–48.

Rubin, Beth A. 2007b. "Time-Work Discipline in the 21st Century." In Beth A. Rubin, ed., *Workplace Temporalities: Research in the Sociology of Work, Vol. 17.* Oxford: Elsevier JAI, pp. 1–26.

Sahlins, Marshall. 1972. *Stone Age Economics.* Chicago, IL: Aldine Publishing Company.

Sandberg, Joanne C. and Daniel B. Cornfield. 2000. "Returning to Work: The Impact of Gender, Family, and Work on Terminating a Family or Medical Leave." In Toby L. Parcel and Daniel B. Cornfield, eds, *Work & Family: Research Informing Policy.* Thousand Oaks, CA: Sage Publications, pp. 161–87.

Sayer, Liana C. 2005. "Gender, Time and Inequality: Trends in Women's and Men's Paid Work, Unpaid Work and Free Time." *Social Forces* 84(1): 285–303.

Sayer, Liana C. 2007. "Gender Differences in the Relationship between Long Employee Hours and Multitasking." In Beth A. Rubin, ed., *Workplace Temporalities: Research in the Sociology of Work, Vol. 17.* Oxford: Elsevier JAI, pp. 403–35.

Schor, Juliet B. 1991. *The Overworked American: The Unexpected Decline of Leisure.* New York: Basic Books.

Schor, Juliet B. 2001. "The Triple Imperative: Global Ecology, Poverty and Worktime Reduction." *Berkeley Journal of Sociology* 45: 2–16.

Schor, Juliet B. 2010. *Plenitude*. New York: Penguin.

Schumpeter, Joseph. 1989. *Essays: On Entrepreneurs, Innovations, Business Cycles, and the Evolution of Capitalism*. New Brunswick, NJ: Transaction.

Segal, Lewis M. and Daniel G. Sullivan. 1997. "The Growth of Temporary Services Work." *Journal of Economic Perspectives* 11(2): 117–36.

Serrin, William. 1986. "Part-Time Work New Labor Trend." *The New York Times* (July 9): A1.

Seyler, D. L., P. A. Monroe, and J. C. Garan. 1995. "Balancing Work and Family: The Role of Employer-Supported Child Care Benefits." *Journal of Family Issues* 16: 170–93.

Shellenbarger, Sue. 2008. "Plans to Expand Paid Leave Have Ally in Obama." *The Courier-Journal* (December 1): D1.

Shelton, Beth Anne. 1992. *Women, Men, and Time: Gender Differences in Paid Work, Housework, and Leisure*. New York: Greenwood.

Shelton, Beth Anne and Daphne John. 1993. "Ethnicity, Race, and Difference: A Comparison of White, Black, and Hispanic Men's Household Labor Time." In Jane Hood, ed., *Men, Work, and Family*. Newbury Park, CA: Sage, pp. 131–50.

Simmel, Georg. [1905] 1950. "The Metropolis and Mental Life." In Kurt Wolff, ed., *The Sociology of Georg Simmel*. New York: Free Press, pp. 409–24.

Simmel, Georg. [1920] 1978. *The Philosophy of Money*. London: Routledge and Kegan Paul.

Sirianni, Carmen. 1987. "Economies of Time in Social Theory: Three Approaches Compared." *Current Perspectives in Social Theory* 8: 161–95.

Sirianni, Carmen. 1991. "The Self-Management of Time in Postindustrial Society." In Karl Hinrichs, William Roche, and Carmen Sirianni, eds, *Working Time in Transition*. Philadelphia, PA: Temple University Press, pp. 231–74.

Sirianni, Carmen and Cynthia Negrey. 2000. "Working Time as Gendered Time." *Feminist Economics* 6(1): 59–76.

Sklar, Kathryn Kish. 1988. " 'The Greater Part of the Petitioners Are Female': The Reduction of Women's Working Hours in the Paid Labor Force, 1840–1917." In Gary Cross, ed., *Worktime and Industrialization: An International History*. Philadelphia, PA: Temple University Press, pp. 103–33.

Smith, Ralph E. 1979. *The Subtle Revolution: Women at Work*. Washington, DC: The Urban Institute.

Smith, Shirley J. 1986. "The Growing Diversity of Work Schedules." *Monthly Labor Review* 109 (November): 7–13.

Smith, Vicki. 1997. "New Forms of Work Organization." *Annual Review of Sociology* 23: 315–39.

Smith, Vicki. 1998. "The Fractured World of the Temporary Worker: Power, Participation, and Fragmentation in the Contemporary Workplace." *Social Problems* 45(4): 411–30.

Smyth, R. Brough. 1878. *The Aborigines of Victoria, Volume 1.* Melbourne: Government Printer.

South, Scott J. and Glenna Spitze. 1994. "Housework in Marital and Nonmarital Households." *American Sociological Review* 59 (June): 327–47.

Steinberg, Ronnie. 1982. *Wages and Hours: Labor and Reform in Twentieth-Century America.* New Brunswick, NJ: Rutgers University Press.

Stier, Haya and Noah Lewin-Epstein. 2003. "Time to Work: A Comparative Analysis of Preferences for Working Hours." *Work and Occupations* 30(3): 302–26.

Stier, Haya, Noah Lewin-Epstein, and Michael Braun. 2001. "Welfare Regimes, Family-Supportive Policies, and Women's Employment along the Life-Course." *American Journal of Sociology* 106(6): 1731–60.

Stiglitz, Joseph E. 2007. "The Economic Consequences of Mr. Bush." *Vanity Fair* (December): 312–15, 375–6.

Stone, Pamela. 2007. *Opting Out: Why Women Really Quit Careers and Head Home.* Berkeley, CA: University of California Press.

Strope, Leigh. 2003. "Flex Time Often Informal." *The Courier-Journal,* January 13: F6.

Strople, Michael H. 2006. "From Supermarkets to Supercenters: Employment Shifts to the One-Stop Shop." *Monthly Labor Review* 129 (February): 39–46.

Sullivan, Oriel and Jonathan Gershuny. 2001. "Cross-National Changes in Time Use." *British Journal of Sociology* 52(2): 331–47.

Sweet, Stephen and Peter Meiksins. 2008. *Changing Contours of Work: Jobs and Opportunities in the New Economy.* Thousand Oaks, CA: Pine Forge Press.

Thompson, E. P. 1967. "Time, Work-Discipline, and Industrial Capitalism." *Past and Present* 38: 56–97.

Thompson, Linda and Alexis J. Walker. 1989. "Gender in Families: Women and Men in Marriage, Work, and Parenthood." *Journal of Marriage and Family* 51 (4): 845–71.

Thorne, Barrie. 2004. "The Crisis of Care." In Ann C. Crouter and Alan Booth, eds, *Work–Family Challenges for Low-Income*

Parents and Their Children. Mahwah, NJ: Lawrence Erlbaum Associates, pp. 165–77.

Thull, Francoise and Marianne Arens. 2000. "The 35-Hour Work-week in France: How a Progressive Idea was Distorted Beyond Recognition." *World Socialist Website*, February 18 (retrieved from <http://www.wsws.org/articles/2000/feb2000/fran-f18_prn.shtml>).

Tilly, Chris. 1991. "Reasons for the Continuing Growth of Part-Time Employment." *Monthly Labor Review* 114 (March): 10–18.

Tilly, Chris. 1996. *Half A Job: Bad and Good Part-Time Jobs in a Changing Labor Market*. Philadelphia, PA: Temple University Press.

Umezaki, Masahiro, Taro Yamauchi, and Ryutaro Ohtsuka. 2002. "Time Allocation to Subsistence Activities among the Huli in Rural and Urban Papua New Guinea." *Journal of Biosocial Science* 34: 133–7.

US Congress, House of Representatives, Committee on Education and Labor. 1979. *To Revise the Overtime Compensation Requirements of the Fair Labor Standards Act of 1938*, Hearings before the Subcommittee on Labor Standards, 96th Congress, 1st Session, on H.R. 1784, October 23–25. Washington, DC: Government Printing Office.

US Department of Commerce. Bureau of the Census. 1997. *Statistical Abstract of the United States*. Washington, DC: Government Printing Office.

US Department of Commerce. Bureau of the Census. 2003. *Statistical Abstract of the United States 2003*. Washington, DC: Government Printing Office.

US Department of Commerce, Bureau of the Census. 2011. *Statistical Abstract of the United States 2011*. Washington, DC: Government Printing Office.

US Department of Health and Human Services. 1999. *Access to Childcare for Low-Income Families*. Washington, DC: Government Printing Office.

US Department of Health and Human Services. 2000. *Third Annual Report to Congress*. Retrieved from <http://www.acf.dhhs.gov>.

US Department of Health and Human Services. 2001. *Trends in the Well Being of Children and Youth*. Washington, DC: Government Printing Office.

US Department of Labor. 2004. *Employment and Earnings*, January. Washington, DC: Government Printing Office.

US Department of Labor. 2005a. "Computer and Internet Use at Work in 2003." *BLS News*, August 2.

US Department of Labor. 2005b. "Contingent and Alternative Employment Arrangements, February 2005." *BLS News*, July 27.

US Department of Labor. 2005c. "Work at Home in 2004." *BLS News*, September 22.

US Department of Labor. 2006. *Women in the Labor Force: A Databook 2006.* (<www.bls.gov>).

US Department of Labor. 2008a. *Employment and Earnings*, January.

US Department of Labor. 2008b. "Involuntary Part-Time Work on the Rise." *Issues in Labor Statistics*, December.

Vinocur, John. 1999. "France's Shift to a 35-Hour Workweek: Is It Breeding Jobs or Higher Taxes?" *International Herald Tribune*, June 1 (retrieved from <http://www.iht.com/IHT/JV/99/jv060199.html>).

Vittoz, Stanley. 1987. *New Deal Labor Policy and the American Industrial Economy.* Chapel Hill, NC: University of North Carolina Press.

von Hippel, C., S. Mangum, D. Greenberger, R. L. Heneman, and J. Skoglind. 1997. "Temporary Employment: Can Organizations and Employees Both Win?" *Academy of Management Executive* (11): 93–104.

Wacker, Mary Ellen and David B. Bills. 2000. "Barriers and Adaptations: Hiring Managers and Contingent Workers." In Randy Hodson, ed., *Marginal Employment.* Stamford, CT: JAI Press, pp. 231–52.

Waldfogel, Jane. 1997. "The Effects of Children on Women's Wages." *American Sociological Review* 62(2): 209–17.

Walsh, John P. 1989. "Technological Change and the Division of Labor: The Case of Retail Meatcutters." *Work and Occupations* 16(2): 165–83.

Walsh, John P. 1991. "The Social Context of Technological Change: The Case of the Retail Food Industry." *Sociological Quarterly* 32(3): 447–68.

Walsh, John P. 1993. *Supermarkets Transformed.* New Brunswick, NJ: Rutgers University Press.

Walsh, John and Anne Zacharias-Walsh. 1998. "Working Longer, Living Less: Understanding Marx through the Workplace Today." In Peter Kivisto, ed., *Illuminating Social Life: Classical and Contemporary Theory Revisited.* Thousand Oaks, CA: Pine Forge Press, pp. 107–43.

Warhurst, Chris, Doris Ruth Eikhof, and Axel Haunschild. 2008. "Out of Balance or Just Out of Bounds? Analysing the Relationship between Work and Life." In Chris Warhurst, Doris Ruth Eikhof, and Axel Haunschild, eds, *Work Less, Live More?*

Critical Analysis of the Work–Life Boundary. Basingstoke, England: Palgrave Macmillan, pp. 1–21.

Warren, Tracey. 2010. "Work Time, Leisure Time: On Women's Temporal and Economic Well-Being in Europe." *Community, Work & Family* 13(4): 365–92.

Weaver, Stewart. 1988. "The Political Ideology of Short Time: England, 1820–1850." In Gary Cross, ed., *Worktime and Industrialization: An International History*. Philadelphia, PA: Temple University Press, pp. 77–102.

Weber, Max. 1958. *The Protestant Ethic and the Spirit of Capitalism*. New York: Charles Scribner's Sons.

West, Candace and Don H. Zimmerman. 1987. "Doing Gender." *Gender & Society* 1: 125–51.

Wharton, Amy. 2006. "Understanding Diversity of Work in the 21st Century and Its Impact on the Work–Family Area of Study." In Marcie Pitt-Catsouphes, Ellen Ernst Kossek, and Stephen Sweet, eds, *The Work and Family Handbook*. Mahwah, NJ: Lawrence Erlbaum Associates Inc, pp. 17–39.

Whipp, Richard, Barbara Adam, and Ida Sabelis. 2002. *Making Time: Time and Management in Modern Organizations*. Oxford: Oxford University Press.

Williams, Claudia. 2011. "Paid Sick Days Legislation Gaining Momentum." *IWPR Quarterly Newsletter* (spring/summer). Washington, DC: Institute for Women's Policy Research, p. 4.

Williams, Joan. 2000. *Unbending Gender: Why Family and Work Conflict and What To Do About It*. New York: Oxford University Press.

Wilson, William Julius. 1987. *The Truly Disadvantaged*. Chicago, IL: University of Chicago Press.

Wise, Lois Recascino. 1989. *Labor Market Policies and Employment Patterns in the United States*. Boulder, CO: Westview Press.

Woloch, Nancy. 1996. *Muller v. Oregon: A Brief History with Documents*. Boston, MA: Bedford Books of St Martin's Press.

Yerkes, Mara and Jelle Visser. 2006. "Women's Preferences or Delineated Policies? The Development of Part-Time Work in the Netherlands, Germany and the United Kingdom." In Jean-Yves Boulin, Michel Lallement, Jon C. Messenger, and Francois Michon, eds, *Decent Working Time*. Geneva: International Labour Office, pp. 235–61.

Zak, Dan. 2008. "Tightwad Spends Less, Enjoys Life More." *The Courier-Journal*, March 30: E2.

Zerubavel, Eviatar. 1981. *Hidden Rhythms: Schedules and Calendars in Social Life*. Chicago, IL: University of Chicago Press.

Zerubavel, Eviatar. 1985. *The Seven Day Circle: The History and Meaning of the Week*. New York: The Free Press.

Index